ANCIENT ALIENS, THE RAPTURE AND THE RETURN OF CHRIST

CHET CATALDO

authorHOUSE®

AuthorHouse™
1663 Liberty Drive
Bloomington, IN 47403
www.authorhouse.com
Phone: 1-800-839-8640

First published by AuthorHouse 5/17/2011

ISBN: 978-1-4634-0006-4 (sc)
ISBN: 978-1-4634-0005-7 (e)

Library of Congress Control Number: 2011908112

Printed in the United States of America

To Jodi, my wife, love and friend

TABLE OF CONTENTS

INTRODUCTION

The end is fast approaching. The world's end will soon be upon us. This is the opinion of experts in almost every field. Included within those who see the possible end of the world are experts amongst the religious and the non-religious. Scientists, who do not hold to a religious persuasion have been announcing that global warming is leading to catastrophic events. These catastrophic events include the death of the world's ocean from red tide, the melting of the glaciers and the resultant devastating flooding of the coastlands, the affecting of weather patterns which will cause a more extreme winter and a more extreme summer, the increasing of earthquakes, and the increase in the number and intensity of hurricanes and typhoons. The medical community is warning of the increase of drug resistant bacteria; the continued spread of HIV, malaria, H1N1, bird flu and other illnesses that have the capability of affecting many of the world's peoples. There is also the increase of world tensions between countries and ideologies that result in terrorist attacks, nuclear buildup and the pursuit of some countries for nuclear capability. All of these and more lead to the view that the world is speeding toward the Apocalypse.

In addition to the opinion of the scientific community, there is also a common teaching that is found in many cultures throughout the world. This common teaching states that soon the Apocalypse will be here. The teaching

2

of the coming Apocalypse found in these many cultures is an interesting phenomenon, because these cultures are separated by time and distance. According to anthropologists they have had no connection or communication with one another. How, then, can different cultures, separated by time and distance, share a common teaching? The answer to that question is found in two concepts. The first is a concept which I call *residual knowledge.* Residual knowledge is a concept that states that cultures share a common seed or core of knowledge from centuries past. The second concept of how so many unrelated cultures throughout the world can share a common teaching is the ever increasing understanding that *Ancient Aliens* visited this planet and shared knowledge with human beings.

This study will look into the concept of residual knowledge and will identify the Ancient Aliens who visited this planet long ago, and who will visit this planet again in the future, just before the Apocalypse.

Another source that tells of the coming Apocalypse is the Bible. This study will take a look at what the Bible has to offer to this discussion. The Bible offers a timeline to the Apocalypse, the end. It is this timeline and various related topics that will be looked at. The timeline to the Apocalypse is not a timeline which states a specific year or day. However, found within the timeline are clues that identify where on the timeline the world is at. Included within the related topics will be the Bible and its reliability, prophecy, the timeline as found in Daniel and its relation to world history, the figure of the Anti-Christ, the present age, the rapture and a look at the events that affect the world in the time just before the Apocalypse.

Included within this study is an investigation of the rapture. It is recognized that the teaching of the rapture of the Church of Jesus Christ is a topic that is either strongly held to or is rejected altogether. Within the Christian Church, there are a number of views concerning the rapture. One view concerning the rapture is that the rapture is a fiction, a figment of the imagination. This view states that all Christians, that is all those who are alive at that time, will go through the Great Tribulation.

However, even to those who hold to the teaching of the rapture, there is disagreement as to when the rapture will occur. There are those who hold to a rapture that occurs before the Great Tribulation. A second view is of a rapture that occurs in the middle of the Great Tribulation. Finally, there is the view of the rapture that will occur at the end of the Great Tribulation.

This study will attempt to answer several questions regarding the rapture. These questions are: Is there a rapture and if so when will the rapture occur? The question regarding the *when* of the rapture is not a question as to year, day or hour. There have been and are those who claim to know the when of Jesus' return and of the rapture. The truth, however, is that no one knows the hour, day or year but the Father alone (Matt 24:36). The question regarding

4

the *when* of the rapture is in reference to the Great Tribulation. Will the rapture occur before, in the middle or at the end of the Great Tribulation? This is the focus of the question regarding the when of the rapture.

The when of the rapture is in reference to what is called in the Bible the Great Tribulation. The phrase *the great tribulation* is in reference to a specific period of time that the Bible singles out and emphasizes. This specific time will be a time of trouble, calamity, death and destruction. Throughout the history of the Christian Church, there have been periods of tribulation. However, these former periods are not called by the Bible, the Great Tribulation. The name The Great Tribulation is reserved for the time of trouble that is coming at the end of the days just before the Apocalypse. Jesus in his description of the time of tribulation that is connected to his Second Coming calls this time period θλῖψις μεγάλη, great tribulation (Matt 24:21). Jesus further describes the Great Tribulation as a time that is unequaled from the beginning of the world until now and never will occur again (Matt 24:21). The Bible further calls the Great Tribulation the Day of God's Wrath (Rev 6:16, 17).

The *when* of the rapture and the Great Tribulation will be found within the context of the general historical outline which is contained within the Bible. This general outline focuses primarily on the nation of Israel and the Christian Church. This means that there will not be found within this general

5

outline most of the historical events of the rest of the world. The reason for this is that the history of Israel and the history of the Christian Church are the histories that are tied to the Apocalypse and the end of the present world. The history of the nation of Israel and of the Christian Church constitutes *salvation history.* In essence, salvation history is the record of God's activities to win a rebellious world back to Him. The histories of the remaining portions of the world contribute to the history of salvation but are not the main ingredients to that history.

The arena of the activities of God in salvation history is primarily this present world, yet salvation history is not limited to this world. The Revelation of John is the primary account of God's activities that are not located within this world. The book of Daniel gives a general outline of the history of the nation of Israel and of the Gentile nations that make up salvation history.

Since the general outline of salvation history is found primarily within Daniel and the Revelation of John, it is important to understand that these books are considered apocalyptic. Apocalyptic writing is a type of writing that contains many symbols. The clue to understanding these symbols are contained within the writing itself. For instance, Daniel's dream of the four beasts in Dan 7:1-14 is interpreted in Dan 7: 15-28; Daniel's vision of the Ram and Goat in Dan 8:1-14 is interpreted in Dan 8:15-27. Symbols and their interpretation are also found within the Revelation of John. As an example: the seven stars found in Rev 1 are angels (Rev 1:20); the seven lamp stands also found in Rev 1 are the seven churches (Rev 1:20); The Great Prostitute of Rev 17:1 is Babylon (Rev 17:5); the seven heads of Rev 17:3 are both hills and kings (Rev 17: 10); the ten horns of Rev 17:3 are kings (Rev 17:12); the waters on which the Great Prostitute sits (Rev 17:1) are peoples, multitudes, nations and languages (Rev 17:15). There are other symbols in both Daniel and Revelation, and the key to understanding these books is that the interpretation of the symbols is found *within* the books themselves. Neither Daniel nor the Revelation of John leave the interpretation of the symbols up to the reader, the interpretation of the symbols is given in the books.

Apocalyptic writing is interpreted by four main methodologies:

1. The view that the events described in the writings have already taken place in history. The message of the writings held relevance to the time of the writings, and were then fulfilled during that particular time. This view states that the events described are past history and have little or no relevance beyond that particular historical period.

2. The view that the events described in the writings, especially in the Revelation of John are symbols of the ultimate victory of good over evil. This methodology holds that the writings are symbolic and contain little that fits within a particular historical period. As symbols, the truths portrayed are time-less and applicable to all historical periods.

3. The view that states that the contents of the Apocalyptic writings are primarily future and have little relevance to the historical period of their writings. This view holds the understanding that the writings, though written in the past, were intended for the future. The future meant by this view is the time of the end of the days.

4. The view that states that the Apocalyptic writings contain both history fulfilled and history yet to be fulfilled. This view understands Daniel and the Revelation of John as containing truths that were relevant in the day of its writing and applicable to the setting of the end times.

The understanding of salvation history is further divided into different views regarding the millennium. Rev 20:2 states that the dragon who is the Devil, was bound for 1,000 years. Scholars hold different views of this 1,000 year period. There are scholars who hold to a literal 1,000 year time period; while other scholars hold to an understanding that the 1,000 years is a long but undetermined period of time. The understanding of the millennium is further divided into three main views. These views are:

1. Amillennialism. This view states that the millennium is the present reign of Christ. Jesus reigns from heaven over his kingdom (Matt 28:18-20; 1 Cor 15:25; Heb 1:3). This view further teaches that following Christ's return there will be a general resurrection, the final judgment and then the reign of

8

Christ over a perfected world. Amillennialism does not hold to a literal 1,000 year period.

2. Pre-millennialism. This view understands that the present form of Christ's reign is heading toward the return of Christ, the first resurrection and the reigning of Christ on earth for a literal 1,000 year period or millennium. This view has two main sub-categories: The first sub-category holds to the view that the rapture and the return of Christ are one event. The second sub-category holds the view that the rapture and the return of Christ are two distinct events. This sub-category is furthered divided by the understanding of the time that separates the rapture and the return of Christ.

3. Post-millennialism. This view holds that the world will eventually become Christian by the preaching of the Gospel, teaching of the Bible and through missionary outreach. After the world is Christianized, there will be a long period of peace and prosperity called the millennium. The return of Christ, the resurrection of the dead, and the final judgment follow this long period of peace and prosperity, which is the millennium.

The millennium is not a topic of this study, but is mentioned only in its reference to the rapture and the Great Tribulation.

CHAPTER 1

THE NATURE OF PROPHECY

The specifics of the timeline to the coming Apocalypse is found primarily within a type of writings in the Bible that are called prophetic. The prophetic writings are the writings, the messages of men and women to whom and through whom God spoke. The messages of the prophets concerned the future.[1] Heschel states that the prophets understanding of the future included the near future and the far distant future.[2] This future view of the prophets, especially Daniel, is agreed with by Josephus.[3] The prophets not only proclaimed the future, but the promise of future salvation was one of the most distinctive features in the message of the prophets.[4] This promise of future salvation is one of the main features of prophetic proclamation that binds the Old Testament with the New Testament.[5] It is within this bond between the Old Testament and the New Testament that the study of the timeline of the coming Apocalypse will occur.

The Prophets, though part of Israel, did not make proclamation of the future that was only for Israel. The future that the prophets proclaimed was for the entire world.[6] What this means is that prophecy had as its intended audience the world and not just Israel. The world-wide scope of prophecy is seen in the many prophetic proclamations made by Israel's prophets against the Gentile nations as well as against Israel herself.[7] Heschel writes that

Israel's history was a drama of God and all the people of the world. He also adds that the hope of the world as well as God's kingship were at stake in Jerusalem.[8] In other words, the prophetic messages that are found in the Old Testament have the entire world as its intended outreach and scope.

The message of the Old Testament and of the Prophets was a message not just intended for the entire world, but was a message that was about Ultimate Reality.[9] This message of Ultimate Reality included a message of how to encounter Ultimate Reality[10] in a personal way. The message of the prophets is not just a message *from* God that will affect the human race. Prophecy proclaims what happens to God as well as what will happen to people.[11] This understanding of prophecy removes the prophetic message from the realm of simply a legalistic utterance from a distant and removed God and brings the prophetic message, the world and God into a closer bond.[12]

The prophetic message came out of an experience that the prophet had with God. This experience of the prophet was a fellowship in the *feelings* of God.[13] God is involved intimately, personally in the prophetic message. The outcomes of the prophetic messages are outcomes that affect God as well as the human race. This understanding of the prophetic message is far different from the understanding which the majority of persons have in the world today. Many in the world do not recognize God's existence. For those who do recognize in some way that God exists, God for them is a distant, hard,

11

un-caring entity who is seen as more of an obstacle to happiness then one who is intimately involved in the life, sorrow and life experiences of people. The prophets tried to communicate with their teaching that the prophetic message was a message in which God is personally and intimately involved.

Since the prophets understanding was of the future, both the immediate future and the distant future, this study will focus its investigation on the prophetic messages that point towards the coming Apocalypse. These messages are found primarily within the writings called Daniel, Matthew and Revelation. There are other books, sources, of course, which discuss the future foretold by the prophets. These other books and sources will be engaged and included within the discussion regarding the coming Apocalypse. However, the historical outline is primarily found in Daniel, Matthew and Revelation.

To understand Daniel, the Revelation of John and other apocalyptic writings as salvation history, it is necessary to understand what the Bible teaches concerning prophecy. The Bible teaches that prophecy is not the result of human interpretation or originates in the human will (2 Pet 1:20). Prophecy, however, is the result of the prophet being carried[14] along by the Holy Spirit (2 Pet 1:21). The verb to prophesy, προφητεύω means to speak under the influence of divine inspiration, with or without reference to future events.[15] What is seen in this definition is that prophecy has two aspects to it. The first

12

aspect is an utterance inspired[16] by God that has reference to the present. The second aspect is an utterance inspired by God that has reference to the future.

The dual nature of prophecy is not found only within the definition of the word προφητεύω. The dual nature of prophecy is also found within the teachings of the Scriptures, the Bible. Paul writes concerning Scripture in general that whatever was written in the past was written to teach us in the present (Rom 15:4). Here can be seen the dual nature of Scripture and prophecy. The dual nature of Scripture is seen in the fact that it was written in the past and is able to teach in the present. To include prophecy in this understanding is not inaccurate. The reason being, prophecy is part of the Scriptures. Therefore, since prophecy is a part of the category called Scripture, what is said about Scripture can be applied to prophecy. Paul continues his discussion regarding the dual nature of Scripture when he says that what happened in the past was written down as warnings to us, that is to the ones reading what Paul wrote (1 Cor 10:1-11, esp. v. 11).

The dual nature of prophecy is seen in the fact that when the prophets who wrote the message given to them by God, they did not always understand the full meaning of the message themselves. Peter wrote concerning prophets and the nature of prophecy that when prophets spoke the message that they were given, the prophetic message was not fully realized in the lifetime of the prophet nor was the message completely fulfilled in the situation in which the prophet spoke (1 Pet 1:10-12). The prophets, Peter wrote, were given to understand that the message they wrote and spoke applied to the prophets situation *and* to the future (1 Pet 1:10-12). Peter also taught the dual nature of prophecy when he told the disciples that many prophets longed to hear and see what the disciples heard and saw (1 Pet 1:10-12).

The dual nature of prophecy especially and of Scripture in general is seen in the example of Abraham. Abraham, the Scriptures tell us, believed God and in believing, he was considered as righteous by God (Rom 4:3). Paul, when he wrote the letter to the Romans and spoke concerning Abraham, based his statement concerning Abraham on Gen 15:6. What is important to understand is that when Paul quoted Gen 15:6 regarding Abraham believing God and being considered righteous, Paul had a wider understanding of Gen 15:6 then just for Abraham. This wider understanding of Gen 15:6 is explained by Paul in Rom 4:23,24 where Paul states that the words it was credited to him, that is Abraham, were not written *for him alone, but also for us,* that is to those of all generations who believe in Christ.

Jesus also stated the dual nature of prophecy when He said that the prophets longed to see and hear what the disciples saw and heard (Luke 10:24). The question to be asked is: how could prophets long to see and hear what the disciples saw and heard, if the prophets did not have some word or partial understanding of the message in his or her lifetime? The prophets then

14

had to understand that the understanding that they had was only partial and not complete, since the prophets longed to see and hear the full meaning which was given to the disciples. When the prophetic message was given to the prophets they understood that the message would be fulfilled only partially in the prophet's lifetime and completely fulfilled in the future.

The writer to the Hebrews helps us understand the meaning of Jesus' words when he wrote that the forebears of the faith only saw from a distance the fulfillment of the promises and the prophetic messages (Heb 11:13). Indeed, the forebears saw from a distance, yet in their lifetimes, saw only a part of the message. They understood that the message would be completely fulfilled in the future. However, the complete fulfillment was what the prophets longed to see and hear.

The teaching that prophecy has a dual nature is not found only within the New Testament, but also in the Old Testament as well. Hab 2:2, 3 states that prophecy was written at one time, yet, had a fulfillment in the future. Ezekiel teaches that the dual nature of prophecy was understood by the people of Israel (Ezek 12:26-28). The prophecy of Daniel was given in a specific time, yet had its fulfillment in the future, a time yet to come (Dan 10:14). The time of complete fulfillment of Daniel's visions and prophecies was the time of the end (Dan 12:4). It is recognized that there is disagreement as to the meaning of the *time of the end* in Dan 12:4. The point at this juncture is to recognize the dual nature of the message of Daniel, that the message had relevance at the time it was given *and* at a later date.[17] The understanding that Daniel has a message for both the time that it was written and for the future is not a recent understanding but is an understanding that Josephus had as well.[18]

The dual nature of prophecy is a key factor in the understanding of salvation history as found within Daniel and the Revelation of John and the identification of the little horn of Dan 7, 8.[19]

The Apocalypse is coming. There is no doubt as to this reality. What will the future look like? How much time remains? These are some of the questions that the future chapters of this book will attempt to answer as we look into the timeline of the coming Apocalypse.

CHAPTER 2

HISTORICAL TIMELINE

Within the Bible is contained a general history of the human race. This general history includes the creation of the human race in the image of God, the Fall of the humanity from God by sin in the Garden of Eden, the Promise of salvation through the gift of God's Son and a general historical timeline for the coming Apocalypse. As we begin to look into the timeline of the coming Apocalypse; it is important to understand that the Bible is God's Word to the human race. This means that the historical timeline that is found within the pages of the Bible is not of human origin but divine and is of utmost importance, for the timeline is part of salvation history.

We begin with a short study of the nature of the Bible. The Bible as God's Word is inspired (2 Tim 3:16). The word inspired is translated from the Greek θεόπνευστος. Θεόπνευστος is a word that is made up of two words. The first word is θεός which means God. The second word is πνεύστος which is means breath or spirit. θεόπνευστος literally means God-breathed.[20] God-breathed means that the Scriptures are the result of a divine action. The Scriptures, being the result of God's action is not simply the collection of religious stories. The Scriptures are the Word of God written[21] and given to the human race.

In 2 Tim 3:16 Paul wrote that *all scriptures* are God-breathed. The *all*

17

scriptures of 2 Tim 3:16 include the Old Testament writings, as well as the extant writings of the New Testament. This is to be understood because Peter includes Paul's writings in the category of *Scripture* (2 Pet 3:16). In addition, Paul states that the Gospel he preached was given to him by a revelation, ἀποκαλύψεως,[22] of Jesus Christ and is not from any human being.

In addition, there are parts of the Scriptures that are *personified.* Gal 3:8 states that the Scriptures *foresaw* that God would justify the Gentiles by faith, and announced the Gospel in advance to Abraham, saying: All nations will be blessed through you (Gen 12:1-3). In Rom 9:17 Scripture is said to *have spoken* to Pharaoh. It was not the *written* Scriptures that foresaw or spoke. It was God who spoke to Abraham and through Moses to Pharaoh. The acts of speaking and foreseeing can be attributed to Scripture only because of the identification of Scripture with God.[23]

Jesus Christ Himself witnesses to the God-breathing of Scripture. When Jesus was tempted by the Devil, Jesus replied to the Devil's temptation by quotations from the Old Testament. Jesus also stated he came not to abolish the Law or the Prophets but to fulfill them (Matt 5:17). The teaching of the Scriptures reveals that Jesus saw his life as the fulfillment of the Scriptures (Luke 24:25-27).

In summary, then, we understand that the Scriptures that are God-breathed are more than the Old Testament. Included with the Old

Testament are the extant writings of the New Testament when Paul wrote to Timothy and all the New Testament writings that accurately point to Jesus Christ, since Jesus is the fulfillment of the Scriptures.

This study will focus on the historical timeline that is found within the pages of the God-breathed Bible that presents a general outline of the world's events. This general outline tells of the coming Apocalypse. This general outline is called *salvation history*. Salvation history is the record[24] of God's activities in the history of the human race, primarily in and through the nation of Israel and the Christian Church. Properly understood, salvation history is the record of God's activities by which God is attempting to win the human race back to Himself.

The general outline found within the Bible will tell the one who longs for the appearing of Christ (2 Tim 4:8) when to look up for salvation is near. As has been stated before, this historical outline will not give a day, hour or even year of the coming Apocalypse. However, the historical outline within the Bible does unfold world events in such a way that it is possible to have an understanding of the process that leads to the end of the world.

This timeline is found in the book of Daniel. In the study of the last days, Daniel gives a timeline from the days of the Babylonian kingdom (Dan 2:36-38) until God's kingdom not only fills the world but also strikes and shatters all other kingdoms (Dan 2:35, 44, 45). This general historical outline is from the time of the kingdom of Babylon to the end of the age.

The historical outline was given in a dream to the king of Babylon. The king of Babylon had a dream concerning a great statue (Dan 2). This statute consisted of a head made of gold, chest and arms of silver, belly and thighs of bronze with legs made of iron and feet partly of iron and partly of baked clay (Dan 2:31-33). While the king was watching, a rock was cut out, but not by human hands. This rock struck the statue on its feet of iron and clay and smashed them (Dan 2:34). When the rock struck the feet of the statue, not only were the feet of the statue destroyed, but the whole statue was destroyed (Dan 2:35). After the entire statue was destroyed, the rock not made by human hands filled the entire earth (Dan 2:35).

Along with the dream that was given, the interpretation of the dream was also given. This is one of the characteristics of apocalyptic writings, that is, along with the symbols, the interpretation of the symbols are also supplied. The interpretation of the dream of the great statue is given in Dan 2:36-45 and is as follows.

The golden head of the great statue is the kingdom of Babylon (Dan 2:38). After the kingdom of Babylon, another kingdom will follow represented by the arms of silver (Dan 2:32, 39). Following this second kingdom, a third kingdom will arise. This third kingdom, symbolized by the belly and thighs of bronze (Dan 2:32, 39) will be followed by the fourth kingdom, symbolized by the legs of iron and the feet of both iron and clay (Dan 2:33, 40-43). In the days of the kingdom of iron and clay, which according to the interpretation is a divided kingdom (Dan 2:41), God will set up a kingdom that will never be destroyed (Dan 2:44). The establishment by God of His kingdom will bring to an end to all the other kingdoms of the world (Dan 2:44). The end of all other kingdoms will be by the destroying of the statue through the striking the feet of iron and clay (Dan 2:45).

Because of the interpretation of the dream, it can be understood that the dream of the great statue in Dan 2 is indeed a timeline from the time of the kingdom of Babylon until the time when God will establish a kingdom that will fill the entire world. In essence then, the book of Daniel presents an historical outline from the time of the kingdom of Babylon to the end of the ages; that is, to coming Apocalypse.

Daniel 2 is the foundation of the book of Daniel; all the remaining visions of the book of Daniel add information to the foundation found within Dan 2. The vision of Dan 4 of the great tree and the vision of the writing on the wall (Dan 5) add information to the foundation of the message as presented in Dan 2. This is done by adding information regarding the eventual fall of the kingdom of Babylon. Beginning in Dan 7 and going to the end of Daniel, are visions that explain in greater detail the vision of the great statue and its destruction found in Dan 2.

The general historical outline presented in Daniel 2 is looked at in greater detail in Dan 7-12. Found within Dan 7 is the vision of four beasts. The vision of the four beasts begins with the description of the first beast. The first beast was like a lion that had wings of an eagle (Dan 7:4). The first beast was followed by a second beast which looked like a bear that was raised up on one side (Dan 7:5). This second beast was followed by a third beast that looked like a leopard that had four wings on its back like a bird (Dan 7:6). Following the third beast was a fourth beast. This fourth beast is described as more terrifying and frightening than all the other beasts (Dan 7:7). Three other details are given regarding this fourth beast. The first detail is that the fourth beast had teeth of iron by which it crushed and devoured its victims (Dan 7:7) and that this fourth beast had ten horns (Dan 7:8). The third detail given regarding this fourth beast is that during the time of this beast, a little horn will arise amongst the ten horns and will uproot three of the ten horns (Dan 7:8). This little horn will, after gaining power, will speak boastful words until the little horn is slain and its body thrown into the blazing fire (Dan 7:11).

In the vision of Dan 7 concerning the four beasts, during the time of the fourth beast, several events are listed. The first event is the setting up of thrones, the seating of the Ancient of Days, the establishing of a court, the opening of books (Dan 7:9-10) and the coming of one like a son of man upon the clouds of heaven (Dan 7:13). The one like a son of man approached the

Ancient of Days and was given authority, power and glory (Dan 7:14). When the one like a son of man was given authority, power and glory, all peoples, nations and people of every language worshipped the one like a son of man (Dan 7:14). The authority of the one like a son of man is everlasting and his kingdom will never be destroyed (Dan 7:14).

The interpretation of the vision of the four beasts is given in Dan 7:15-28. The interpretation of the four beasts is that the four beasts are four kingdoms (Dan 7:17). A further explanation of the first three beasts is not given in Dan 7. The interpretation of the fourth beast is given in greater detail, however. The fourth beast is a kingdom, since the interpretation of the four beasts is that they are kingdoms (Dan 7:17). This fourth kingdom will be a kingdom that is different than all the other kingdoms of the earth (Dan 7:23). One of the characteristics that sets this kingdom apart from all the other kingdoms is that the fourth beast will devour and control the whole earth (Dan 7:23). The ten horns that are on the fourth beast are ten kings who will come from the fourth beast (Dan 7:24). The little horn which will arise after the ten horns is another king who will subdue three of the ten kings (Dan 7:24). This little horn will speak against the Most High and oppress the saints of the Most High (Dan 7:25). The oppression of the saints of the Most High will last for a time, times and half a time (Dan 7:25). During this time of oppression, the saints of the Most High will be handed over to the little horn

(Dan 7:25). During the time of the oppression of the saints of the Most High, the little horn will try to change set times and laws (Dan 7:25). After the time of oppression, the saints of the Most High will be given the power of the kingdoms of the earth (Dan 7:27). Likewise, after the time of the oppression of the saints of the Most High, the court will sit and the power of the little horn will be taken away and the kingdom of the Most High will be established. The kingdom of the Most High will be an everlasting kingdom and will fill the whole earth (Dan 7:27).

A further vision is found in Dan 8. Within this vision are a ram with two horns (Dan 8:3) and a goat with a prominent horn between its eyes (Dan 8:5). The goat attacks the ram and destroys the two horns (Dan 8:7). After the goat destroyed the horns of the ram, the goat grew in power until the prominent horn was broken off and four horns took the place of the prominent horn (Dan 8:8). After the four horns were in place, out of one of the four horns came another horn, which started out small but grew in power (Dan 8:9). The growth of the small horn was such that it reached the host of heavens and trampled them (Dan 8:10). This small horn set itself up as great as the Prince of the host; it took away the daily sacrifice, brought low the sanctuary of the Prince of the host (Dan 8:11), the small horn prospered in all it did and threw truth to the ground (Dan 8:12). The growth of the small horn was in part due to the rebellion of the people of the earth (Dan 8:12) and especially of the people of the host. The length of time that the sanctuary will be desecrated and the small horn will prosper will be 2,300 days (Dan 8:14).

The interpretation of the vision of Dan 8 is given in Dan 8:15-27. The two-horned ram is the kingdom of Media and Persia (Dan 8:20) and the goat is the kingdom of Greece (Dan 8:21). The prominent horn between the eyes of the goat is the first king of Greece (Dan 8:21) and the four horns that replace the prominent horn which was broken off represent four kingdoms that will come out of the kingdom of the prominent horn. These four kingdoms will be Greek kingdoms but, in comparison to the kingdom of the prominent horn will be lesser kingdoms (Dan 8:22). The small horn which comes out of one of the four horns is a king (Dan 8:23) who will become strong; will cause destruction and will succeed in all that he does (Dan 8:24). This small horn will cause deceit to prosper, take his stand against the Prince of princes and he will destroy many (Dan 8:25).

At this point a summation and explanation of what is clear will be given. It is clear that the historical outline given in Daniel begins with the Babylonian kingdom, since the head of gold on the great statue is the king of Babylon (Dan 2:24-36). After the Babylonian kingdom will arise another kingdom, a kingdom represented by the silver arms and chest. In history, it is a fact that the Babylonian kingdom fell to a kingdom comprised of a union of the Medes and the Persians in approximately 539 BCE under Cyrus. The kingdom of the Medes and the Persians is the two-horned ram of Dan 8 (Dan 8:20) that is conquered by the shaggy goat with the prominent horn (Dan 8:7).

According to Dan 2, after the kingdom of silver, a kingdom of bronze will arise and replace the kingdom of silver (Dan 2:32). The kingdom of silver which was the kingdom which replaced the kingdom of gold was the kingdom of the Medes and the Persians. Since the kingdom of silver is the kingdom of the Medes and the Persians, also represented by the kingdom of the ram (Dan 8:20); the kingdom of bronze which replaces the kingdom of silver must be the kingdom of Greece. This is seen in that the kingdom of Greece, represented by the kingdom of the shaggy goat with the prominent horn (Dan 8:21) conquers the kingdom of the ram which is the kingdom of the Medes and the Persians (Dan 8:20). History records that the kingdom of the Medes and the Persians was conquered by the armies of Greece under Alexander the Great in approximately 330 BCE.

The kingdom of Greece is described in Dan 8 as the shaggy goat with the prominent horn that was broken off and is replaced by four horns (Dan 8:21). The kingdom of the shaggy goat is represented by two further symbols. The first symbol is the prominent horn. The second symbol is the four horns that replace the prominent horn after the prominent horn was broken off. The four horns that replace the prominent horn are kings that come out of the same nation as the prominent horn (Dan 8:22).

Alexander the Great was the prominent horn of Dan 8. This fact is seen in that Alexander the Great was the Greek king who conquered the Medes and the Persians. According to the vision in Dan 8, the prominent horn of the Greek Empire, Alexander, was broken off and replaced by four horns from the same nation as the prominent horn. History records that Alexander died in 323 BCE. After Alexander's death, the empire was divided up into four main divisions. Those four divisions were headed up by Alexander's four main generals: Antipater and Cassander governed Macedon and Greece; Lysimachus ruled Thrace and Asia Minor; Syria was governed by Seleucus I; and Egypt and the Holy Land were under the control of Ptolemy I[25].

According to the historical outline found in Daniel, the kingdom of silver was replaced by the kingdom of bronze (Dan 2:32, 39). Since the kingdom of silver was the kingdom of the Medes and the Persians which replaced the kingdom of gold, the Babylonian kingdom; the kingdom of bronze was the Greek kingdom under Alexander the Great, which replaced the kingdom of the Medes and the Persians. According to the vision of Dan 2, the kingdom of iron replaced the kingdom of bronze (Dan 2:33, 40). History records that the Roman Empire conquered the various kingdoms that were once the kingdom of Alexander the Great, the kingdom of bronze, in approximately 63 BCE. Thus it is to be seen that the kingdom of iron in Dan 2 is the Roman Empire.

Within Dan 7 is a vision of four beasts. The first beast was like a lion (Dan 7:4); the second beast was like a bear (Dan 7:5); the third beast was like a leopard (Dan 7:6) and the fourth beast is simply described as a beast that was terrifying, frightening, very powerful, had teeth of iron and had ten horns (Dan 7:7). As the vision of the fourth beast is seen, a little horn is said to arise up among the ten horns (Dan 7:8). This little horn had eyes like a person and spoke boastfully (Dan 7:8). Dan 7 states that during the days of the little horn (Dan 7:11) that the Ancient of Days took his seat, books were opened and court was in session (Dan 7:9-11).

The interpretation of Dan 7 is a bit more difficult. However, since Dan 2 is the foundation of the historical timeline found within Daniel and all the other visions add new information to the timeline that is found within Dan 2; Dan 7 must also fit within the timeline of Dan 2 and add information to the information found within Dan 2.

The four beasts of Dan 7 are four human kingdoms (Dan 7:17). The understanding of what these four kingdoms are will begin with the fourth kingdom and then move backward to the first kingdom. Dan 7:9-14 states that in the days of the fourth kingdom, not only did the Ancient of Days take His seat, open the books and open court; but one like a son of man was given a kingdom that will never pass away (Dan 7:13, 14, 27). Dan 7:9-14 is a description of heaven[26] at the end of the age. This is further seen in that the

28

books which are opened are opened at the Day of Judgment (Rev 20:11-15) which occurs after the return of Christ.

What is seen is that the fourth beast, the fourth kingdom will be in existence on the earth when the court of God is in session and the books are opened (Dan 7: 26, 27). According to Dan 2, the kingdom of God, symbolized by a rock not made by human hands (Dan 2:44, 45) will be established on earth after striking the iron feet of the fourth kingdom of the Great Statue. The fourth kingdom, the iron kingdom is the Roman Empire. Not all agree with this, however. Montgomery disagrees with this understanding of the fourth beast and says that the fourth beast is the Greek kingdom.[27] While he holds the view that the fourth beast is the Greek kingdom; he recognizes that the traditional view of the fourth beast is that the fourth beast is the Roman Empire.[28]

The view that the fourth beast is the Greek kingdom can not be accurate. The reason for this is because part of Montgomery's reasoning for holding that the fourth beast is the Greek kingdom is his position that the third beast is the Persian kingdom[29] and the second beast is the kingdom of the Medes.[30] Montgomery, while holding to this view, admits that his understanding of the second and third kingdoms differ from the traditional view of these kingdoms. Montgomery himself states the view that the traditional view of the second kingdom is a combined kingdom of the Medes and the Persians[31] and that the traditional view of the third beast is that it is Greece.[32]

However, according to Montgomery, the fourth kingdom is Greek. For Montgomery to arrive at his position, he must depart from the teaching of the book of Daniel. Montgomery divides the kingdom of the Medes and the Persians into two kingdoms while the book of Daniel maintains the position that the kingdom of the Medes and the Persians was one kingdom (Dan 8:20). Since the book of Daniel maintains the position that the Medes and the Persians were one kingdom in Dan 8, this same understanding must be true for Dan 7.

Since the kingdom of the Medes and the Persians was one kingdom and this kingdom is the second kingdom, this then will cause the third beast to be Greece and the fourth beast to be Rome, since Rome followed Greece in the history of the world. The fourth beast of Dan 7 must be the kingdom of Rome. The reason for this position is as follows: The fourth kingdom of Dan 2 is Rome. This understanding comes out of both the vision of the Great Statue in Dan 2 and history. The Great Statue of Dan 2 begins with Babylon then is followed by the kingdom of the Medes and the Persians. The kingdom of the Medes and the Persians is followed by a third kingdom, the kingdom of bronze. As has been stated previously, history states that the Greek empire under Alexander the Great conquered the kingdom of the Medes and the

Persians. The third kingdom, the Greek, was followed by the fourth kingdom, which history tells us was the Roman kingdom. It is to further to be seen that the fourth empire in Dan 2 is described as a kingdom of iron (Dan 2:33) while the fourth beast of Dan 7 is described as a beast with great iron teeth (Dan 7:7). Secondly, the fourth kingdom of Dan 2 is the legs and the feet of the statue (Dan 2:33). In following the symbolism of the vision, feet have ten toes. This is consistent with the teaching concerning the fourth beast of Dan 7. The fourth beast of Dan 7 has ten horns (Dan 7:7). Thirdly, it is in the days of the fourth beast that God will establish His reign on earth (Dan 7:23-27). This understanding is consistent with the teaching of Dan 2, which states that it is in the days of the fourth empire, the Roman empire, that God will establish His kingdom on the earth (Dan 2:44-45). Another reason that leads to the understanding that the fourth beast in Dan 7 is Rome is the similarity of the number of kingdoms in Dan 2 and Dan 7. The fact that there are four kingdoms mentioned in Dan 2 and four kingdoms mentioned in Dan 7 leads to the position that the four kingdoms being described are the same kingdoms. In addition to all the above, the traditional view amongst the scholars is that the fourth beast is Rome.[33]

Since the fourth beast in Dan 7 is Rome; the third beast would be Greece, the second beast would be the kingdom of the Medes and Persians, and the first beast would be Babylon. The above statement is further supported by the fact that the first beast in Dan 7 is described as having wings like an eagle (Dan 7:4) and Babylon in Ezekiel 17:3 is described as a great eagle. This is confirmed by comparing Ezekiel 17: 3 with Ezekiel 17:12. In addition the description of the first beast after its wings were torn off and it was lifted up from the ground so that it stood on two feet like a man with a human heart, fits the description of what happened to Nebuchadnezzar, the king of Babylon (Dan 4). Since the first beast is Babylon and the fourth beast is Rome. Then, it follows logically that the second beast is the kingdom of the Medes and the Persians and the third beast is the Greek Empire.

What is to be seen is that the four kingdoms of Dan 2: the Babylonian, Medes/Persian, Greek and Roman not only are the same four kingdoms of Dan 7, but the kingdoms in Dan 7 follows the same order as the kingdoms in Dan 2. In addition, the order of the kingdoms in Dan 2 is confirmed by history. The Babylonian kingdom was followed by a kingdom of the Medes and the Persians, which was followed by the Greek Empire and eventually was followed by the Roman Empire.

The historical timeline in Daniel continues with the prophecy concerning the seventy sevens (Dan 9:24-27). Dan 9:24-27 is the vision of the seventy-sevens or seventy sets of years. The meaning of the seventy sevens or seventy sets of years is found in Lev 25:8. Lev 25:8 gives the principle that in Israel there were Sabbaths of years. Sabbaths of years were the multiplying of seven times seven. A period of seven Sabbaths of years amounts to 49 years. This means that the seventy sevens of Dan 9:24 covers a period of 490 years.

The seventy sevens or 490 years is further broken down into three time periods. The first time period covers the first sevens of the vision. This time period begins with the issuing of the decree to restore and rebuild Jerusalem. The second time period is from the end of the first time period and ends with the coming of the Anointed One (Dan 9:25). The first two time periods total 69 sevens. The 69 sevens are found by adding the seven sevens and the 62 sevens of Dan 9:25. What this tells us is that from the decree to restore and rebuild Jerusalem until the coming of the Anointed One, there will be a 483 year period. The number 483 is found by multiplying 69 times 7. This process is according to the Sabbath of years principle found in Lev 25:8.

The third time period found in the prophecy of the seventy sevens is the final seven or 70th Seven (Dan 9:27). During this final seven, the Abomination of Desolation is set up, the temple is desecrated and the saints of God will be persecuted. The final seven when added to the previous 69 sevens results in a total of 70 sevens.

The understanding of the vision of Dan 9:24-27 is found in two main views. One view is that Dan 9:24-27 covers the time of the Exile and ends with the death of Onias III.[34] This view states that the beginning point is 587 BCE, the year of the Exile and ends in 171 BCE the assassination of Onias III. The second view is that this vision begins with the decree to restore and rebuild Jerusalem (Dan 9:25) and the starting point of this vision is either the letter of Artaxerxes to rebuild Jerusalem (Ezra 7:1 1) which was sent in 458 BCE or the commission given to Nehemiah to rebuild Jerusalem (Neh 2:1-8) which occurred in 444 BCE and ends with the Second Coming of Christ.[35]

To understand the vision found in Dan 9:24-27, we begin with the understanding that Dan 9:24 states that there were several *events* that were to be fulfilled during the period of time covered by the seventy sevens, the time covered by Dan 9:24-27. These events are: to finish transgression, to put an end to sin, to atone for wickedness, to bring in everlasting righteousness, to seal up vision and prophecy and to anoint the most holy[36].

To finish transgression and put an end to sin refers to the national repentance of Israel (Deut 30:1-5). It was because of sin that Israel was sent into captivity and it will be repentance that will signal the end to that captivity. However, a time of national repentance has not yet occurred within Israel. The Exile was not merely for disobedience and idol worship, but Israel was sent into captivity because as a nation, they did not understand that righteousness comes from God which is by faith (Rom 10). Israel pursued a law of righteousness and for that reason did not attain righteousness, which is by faith (Rom 9:30-32).

The teaching that righteousness was by faith is not just a New Testament teaching but is also found in the Old Testament. The Scriptures say that Abraham *believed* God and it was reckoned to him as righteousness (Gen 15:6). A time of national repentance still lies in the future. Paul does refer to a time in the future when all Israel will be saved (Rom 9-11, esp. 11:25, 26).

The next *event* listed was to atone for wickedness (Dan 9:24). Lev 17:11 states it is the blood that accomplishes atonement. There were many sacrifices in the Old Testament era that had reference to atonement. However, these sacrifices, according to the writer to the Hebrews were only shadows of the good things, not the realities themselves (Heb 10:1). It is further stated that *it is impossible for the blood of bulls and goats to take away sins* (Heb 10:4). This is clearly a reference to the animal sacrifices of the Old Testament era. Paul echoes this when he wrote that the Law and the Prophets testify to righteousness being apart from law; that is, apart from the animal sacrificial system (Rom 3:21). The Gospel, Paul wrote, which states that righteousness is by faith is not a New Testament era message. God promised beforehand the Gospel in the Holy Scriptures (Rom 1:2, 3). The Gospel by which God intends to justify the Gentiles was announced in advance to Abraham (Gal 3:8). Paul further states that it is Jesus Christ who is the sacrifice of atonement (Rom 3:25) and that the purpose of the Law was to point people to Jesus Christ (Gal 3:24). The relation of the Law and the Prophets to the New Testament is clearly seen in the words of Jesus when He said that He is the fulfillment of the Law and the Prophets (Matt 5:17).

Associated very closely with the atoning for wickedness is to bring in everlasting righteousness (Dan 9:24). Righteousness means to be rightly related to God.[37] It is in the Gospel which God promised in the Law and the Prophets that righteousness is to be found (Rom 1:17). As was stated above, the Law and the Prophets testify that righteousness is apart from the law (Rom 3:21) and is by faith (Gen 15:6; Rom 3:22; 4:23). Righteousness comes from God (Rom 3:22) and is the presence of Jesus Christ in the heart and life of a person (1 Cor 1:30).

Dan 9:24 refers to the bringing in of *everlasting* righteousness. God is the only one who is or one can say has everlasting, eternal righteousness (Ps 112:9; 2 Cor 9:9). Jesus is the Righteous One (1 John 2:1) and when He comes He will bring in everlasting, eternal righteousness.

What we are to understand from the above is that the teaching that righteous by faith is a New Testament teaching is inaccurate.[38] We are told that Abraham believed God and it was credited to him as righteousness (Gen 15:6). Thus, the teaching concerning righteousness is a teaching that is fundamental to the relationship which God has with His creation. To understand the phrase "the bringing in of eternal righteousness," we will need to look at how a person becomes righteous. Jesus is the Christ, the one who was sent to rescue the human race from the results of the Fall. What will now be examined is how Jesus has rescued the one who believe in His name.

The answer to the question of how Jesus rescues is found specifically stated in 2 Cor 5:21. In this verse, Paul states clearly that the death of Jesus on the Cross of Calvary was: 1. or sin; 2. as a substitute for us. To discuss point 1 above that Jesus' death on the Cross was for sin; it is possible to list passage after passage. However, tt is necessary to list only a few which clearly state that Jesus died for sin.   Jesus, the writer to the Hebrews states, died to cleanse heaven by the removing of sin (Heb 9:23-28). Found within this passage is a clear statement that Jesus died to do away with sin by the sacrifice of Himself (Heb 9:26).   According to the Gospel of Matthew, Jesus is claimed to have said that he came to give his life a ransom for many (Matt 20:28). John the Baptist claimed that Jesus was the Lamb of God which took away sin (John 1:29).

Jesus' death on the Cross was not accidental. His death was the answer to sin. Not only did Jesus die for sinners,[39] but He also died to cleanse heaven from sin (Heb 9:23). What is to be understood from this statement is that sin is not solitary, nor is it individualistic. Sin touches and contaminates all of creation. The stench of sin reaches even to heaven itself. Jesus died for sin; to remove sin from all of creation and not just for the sinner.

The second point listed above is that Jesus died as a substitute for the

37

sinner. Peter wrote that Jesus bore our sin on His body on the tree (1 Pet 1:24). Paul, echoing Peter writes that at the right time Jesus died for the ungodly (Rom 5:6). In the death of Jesus, the sinner died. Jesus is the Lamb of God (John 1:29). The meaning of the Lamb of God is found in the Feast of the Day of Atonement (Lev 16). During the Day of Atonement, the High Priest would take two goats. Lots were cast for the goats as to which one was sacrificed and which one bore the sin of the people into the wilderness. The goat that was chosen for sacrifice was sacrificed on the altar as a sin offering (Lev 16:9) and its blood was carried into the Holy of Holies and sprinkled on the atonement cover of the Ark (Lev 16:15). The blood of the goat which was a sin offering made atonement, cleansed the Most Holy Place (Lev 16:16). It is clearly stated that the sin, the uncleanness and rebellion of the Israelites contaminated the Most Holy Place. Here is a clear reference to Heb 9 and how the blood of Jesus cleanses heaven itself.

The High Priest would then return to the altar area, which was outside and bring forward the live goat. As the High Priest stood before the people of Israel, the High Priest would lay his hands upon the head of the live goat and confess over it all the wickedness and rebellion of the people, all their sins (Lev 16:20, 21). The act of the High Priest laying his hands upon the head of the live goat and confessing over the goat the sins of the people was to put the sins of the people on the live goat (Lev 16:21). The live goat would then be lead alive into the wilderness bearing the sins of the people to a solitary place (Lev 16:22).

The sacrificial system that was given to Israel by God was given, not as the final answer to sin,[40] but to point the world towards Jesus (Heb 9:11-28). In fact, before Christ came into the world and died on the Cross, God left the sins unpunished (Rom 3:25). It was Jesus as the Lamb of God (John 1:29) bore the sins of the people (1 Pet 1:24) and by His death: cleansed heaven (Heb 9:23) and freed the believing sinner from their sins (Rev 1:5; Heb 9:28).

The purpose of the people who belong to God spiritually during the *gap,* the period of time between the 69th seven and the 70th seven is to make disciples of Jesus Christ (Matt 28:18-20). One part of making disciples for Jesus Christ is the spreading of the message of salvation. The message of salvation will lead a person to either accept or reject the subject of salvation. The subject of salvation is Jesus Christ. When a person responds positively to Jesus Christ, then that person experiences salvation.

The experience of salvation[41] begins when an individual believes in Jesus Christ as Lord and Savior. This experience has several aspects that are included within the parameters of the term *salvation.* Before the aspects or images[42] of salvation are examined; it is needful to understand the purpose and the how of salvation. Salvation contains many aspects. The reason for this is that sin is that sin causes the disruption of the Creation and of the human

39

race in a number of dimensions. Salvation, God's answer to sin must deal with the total destruction caused by sin.

The first aspect or image that will be looked at is justification. Justification is a term that can be understood from two perspectives.[43] One perspective is that justification means that God declares the sinner righteous.[44] Justification is a legal term whereby a judge declares a person guilty or not guilty.[45] Here is seen one perspective on the term justification.

The other perspective of the term justification is that not only does God declare the sinner righteous, but God makes the sinner righteous.[46] R.E. Cushman writes in his understanding of justification that justification is God's acceptance of the sinner, for Christ's sake, in forgiveness of sins and is also reconciliation, because it is a reunion which replaces willful self-alienation from God.[47]

Within the two perspectives of justification there is much overlapping. Wesley who believed that justification was both the declaring of the sinner as righteous and at the same time the making of the sinner righteous.[48] Yet, for Wesley, justification was more than a mere declaration. Justification was being saved from the guilt of and the consequences of sin.[49] Justification for Wesley was also forgiveness and being accepted by God.[50]

Brunner, in defending the emphasis on the declaration by God that the believing sinner is righteous[51] states that God is the one who makes the declaration and in essence, no is able to stand up to or refute God's declaration. God, according to Brunner, says: You are right with me, just as you are.[52]

The statement of Brunner carries within it elements that can be agreed with and elements that most be viewed with the eye of caution. The elements that can be agreed with are: God does, in Christ, state to the believing sinner: You are right with me, just as you are. As Christian Believers we are accepted, acceptable in Christ (Rom 15:7). In justification, God does declare the believing sinner righteous; that is right with me (Rom 4:23, 24).

The element that needs to be viewed with caution in Brunner's statement is the view that God arbitrarily declares the believing sinner righteous. If justification was *only* the declaring of the believing sinner righteous without the believing sinner actually being righteous, then God would be declaring that which is not true to be true. This is not the case. God is able to declare the believing sinner righteous, not simply because God chooses to, but because of what Christ has done for the sinner. The basis for the declaration of God that a believing sinner is righteous is the work of Christ Jesus and the believing sinner's faith in Christ. (Rom 5:1).

The Bible teaches that Jesus bore our sins on the Cross (1 Pet 1:24). The meaning of this is that Jesus bore the legal responsibility for our sins; he voluntarily accepted liability for our sins.[53] Jesus did not become as we are, that is He did not become a sinner (Heb 4:15). Jesus, while being pure and holy, accepted legal responsibility for our sins while not being contaminated by the sins of the human race.

While Jesus accepted liability for our sins, the believing sinners were set free from the punishment that is due them (1 John 4:18). In Jesus, our sins were condemned so that we might be freed from them (Rom 8:1-4). God condemned our sins in Christ (Rom 8:3) so that the righteous requirements of the law might be fully met in us (Rom 8:4). What this means is that in Christ, God condemned our sin so that in Christ we might become righteous.

The death of Jesus on the Cross also freed the believing sinner from the curse of the law (Gal 3:13, 14). The curse of the law was God's punishment for sin (Deut. 21:23). Christ, in dying in our place and for our sins, took the curse upon Himself. By this act of Jesus, the believing sinner is freed from the curse of the law, freed from God's punishment and rejection. When one is no longer under punishment and rejection of God, one is now accepted by God as His child (Gal 3:13, 14).

Because Jesus Christ died as a substitute for the sinner and the sinner accepts by faith, Jesus as Lord and Savior, God is able to declare that person righteous (Rom 5:1). God does not arbitrarily declare someone righteous. The declaration that a believing sinner is righteous is made only upon the faith of the believing sinner (Rom 5:1).

The aspect of justification as the declaring by God that the believing sinner is righteous is seen in Rom 4:23, 24. In these verses Paul writes that God credited righteousness to Abraham and to the one who believes in Jesus the Lord. Justification, the state of being righteous with God, is seen as God crediting, God declaring the believing sinner to be righteous.

The idea behind the word credited or some Bible translations use the term reckoned is the keeping of records and the charging to the account of someone.[54] The understanding that justification is in part the declaring by God of the believing sinner righteous is furthered by the understanding that the word *credited* also means to consider, or to look upon as.[55] When a believing sinner believes in Jesus Christ, God reckons, credits to them, imputes the righteousness of Christ to the believing sinner. In other words, the righteousness of Christ is applied to the account of the believing sinner. Because righteousness has been credited, reckoned to the account of the believing sinner, God declares the believing sinner righteous.

The above discussion leads to the understanding that justification does indeed contain the element of God's declaring the believing sinner righteous. Yet, that is not the end of the discussion.

The teaching of Scripture is that righteousness is not just a declaration of God but is also the experience of the believing sinner. Righteousness is also imparted or given to the believing sinner when the believer enters into a living

43

relationship with Christ. Paul writes that Christ has become for us wisdom from God, this is our righteousness, holiness and redemption (1 Cor 1:30). The emphasis here is on the phrase *has become* for the believer. When a sinner believes in Jesus Christ as Lord and Savior, the Holy Spirit indwells the believer (Rom 8:9-11). The experience of the believing sinner is that once he or she accepts Jesus Christ as Lord and Savior and the Holy Spirit indwells, the mortal body of the believing sinner is dead because of sin, yet the spirit of the believing sinner is alive because of righteousness (Rom 8:10). The believing sinner's experience is to be understood in two aspects. The first is that the believing sinner lives in a dead body. A dead body does not mean, in this context, that the body is not functioning. In this context a dead body means dead in that it is sinful. At the same time that the believing sinner's body is dead, his or her spirit is alive because of righteousness. The spirit of the believing sinner is in a different life experience than the body of the believing sinner. The spirit of the believing sinner is alive because of righteousness. The living spirit of the believing sinner is righteous.

The spirit of the believing person is righteous. To understand this, it is to be understood that the Holy Spirit being the Spirit of God and of Christ is the righteousness that is imparted, given to the believer. When the Holy Spirit is given to the believing sinner, the righteousness of Christ is also given to the believer. Paul wrote that Christ has become righteousness for the one who

44

believes in Christ (1 Cor 1:30). Christ *has become*[56], not will become, the believing sinner's righteousness.

When a believing sinner believes in Jesus Christ as Lord and Savior, God declares that believing sinner righteous. At the moment of belief,[57] the Holy Spirit indwells the believing sinner and the believing sinner becomes righteous. Thus, it can be seen that justification means God both declares the believing sinner righteous and imparts, or gives to the believing sinner, the actual righteousness of Christ. The double aspect of justification must be the truth. If it were not, if justification meant only that God declared the believing sinner righteous without any actual change in the believing sinner, then God would be declaring true that which was not true. If justification were only God declaring the believing sinner righteous, when in fact the believing sinner was not righteous, then not only would God be declaring true that which was not true, but God would be seen as a liar and God's holiness as arbitrary.

At the moment of justification, God declares the believing sinner righteous and at the same time that believing sinner, in Christ, becomes righteous. In Christ, Christ has become the believing sinner's righteousness. When a believing sinner is justified; when a believing sinner becomes righteous; that believing sinner is also accepted by God as His child. A believing sinner becomes God's child through the new birth.

Because the Law and the Prophets testify to the righteousness that is found in the Gospel, which is by faith; the bringing in of everlasting righteousness (Dan 9:24) cannot be fulfilled in the time of Antiochus Epiphanes, nor within the time frame of the Exile, but must refer to the future, that is to the Second Coming of Jesus Christ when He brings *everlasting, eternal* righteousness to the world.

The next *event* that must be filled within the time period that is covered by Dan 9:24-27 is the sealing up of vision and prophecy (Dan 9:24). Vision and prophecy exist until the perfect has come (1 Cor 13:9, 10). Vision and prophecy are thus temporary activities waiting for the arrival of perfection. Paul tells when vision and prophecy will be sealed. Vision and prophecy will cease when love has arrived in full (1 Cor 13:8-12). Love will have come in full at the Second Coming of Jesus Christ (1 Cor 13:12). Thus, it seems that the sealing up of vision and prophecy refer to the Second Coming of Jesus Christ.

The final *event* which must occur before the end of Daniel's 70 sevens is the anointing of the most holy (Dan 9:24). There is debate over whether the most holy refers to the most holy place[58] or to the most holy one. There are rare occasions when places or things were anointed (Ex 30:26). Anointing, however, was primarily used in reference to people. Aaron and his sons were anointed (Ex 30:30); the king of Israel was anointed (1 Sam 15:1). The cloud of uncertainty is removed as to the meaning of the most holy in Dan 9:24 by the statement that the Anointed One will come (Dan 9:25). In Dan 9:25 the reference is to the Anointed One, the ruler. The Anointed One, the ruler is a person and not a place or thing. Thus, the meaning of Dan 9:24 concerning the anointing of the most holy, refers to a person, the Anointed One. The understanding that Dan 9:24 refers to the Anointed One is also seen in that the word *Messiah.* The word Messiah comes from the Hebrew that is translated *anointed.* The Messiah is a person and not a thing or place. So, once again there is evidence that the meaning of the anointing of the most holy in Dan 9:24 refers to a person.

There is further evidence that Dan 9:24 is referring to a person, that is the Anointed One in comparing the Greek word for Christ with the Hebrew for Messiah. The Greek word translated Christ means Anointed One.[59] In fact, Louw and Nida, translate Christ as not only Anointed One but as Messiah as well.[60] What this means is that the Hebrew *Messiah* and the Greek *Christ* both mean *The Anointed One.*

The identity of the Anointed One is also known. Jesus is called the Christ (Matt 1:17). Thus, Jesus is the Christ, the Messiah, the Anointed One. The fact that Jesus was not anointed king at His first appearance, means that the anointing of the Most Holy One in Dan 9:24 refers to the Second Coming of Jesus Christ.

The view that states that Dan 9:24-27 refers to the Exile also states that the point of departure, the beginning point of the calculation for the seventy sevens is the beginning of the Exile in 587 BCE[61] and the end of the seventy sevens is 171 BCE at the assassination of Onias III.[62] However, in answer to this view, the structure of the message of Dan 9:24-27 is to be noticed. When the structure of Dan 9:24-27 is noticed, what is seen is that Dan 9:24 is the conclusion to the message of Dan 9:24-27 and Dan 9:25-27 gives the details to the message.[63] What this would mean is that the fulfillment of the *events* found in Dan 9:24 and the details given in Dan 9:25-27 must occur within the same time period. Since the fulfillment of the *events* of Dan 9:24 were found to refer to the Second Coming of Jesus Christ, the seventy sevens of Dan 9:24-27 must also be in reference to the Second Coming of Christ.

The view that the prophesy of the seventy sevens of Dan 9:24-27 refers to the end of the age and Jesus' Second Coming is confirmed by Jesus Christ Himself in Matt 24. The context of this passage is thus: Jesus and His disciples had just left the Temple in Jerusalem (Matt 24:1) and Jesus makes a remark concerning the future destruction of the Temple (Matt 24:2). History bears out the truth of Jesus' words concerning the destruction of the Temple in Jerusalem. It is a well known historical fact that the Temple was destroyed in 70 CE by the Romans under Titus. The disciples then ask Jesus about the end of the age and the sign of His coming (Matt 24:3). The context, therefore, of all that follows in Matt 24 is in answer to the disciples' question regarding the *when* of Jesus' coming and the end of the age, that is the when of the coming Apocalypse.

The disciples asked Jesus what would be the signs of His coming (Matt 24:3). What is obvious is that the disciples could not be asking Jesus about His first coming or His birth. The reasons for this is obvious: Jesus was already right before their eyes. In addition, the reference to Jesus' coming is in relation to the end of the age (Matt 24:3). This is seen the question that the disciples asked Jesus. They asked Jesus what would be the signs of the end of the age and His coming (Matt 24:3). Thus, the coming of Jesus is associated with the end of the age.

The beginning sign of the end of the age is seen as the destruction of the Temple (Matt 24:2). The destruction of the Temple is followed by the coming of false Christs (Matt 24:4, 5); wars and rumors of wars (Matt 24:6); the rise of nation against nation (Matt 24:7); famines and earthquakes (Matt 24:8); the persecution of the saints (Matt 24:9); apostasy, which is the turning away of the faith by believers (Matt 24: 10); the rise of false prophets (Matt 24;11); the increase of wickedness (Matt 24:12); the loss of passion for Christ, which is the love turning cold (Matt 24: 12); the world wide preaching of the Gospel (Matt 24:14).

The next sign that Jesus mentions that leads to His Second Coming is the setting up of the Abomination of Desolation (Matt 24:15) which is followed by a time of great distress (Matt 24:21). It is immediately after the time of the great distress that the Second Coming of Jesus occurs (Matt 24:29, 30). Notice the word *immediately after the distress of those days* in Matt 24:29. What Jesus said is that immediately after the Great Distress or Great Tribulation, the Son of Man will appear (Matt 24:29, 30).

The Second Coming of Jesus is associated with the setting up of the Abomination of Desolation (Matt 24:15). Jesus connects the Abomination of Desolation that is associated with His Second Coming to the prophecy and vision found in the book of Daniel (Matt 24:15). What is important at this point to understand is that Jesus identified one of the signs of His Second Coming as the setting up of the Abomination of Desolation that Daniel foretold (Matt 24:1-30, esp. 29, 30). It is important for the reader to understand that it is Jesus who connects the Abomination of Desolation mentioned in Daniel to the end of the age and His Second Coming.

A further discussion regarding the identity of the Abomination of Desolation will be made in the next chapter of this study. What is to be understood at this point is that within the historical timeline found in Daniel is a discussion regarding the setting up of the Abomination of Desolation.

The context of Jesus' remarks concerning the Abomination of Desolation is in agreement with the context of Daniel's mention of the Abomination of Desolation (Dan 9:27). Daniel's second mention of the

Abomination of Desolation is in the context of the prophecy of the seventy sevens (Dan 9:24-27). Daniel is told by the angel Gabriel (Dan 9:21) that there would be a time period of seventy sevens that began at the decree to rebuild and restore the city of Jerusalem (Dan 9:25) and would end with the death of the Abomination of Desolation (Dan 9:27).

The seventy sevens are thus broken down. There will be seven sevens and 62 sevens for a total of 69 sevens or 483 years from the decree to rebuild Jerusalem until the coming of the Anointed One (Dan 9:25). If the decree to rebuild Jerusalem is the letter of Artaxerxes (Ezra 7:11 in 458 BCE) or the commission to Nehemiah (Neh 2:1-8 in 444 BCE) the end of the 69 sevens leads up to either 25 CE or 39 CE. What is to be noticed is that both dates, 25 CE and 39 CE are in the time of Jesus' first coming. This is in agreement with the discussion that Anointed One is Jesus Christ.

After the coming of the Anointed One, which is after the first 69 sevens, the final seven occurs, which is the time frame for the Abomination of Desolation (Dan 9:27). Dan 12 states that the time of the setting of the Abomination of Desolation (Dan 12:11) is in the time of the end (Dan 12:4). The time of the end is understood as during the time of distress that has not happened since nations came into existence (Dan 12:1).

The Great Distress or Great Tribulation is mentioned by Jesus in his discussion with the disciples in answer to the disciples' question concerning the end of the age and His Second Coming (Matt 24:1-30). In His discussion with the disciples regarding His Second Coming (Matt 24:3, 29, 30), Jesus states that there will be a time of distress, unequaled from the beginning of the world until now (Matt 24:21). This time of distress, Jesus said will occur once and never again (Matt 24:21). Because there will only be one time of great distress, the times of distress mentioned in Dan 12:1 and by Jesus in Matt 24:21 must be the same distress. This is confirmed by the fact that both Daniel and Jesus mention the setting up of the Abomination of Desolation and the time of great distress in the context of the end (Dan 12:4,11; Matt 24:15, 21, 29, 30).

What is to be understood is that the Abomination of Desolation will be set up (Matt 24:15) during a time of great distress (Dan 12:1,11; Matt 24:21) which immediately precedes the time of Christ's Second Coming (Matt 24:29, 30) which in Daniel is called the end (Dan 12:4).

The time of the setting up of the Abomination of Desolation is further clarified in Dan 9:26, 27). According to Dan 9:24-27, after the first seven, the streets and wall was rebuilt (Dan 9:25). See Neh 6:15 for the fulfillment of the building of the walls and the streets of Jerusalem. After 62 more sevens history will see the Anointed One cut off (Dan 9:26). This brings a total of 69 sevens. After the 69 Sevens, there remains one seven, the 70th.

The coming Apocalypse will occur after the final Seven, the 70th

Seven. During the last seven, the 70th seven the major sign that will occur is the setting up of the Abomination of Desolation. The Abomination of Desolation will be set up half way through the last 7 years. Dan 9:27 states that in the *middle of the seven,* the Abomination of Desolation will be set up. The seven referred to is the final seven, the 70th seven. The setting up of the Abomination of Desolation will be after a total of 69 ½ sevens. After the setting up of the Abomination of Desolation there remains one-half of a seven, that is 3 ½ years.

Jesus stated that the Abomination of Desolation will be set up immediately preceding the great distress or tribulation. The great distress of tribulation mentioned by Jesus is the one that is immediately followed by His Second Coming (Matt 24:15-30). Since, according to Daniel, the Abomination of Desolation is set up in the middle of the 70th sevens, which is after 3 ½ years, this means that after the setting up of the Abomination of Desolation, there will remain 3 ½ years before the Second Coming of Jesus Christ.

The historical timeline found in Dan 9:24-27 states that there will be seventy sevens that are decreed for *Daniel's people and for the holy city* (Dan 9:24). These seventy sevens are broken down in this manner. There will be 69 weeks from the decree to rebuild and restore the holy city of Jerusalem until the coming of the Anointed One (Dan 9:25). Within the prophecy of the seventy weeks, after the first 69 weeks, there is found a description of the cutting off of the Anointed One (Dan 9:26), which according to the timeline is the crucifixion of Jesus[64] followed by the description of a coming people and ruler who will destroy the city and the sanctuary (Dan 9:26).

The order of this prophecy is the same order that is found in the words of Jesus and in history. Jesus told the disciples that there would come a day when the temple would be destroyed (Matt 24:2). The words of Jesus were fulfilled when the Romans under Titus came to Jerusalem in 70 CE and destroyed both the city and the temple. The destruction of Jerusalem and of the temple occurred after the death, the crucifixion of Jesus. The order of Dan 9:26 of the cutting off of the Anointed One followed by the coming of a people and a ruler who would destroy the city and the temple is seen both in the words of Jesus and in history.

After the statement of the coming destruction of the temple (Dan 9:26), there is then a discussion concerning the Abomination of Desolation (Dan 9:27). This does seem to present a difficulty within the historical timeline. This difficulty is seen in the fact that Jerusalem and the Temple were destroyed in 70 CE and the setting up of the Abomination of Desolation is 7 years before the Second Coming of Jesus Christ. If a strict following of the 70 weeks is followed, then the Abomination of Desolation and the Second Coming of Jesus Christ would have occurred 7 years after the death of Jesus. Since Jesus did not come again 7 years after His death on the Cross and there

54

is no historical statement or evidence that the Abomination of Desolation was set up 3 ½ years after the crucifixion of Jesus, this does seem to present a difficulty with the historical timeline. This difficulty is resolved when it is seen that there is a *gap* in the timeline between the end of the 69th seven and the beginning of the 70th seven.[65] This gap is found in Dan 9:26 which is a description of events that will occur after the 69th week and before the beginning of the 70th week as found in Dan 9:27. This gap is seen in the words: *And after the 62 sevens*[66] of Dan 9:26 and the discussion regarding the 70th seven in Dan 9:27. The *gap* of time then follows the end of the 69th seven and the beginning of the 70th seven.

Why is there a gap in time found in the historical timeline of Dan 9:24-27? The answer to that question is found in the words of the angel Gabriel to Daniel at the beginning of the prophecy of the 70 weeks. Gabriel told Daniel that there is decreed for *your people and your holy city* (Dan 9:24) 70 sevens. What the words of Gabriel to Daniel mean is that the primary focus of the prophecy of the 70 sevens will be Daniel's people and Daniel's people's holy city. Daniel was a member of the nobility of the nation of Israel (Dan 1:3-6), so Daniel's people would have been the people of Israel. The holy city of Daniel's people would be Jerusalem. Thus, according to the words of Gabriel, the angel, the primary focus of the prophecy of the 70 sevens was the nation of Israel. This focus is reiterated by Paul in Rom 9-11 where he states that in the plan of God, all Israel will be saved.

The *gap* that is found between the 69th seven and the 70th seven is in agreement with the theme of all of Daniel's prophecies. Daniel's prophecies were concerning a period of time that began with the Babylonian kingdom and ended with the Second Coming of Christ when Jesus would establish His kingdom throughout this world (Dan 2, 7). The kingdoms covered by Daniel's prophecies were the Babylonian, Medo-Persian, Greek and Roman. These kingdoms were comprised of people that are called Gentiles. The period of time that the prophecies of Daniel cover can be named, *the time of the Fullness of the Gentiles.*[67] The angel Gabriel told Daniel that in the midst of *The Times of the fullness of the Gentiles* there is decreed, the Hebrew means *to cut,*[68] a period of 490 years that are cut out of the Times of the Gentiles to bring about the final restoration of Israel.[69] In other words, in the midst of the Times of the Fullness of the Gentiles, where the primary focus of God is on the Gentiles, there is a period of time decreed, cut out of, separated from; where the primary focus of God will be upon Daniel's people, the Nation of Israel, that is the Jewish people.

The idea of a *gap* in the historical timeline that is seen to be between Dan 9:25 and Dan 9:27 is not a strange addition to the prophecies of Daniel. The reason for this is seen in the fact that the focus of Daniel's prophecies was the Gentile nations and the very inclusion of the prophecy of the seventy

56

sevens constitutes a *gap* in the flow of the prophecies themselves. What this means is that as Daniel prophesied concerning the Gentile nations, the inclusion of the seventy sevens, which is a prophecy concerning the nation of Israel, interrupts the flow of Daniel's prophecies concerning the Gentile nations. Thus, the existence of a *gap* in the timeline that is described by the prophecy of the seventy sevens, the prophecy concerning Israel, is consistent with what has already occurred in the prophecies of the Gentiles.

Because the primary focus of the prophecies of Daniel is the Gentile nations and the prophecy of the seventy sevens is concerning the nation of Israel, the *gap* in the historical timeline found within the prophecy of the seventy sevens (Dan 9:26) *reconnects* the prophecies of Daniel with their primary focus and that is the Gentile nations.

The book of Daniel presents an historical timeline that begins with the nation of Babylon and ends with the Second Coming of Christ. This historical timeline covers primarily the Gentile nations that controlled the Holy Land and its surrounding area. Within the timeline concerning the Gentile nations is found a prophecy concerning the nation of Israel (Dan 9:24-27). The prophecy concerning Israel contains within it a *gap* that connects the prophecy concerning Israel to the prophecy concerning the Gentile nations. What is seen in this interwoven prophecy concerning the Gentile nations and Israel is God's concern for the whole world (John 3:16).

The timeline to the coming Apocalypse, seen by many as doomsday, can also be seen as a message in which God is personally and intimately involved—a call to repentance and a return to God.

CHAPTER 3

THE IDENTITY OF THE LITTLE HORN

The historical outline of the coming Apocalypse that is found within Daniel gives details that help the reader understand the times. Two of the details found within the timeline to the coming Apocalypse that Daniel wrote concerning and are key signs in the outline are both named *the little horn*. The first reference to the little horn is Dan 7:8. The second reference to the little horn is found in Dan 8:9. In the symbolism of Daniel, a horn represents a king (Dan 7:24). The discussion of the identity of the little horn of Dan 7 will be done first, and afterwards the identity of the little horn of Dan 8 will be conducted.

There is a great debate over the identity of the little horn in the Book of Daniel. One view concerning the identity of the little horn is that the little horn is Antiochus Epiphanes. The second view is that the little horn is the Anti-Christ of the last days. Part of the confusion concerning the identity of the little horn stems from the identifying of the little horn of Dan 7 with the little horn in Dan 8.[70] This confusion is based on the similarities of character and action that exist between the little horn of Dan 7 and the little horn of Dan 8.

The similarities that exist between the little horn of Dan 7 and Dan 8 are: The little horn of Dan 7 is said to speak against the Most High (Dan 7:25).

The little horn of Dan 8 will also be one who takes his stand against the Prince of princes (Dan 8:25). The little horn of Dan 7 will oppress the saints (Dan 7:25), while the little horn of Dan 8 will also attempt to destroy the holy people (Dan 7:24). The little horn of Dan 7 will attempt to change the set times and the laws (Dan7:25), while the little horn of Dan 8 will cause deceit to prosper (Dan 8:25). A final similarity that exists between the little horn Dan 7 and Dan 8 is that both the little horn of Dan 7 and 8 will desecrate the temple in Jerusalem.

Although the characters and the actions of the little horn of Dan 7 are very similar to the character and actions of Dan 8; the little horn of Dan 7 and the little horn of Dan 8 are not the same individual. The reason that they cannot be the same individual is found in the time of their rising to power.

The *time of the rising to power* of the little horn of Dan 7 is in the days of the fourth kingdom in Daniel's vision (Dan 7:23-27). The rise to power of the little horn in Dan 7 is associated with the Second Coming of Jesus Christ (Dan 7:7,8, 21, 22) when the judgment seat of God is set up and the saints are given the kingdom (Dan 7:23-27).

The *when* of the Dan 8 little horn is during the *latter days of the reign of their reign* (Dan 8:23). What needs to be asked is: who is meant when the Bible says their reign? The answer is found in Dan 8:22 where it is foretold that there will be four horns that replace the prominent horn that was broken

60

off. In other words, *their reign* refers to the reign of the four horns. The four horns are four kingdoms that comprised the kingdom of the prominent horn (Dan 8:21-23). The four horns are the four generals of Alexander the Great who divided his kingdom amongst themselves after the death of Alexander. What this means is that the little horn of Dan 8 rises to power in the *latter part* of the reign of the four kings that ruled the four divisions that were once the empire of Alexander the Great. In other words, the little horn rises to power during the final days of the Greek Empire, which is the third kingdom in the visions of Daniel.

The little horn of Dan 8:9-12 comes out of the Greek nation,[71] which is the third kingdom in the historical outline of Daniel (Dan 8:22, 23). The actions of the little horn of Dan 8 and the actions of a Greek king named Antiochus Epiphanes will show that the little horn of Dan 8 is indeed Antiochus Epiphanes.[72] The following is the account of the actions of Antiochus Epiphanes in relation to the temple in Jerusalem.

> The king, Antiochus Epiphanes, came up to Jerusalem, and, pretending peace, he got possession of the city by treachery; at which time he spared not so much as those that admitted him into it, on account of the riches that lay in the temple; but, led by his covetous inclination, (for he saw there was in it a great deal of gold and many ornaments that had been dedicated to it of very great value) and in order to plunder its wealth, he ventured to break the league he had made. So he left the temple bare, and took away the golden candlesticks, and the golden altar of incense and table of shew bread, and the altar of burnt-offering and did not abstain from even the veils which were made of fine linen and scarlet. He also

emptied it of its secret treasures, and left nothing at all remaining; and by this means cast the Jews into great lamentation, for he forbade them to offer those daily sacrifices which they used to offer to God, according to the law. And when he had pillaged the whole city, some of the inhabitants he slew, and some he carried captive, together with their wives and children, so that the multitude of those captives that were taken alive amounted to ten thousand. He also burnt down the finest buildings; and when he had overthrown the city walls, he built a citadel in the lower part of the city, for the place was high, and overlooked the temple on which account he fortified it with high walls and towers, and put into it a garrison of Macedonians. However, in that citadel dwelt the impious and wicked part of the Jewish multitude, from whom it proved that the citizens suffered many and sore calamities. And when the king had built an idol altar upon God's altar, he slew swine upon it and so offered a sacrifice neither according to the law, nor the Jewish religious worship in that country. He also compelled them to forsake the worship which they paid their own God and to adore those whom he took to be gods; and made them build temples and raise idol altars in every city and village and offer swine upon them every day. He also commanded them to not circumcise their sons and threatened to punish any that should be found to have transgressed his injunction. He also appointed overseers, who should compel them to do what he commanded. And indeed many Jews there were who complied with the king's commands, either voluntarily or out of fear of the penalty that was denounced; but the best men, and those of the noblest souls, did not regard him, but did pay a greater respect to the customs of their country than concern as to the punishment which he threatened to the disobedient; on which account they every day underwent great miseries and bitter torments; for they were whipped with rods and their bodies were torn to pieces; and were crucified while they were still alive and breathed; they also strangled those women and their sons whom they had circumcised, as the king had appointed, hanging their sons about their necks as they were upon the crosses. And if there were any sacred book of the law found, it was destroyed; and those with whom they were found, miserably perished also.[73]

In comparing the actions of the Antiochus Epiphanes and the little horn of Dan 8 it will be seen that the actions of Antiochus Epiphanes and the actions of the little horn of Dan 8 are similar. The little horn will take away the daily sacrifice (Dan 8:11). The little horn would also bring low the place of the sanctuary, which Antiochus Epiphanes did by desecrating the temple when he placed a pagan idol on the altar in the temple and when he sacrificed pigs on the altar in the temple. The little horn would also destroy the holy people (Dan 8:24), which Antiochus Epiphanes attempted to do by killing many of the Jews and by taking ten thousand of the Jews captive. As it can be seen from the above description, Antiochus Epiphanes did desecrate the temple and the city of Jerusalem. When Dan 8:9-14, 23-26 is compared with the actions of Antiochus Epiphanes, it can be seen that Daniel foretold[74] the coming of Antiochus Epiphanes and what he would do. Thus, it can be seen that the little horn of Dan 8 is a king, who arises amongst the four horns (Dan 8:21-25) of the third kingdom, that is of the Greek kingdom. Antiochus Epiphanes was a Greek king[75] who ruled part of the Greek empire established by Alexander the Great.

The phrase *little horn* is also mentioned in Dan 7. The identity of the little horn of Dan 7 is not the same king as the little horn of Dan 8. In other words the little horn of Dan 7 is not Antiochus Epiphanes. Antiochus Epiphanes was a Greek king, which is the third kingdom in Daniel's vision.

The little horn of Dan 7 rises from the ten kings that are part of the fourth kingdom, that is the kingdom of Rome (Dan 7:7-8). In addition, the little horn of Dan 7 is said to arise in the days when God hands the kingdom over to His saints (Dan 7:27), which is the end of the age (2 Esdras 11:36-45; 12:11). It is during the days of the fourth kingdom that the Messiah will return (Dan 7:13-14; 2 Esdras 12:31, 32) and judge the world. The when of the handing of the kingdom to the saints is further clarified and is stated to be in the days associated with the Second Coming of Christ (Luke 1:29-33; Rev 11:15; 22:5; 2 Esdras 12: 31-33). The time of the little horn of Dan 8 is not associated with the time when the saints of God are given the God's kingdom. The identity of the little horn of Dan 7 is an individual who will arise in the days just before the establishment of the kingdom of God on the earth (Dan 7:23-27). The *when* of the Dan 7 little horn is in the last days, the days associated with the Second Coming of Jesus Christ. The identity of the little horn of Dan 7 is given further clarification in Dan 9:24-27.

The identity of the little horn in Dan 8 has been discovered to be Antiochus Epiphanes. The identity of the little horn of Dan 7 is of a different person. The little horn of Dan 7 will be a person who will speak against the Most High (Dan 7:25); will oppress the saints of God (Dan 7:25) and try to change the set times and laws (Dan 7:25). The little horn of Dan 7 will persecute the saints of God for 3 ½ years (Dan 7:25). Although the actions of

64

the little horn of Dan 7 is similar to the actions of the little horn of Dan 8, the time of their rising is different. The little horn of Dan 8 rises to power in the days of the Greek Empire while the little horn of Dan 7 rises to power in the days just before the Second Coming of Christ.

The little horn of Dan 7 will rise to power immediately before God takes His judgment seat (Dan 7:25, 26) and just before the kingdom of God is handed to the saints (Dan 7:27). The saints will receive the kingdom from the Lord Himself (James 2:5) after the Second Coming of Jesus Christ (Matt 25:31-34). Because the little horn of Dan 7 rises to power in the days immediately preceding the Second Coming of Christ (Matt 24:15, 29); the little horn of Dan 7 must be a leader that rises to power in the Last Days and thus cannot be Antiochus Epiphanes.

The character of the little horn of Dan 7 will help identify who the little horn of Dan 7 is. The little horn of Dan 7 is one who both opposes God and hates God. The little horn's opposition to God will be seen in that the little horn will speak against God (Dan 7:25). The little horn will say things against God that have not been heard before (Dan 11:36), except, perhaps, what was said and heard in the Garden of Eden (Gen 3: 4-5).

The little horn's hatred of God will cause the little horn to turn people toward himself. This the little horn will do by claiming to be the source of goodness (Dan 11:36; Gen 3:4, 5). The task of turning people towards himself will not be a difficult task for the little horn. People are looking for that which will make them wise, what is good for food and that which will make them happy in everything other than God (Gen 3:6). To the vast majority of the human race, God is the one who hinders them from happiness, health and prosperity.[76] It will not be a difficult task for the little horn to turn people toward himself. He will do this by saying from a public forum the very things that the human race feels in their hearts and says in their homes. In a very short time, the little horn will become in the eyes of the human race, their champion.

In addition to hating God, the little horn of Dan 7 will hate the people of God, the saints. The hatred for the people of God is not a new phenomenon. It is not a huge leap from hating God to hating the people who are associated with the God that people hate. In fact, it is not a leap at all. It is more of a turning of the head from the God who is withholding life, liberty and happiness from you to the people who are hindering you from life, liberty and happiness. Throughout history, the Jewish people have been hated because in some people's minds they were the ones who prevented others from enjoying prosperity. In today's political world, Evangelical Christians are hated by those who claim that Evangelical Christians are preventing them from receiving what they say is due them, their legal rights and what they want.

The hatred of the little horn for both God and the people of God will cause the little horn to attempt to kill the saints (Dan 7:21, 25). The persecution of the saints of God will be supported by and encouraged by the vast majority of the human race. Again, this will not be a new phenomenon. After the little horn rises to power the little horn of Dan 7 persecutes the saints for 3 ½ years (Dan 7:25). The persecution of the saints by the little horn of Dan 7 will only end when God returns to the earth and defeats the little horn (Dan 7:21, 22).

Throughout the Book of Daniel a 3½ year period is a prominent feature of the prophecies regarding the Last Days. A 3½ year period is mentioned in Dan 7:25; 9:27; and 12:11, 12. In Dan 7:25, the 3½ year period is the time when the little horn of Dan 7 persecutes the saints of God. During the 3½ year period in Dan 7:25, the little horn will not only persecute the saints of God, but the little horn will speak against the Most High and attempt to change the set times and laws, which is to say will attempt to change fundamental truths. In other words, during the 3½ year period of Dan 7:25 there will be a concentrated effort by the one in power to make right wrong and wrong right.

In Dan 9: 24-27, the final seven is divided into two 3½ year periods. At the beginning of the final seven, a covenant is confirmed or established (Dan 9:27). In the middle of the final seven, that is after 3½ years, sacrifice and offering will be forbidden and the Abomination of Desolation will be set up (Dan 9:27). Dan 12: 11-12 tells us that the Abomination of Desolation will stand in the temple for 3½ years.

Jesus identifies a person who will rise to power near a time of great tribulation. This tribulation is just before the Second Coming of Christ (Matt 24:15, 21). This person, Jesus identified with the Abomination of Desolation that Daniel foretold (Matt 24:15).

The Abomination of Desolation is mentioned several times by Daniel in his prophecy (Dan 9:27; 11:31; 12:11). There is also the reference to the rebellion or transgression that causes desolation in Dan 8:11-13. Dan 8:11-13 is a description of the actions of Antiochus Epiphanes when he erected a pagan altar on the sacred altar in the temple of Jerusalem in 168 BCE. However, because Jesus connected the Abomination of Desolation that is found in the prophecy of Daniel (Matt 24:15) with the end of the age and His Second Coming (Matt 24:3, 15), the Abomination of Desolation mentioned by Jesus cannot refer to Antiochus Epiphanes.

A further clarification is given at this point. Why would Jesus, in the context of a discussion regarding the end of the age and His Second Coming, which had not occurred at the time of the discussion, tell His disciples that one of the signs of the end of the age and His Second Coming is when they see (Matt 24:15 Jesus said when *you* see) the Abomination of Desolation standing in the Holy Place (Matt 24:15)? The pronoun '*you*' is vital in understanding the identity of the Abomination of Desolation and Daniel's prophecies.

Antiochus Epiphanes desecrated the Temple in 168 BCE. If the birth

68

of Jesus is 3,4 BCE and at the time of this discussion with the disciples, Jesus

was 33 years old, then that would mean that the discussion Jesus had with the

disciples regarding the Abomination of Desolation occurred close to 200 years

after the action of Antiochus Epiphanes. Why then would Jesus in answering

the disciples' questions regarding the end of the age and His second coming,

which is in the long distant future, tell them that one of the signs of that long

distant future was 200 years in the past?

It is important to reiterate that the context of Jesus' remark concerning

the Abomination of Desolation is the days immediately prior to the end of the

age and His Second Coming (Matt 24:1-3). If the Abomination of Desolation

is Antiochus Epiphanes, then Jesus' Second Coming would have to be

approximately 200 years before His first Coming. Furthermore, Matt 24 is an

historical timeline that began with destruction of temple in 70 CE (Matt 24:2)

and ends with the return of Christ (Matt 24:29, 30). What this means is that the

setting up of the Abomination of Desolation must occur after the destruction

of the Temple, which occurred in 70 CE. Therefore, the Abomination of

Desolation cannot be Antiochus Epiphanes. The reason that the Abomination

of Desolation cannot be Antiochus Epiphanes is that if the Desolation of

Abomination was Antiochus Epiphanes the historical timeline that Jesus

outlined in Matt 24 would not only be disrupted but would make no sense at

all. If Antiochus Epiphanes was the Abomination of Desolation, then the setting up of the Abomination of Desolation would disrupt and not fit within the historical timeline of Matt 24. While the actions of Antiochus Epiphanes are similar to the actions of the Abomination of Desolation, Antiochus Epiphanes is not the Abomination of Desolation.

The little horn of Dan 7 rises to power in the days that immediately precede the seating of God's court (Dan 7:9-10) and the giving of the kingdom to the saints (Dan 7:25). Paul reiterates this teaching when he states that just before the Coming of the Lord there will arise the man of lawlessness (2 Thess 2:3). The phrase *the man of lawlessness* comes from the Greek ἀνομίας. Ἀνομίας means to behave with complete disregard for the laws or regulations of a society.[77]

The action of the man of lawlessness is identical to the actions of the little horn of Dan 7. The idea behind ἀνομίας in the phrase the man of lawlessness does not refer to one without law, but refers to one who lives in a manner that is contrary to law.[78] This is in agreement with the little horn of Dan 7. The little horn of Dan 7 will attempt to change the set times and the laws (Dan 7:25). The man of lawlessness will set himself up in the temple proclaiming to be God (2 Thess 2:4). This man will oppose God and will exalt himself above everything that is worshipped (2 Thess 2:4). The little horn of Dan 7 will oppose God (Dan 7:25) and he speaks boastfully against God (Dan 7:8).

In addition, the timing of the rise to power of the little horn of Dan 7 is identical to the time when the man of lawlessness rises to power. The little horn of Dan 7 rises to power just before the kingdom is given to the saints (Dan 7:27). The man of lawlessness rises to power in the days immediately preceding the Second Coming of Christ (2 Thess 2:1-4). A further fact is seen in the comparison of the little horn of Dan 7 with the man of lawlessness. The man of lawlessness will be overthrown by the return of the Lord Jesus (2 Thess 2:8) and the power of the little horn of Dan 7 will be taken away by God (Dan 7:26).

In comparing the time of the rise to power, the actions of the little horn of Dan 7 and the man of lawlessness of 2 Thess 2, and the fact that both will be overthrown by God; it will be seen that the little horn of Dan 7 and the man of lawlessness are one and the same.

A further key to understanding the identity of the little horn of Dan 7 is the connection that Jesus made with the Abomination of Desolation of the Last Days with the prophecy of Daniel. Jesus stated that one of the signs of His Second Coming was the setting up of the Abomination of Desolation in the holy place, that is the temple (Matt 24:15). Jesus connected the Abomination of Desolation that will be set up immediately preceding His Second Coming with the prophecy in Daniel (Matt 24:15). According to Dan 9:27, the Abomination of Desolation will be set up in the middle of the final seven of

Daniel's seventy sevens (Dan 9:27). Thus, the Abomination of Desolation which Jesus spoke about and the Abomination of Desolation which Daniel prophesied about are one and the same.

The Abomination of Desolation will be set up in the temple in the days immediately preceding the Second Coming of Jesus Christ. As was stated earlier, the man of lawlessness will set himself up in the Temple proclaiming to be God in the days immediately preceding the Second Coming of Jesus Christ (2 Thess 2:4). Thus, it will be seen because of the time when they are set up and in their opposition to God, that the man of lawlessness and the Abomination of Desolation are one and the same.

The identification of the little horn of Dan 7 with the man of lawlessness and the Abomination of Desolation is seen in the book of Revelation. John in his vision states that he saw a beast rising from the sea (Rev 13:1). The beast is said to rise from the sea (Rev 13:1). This ties the beast to Daniel's vision of the four beasts (Dan 7). Daniel, when he saw the four beasts, he saw all four beasts rising from the sea (Dan 7:3). The first understanding of the beast from the sea is that the beast from the sea is the summation of the beasts of Daniel.[79] This is seen in the resemblance of the beast from the sea with the four beasts of Daniel. The beast of the sea resembled a leopard, but had feet like those of a bear and a mouth like that of a lion (Rev 13:2). In Daniel's vision of the four beasts, the first beast was like a lion (Dan 7:4), the second beast was like a bear (Dan 7:5) and the third beast was like a leopard (Dan 7:6). The same characteristics that are seen in full in the fourth beast also describe the beast from the sea.

The idea that the fourth beast is both a separate kingdom and is also the summation of the first three kingdoms is also seen in Dan 2:45 where the rock not made by human hands strikes the feet of the Great Statue and breaks into pieces the iron, the bronze, the clay and the gold.

When the actions of the little horn of Dan 7 and the actions of the beast from the sea are compared, it will be seen that the actions of the little horn of Dan 7 and the beast from the sea are identical. The little horn of Dan 7 will speak against the Most High (Dan 7:25). The beast from the sea speaks proud words and blasphemies God (Rev 13:6). The little horn of Dan 7 oppresses the saints of God (Dan 7:25) and the beast from the sea persecutes the saints (Rev 13:7). The little horn of Dan 7 rises to power in the days when the Abomination of Desolation is set up, which is the end time (Dan 7:8-11). The beast from the sea rises to power in the days preceding the Second Coming of Christ because the beast will make war against Christ Himself (Rev 17:12-14). A further identification of the little horn of Dan 7 and the beast from the sea is that the beast from the sea has an image of himself is set up in the Temple and all people on the earth are forced to worship this image (Rev 13:14). This fact identifies the beast from the sea with the Abomination of

Desolation, which is also set up in the Temple in the days immediately preceding the Second Coming of Christ (Matt 24:15-30).

Because the man of lawlessness and the little horn of Dan 7 are one and the same; and the man of lawlessness and the Abomination of Desolation are one and the same; it is to be seen that the little horn of Dan 7 is the Abomination of Desolation.

Our study has led us to the understanding that Daniel prophesied concerning two persons of great evil. These two persons are both called little horn. The little horn of Dan 8 rises to power during the days of the kings of the third empire, which is the Greek Empire that was founded by Alexander the Great. The identity of the little horn of Dan 8 is Antiochus Epiphanes. The little horn of Dan 7 is not Antiochus Epiphanes because he rises to power in the days of the fourth kingdom, which is the Roman Empire. The identity of the little horn of Dan 7 is found in the one who is the Abomination of Desolation who rises to power in the days immediately preceding the Second Coming of Christ; that is the Anti-Christ.[80]

The designation Anti-Christ is understood in several ways. There are those who say that the Anti-Christ is used as an image of essential human evil.[81] Those who hold this view state that the idea of a person who is called Anti-Christ is a legend that had its origin in the Early Church.[82] The second view of Anti-Christ is of a person and persons who are opposed to Jesus

74

Christ.

The New Testament uses the name Anti-Christ to mean one who is opposed to Christ and one who usurps the role of Christ.[83] The term Anti-Christ is a designation that is composed of ἀντι and Χριστός. Χριστός means Christ. ἀντι can have one of two meanings. One meaning is *instead of* and the second meaning is *against*.[84] The New Testament uses the designation Anti-Christ to describe both a category of people and a single person.

The designation ἀντίχριστος is found only in the Epistles of John. John wrote that one of the characteristics of the last hour is that many anti-Christs will appear in the earth (1 John 2:18). The many anti-Christs who come in the last hour are all the people who deny that Jesus has come in the flesh (2 John 7) and who deny that Jesus is the Christ (1 John 2:22). Furthermore, the spirit of the Anti-Christ is seen in its denial that Jesus is from God (1 John 4:3). In other words, everyone who denies Jesus is both God and Man are anti-Christ.

The coming of these many anti-Christs is a sign that shortly there will follow the One who is called The Anti-Christ (1 John 2:18). The one who is called The Anti-Christ is one who is the summation of all sin and opposition to God.[85] The teaching that the Anti-Christ is both a category of people and a final single opponent of God leads to the second understanding of the beast from the sea. The beast from the sea represents both the final world Empire and a final single ruler who is the opponent of God[86] who will lead the forces of evil against God (Rev 17:12-14).

The teaching that there is one sinful person that leads the forces of sin and darkness against God at the end of this age is also found in many ancient documents. The War Scroll[87] states that Belial, the angel of Malevolence will lead his company of evil spirits and angels against God. Belial's company of spirits or angels of darkness also share in his evil purpose--which is to bring about wickedness and iniquity.[88] The Hopi also teach that there will be one demonic being who leads the evil against the good.[89] The Koran states that in the last days a false Prophet will rise up to lead the evil forces against the good.[90] The Sibylline Oracle talks of the coming and the destruction of the Anti-Christ.[91] In addition, the Revelation of Esdras states the adversary of the human race will rise up from Tartarus in the last days.[92]

The inclusion of teachings from various religions and cultures does not mean that this study accepts all teachings as truth. It is to be recognized, however, that there are *similar* teachings found within different cultures and religions. These similar teachings are due to residual knowledge. Residual knowledge is the knowledge of the truth that was retained by the people of the earth after the confusion of languages at the Tower of Babel (Gen 11). After God confused the languages at the Tower of Babel and people scattered all over the earth, the people's understanding of the truth remained. After the passing of time, however, the clear understanding of the truth began to wane to the point where there remained only a seed or germ or partial understanding of the truth. The seed of truth was enhanced with ideas and thoughts developed by the people as they passed their teachings from generation to generation. These enhanced teachings, however, may or may not have had any connection to the truth. Furthermore, as the various scattered groups began to develop their own culture, the culture that was developed was developed around the idea of a seed of truth surrounded by the enhanced ideas and thoughts of the people. The seed of truth that is common to cultures who have not had any connection to each other since the time of the Tower of Babel but which account for common ideas is called the concept of *residual knowledge.*

The idea of residual knowledge explains why different cultures share the teaching of an evil person rising in the last days to lead the forces of evil against the forces of good. Residual knowledge also explains both the creation stories and the flood stories that are found in many cultures around the world. Residual knowledge explains why the Mayan in their Long Calendar, teach of a world-changing event in 2012.[93] In addition, the idea of residual knowledge would explain the stories of the so-called gods and goddesses[94] cavorting with humans in Greek and Roman mythologies,[95] and other common ideas found in seemingly unrelated cultures.[96] The concept of *residual knowledge* would also explain why the Magi, a group of scholars from Persia would recognize the star which proclaimed the birth of a Jewish king.

Although there has remained the seed of truth within the teachings of many cultures, as time has passed; the truth has been altered and changed to the point where it is only the germ of the teaching that has any connection to the truth. The clear and undeniable truth is found only in Jesus Christ (John 14:6) and in the laws and prophets which he fulfilled (Matt 5:17).

A second reason why many unrelated cultures share common teachings is found in the teaching of many cultures of *Ancient Aliens* who came to earth, shared knowledge with the human race and left. Found within many cultures is a knowledge that is far ancient, and in many cases far superior, to that which is known today. The cultures, themselves, state that this knowledge was given to humans by aliens who came to the earth. These aliens gave this knowledge to humans and then left. These human cultures record that they worshipped these aliens as gods. This is in agreement with the teaching that the Fallen Angels came to earth to lead the human race away from God and that in leading the human race away from God, the Fallen Angels also accepted human worship.[97]

Many of the world's cultures carved the teachings given to them on stone. It may be stated that the ones who gave this knowledge to humans were aliens, however, it is more accurate to say that the ones who came to the earth gave knowledge to humans and then left were angels. These angels, called

78

Watchers, descended to earth to teach the human race in the way of righteousness.[98] These Watchers not only taught humans in the way of righteousness, but some of these Watchers also taught charms and enchantments to humans.[99]

The Fallen Angels, who were called Watchers and who came to earth, revealed the secrets of heaven to human beings.[100] The secrets of heaven would certainly be knowledge far beyond human knowledge, which the various cultures around the world claim that the aliens gave to humans. What is seen in these two references is that angels, both Godly and Fallen, came to the earth, interacted with humans, gave knowledge to the human race and then left the earth. The knowledge and abilities of angels would explain the various cultural teachings of the superior knowledge and strength of the aliens. However, the point here is that the teaching of many of the world's cultures that aliens did come to earth and share knowledge with human beings is indeed, in essence true. The residual knowledge of angels coming to earth and sharing knowledge with human beings was retained. However, after the passing of time, the specifics were forgotten and the story was filled in by the various cultures to explain the core of the teaching that angels came to earth and interacted with human beings.

There are found in many places around the world writings that are carved on rocks that describe the coming to earth of superior beings and in addition some of the teachings that they gave to the human race are also carved on these rocks. These carvings on rock and stone are in accordance with what happened to the teachings of the Watchers, The Fallen Angels. There is recorded in the *Book of Jubilees* the story of Kainam who went out to find a place for himself and while on his journey found carved on a rock teachings of the Watchers.[101] The teachings that Kainam found carved on the rock concerned the sun, moon and stars.[102] The knowledge of the heavens given to human beings would explain the Mayans knowledge of the heavens and their predictions contained in the Mayan Long Calendar. The knowledge of heaven given to humans by the Watchers would also explain the Sumerian teaching of the 3rd century before Christ by Berossus that *all the things that make for the amelioration of life* were given to men by Oannes.[103] Oannes, according to Sumeran teaching, was a half-man, half-fish who rose out of the Persian Gulf and settled in the towns of Sumer.[104] The giving of the knowledge of the heavens to human beings would also explain the ability of the Magi, who upon seeing the star in the heaven knew that it signaled the birth of a king (Matt 2:1-3). The clear conclusion to be drawn from this discussion is that the content of the teachings the Watchers gave to humans is consistent with the teachings received and recorded from the aliens by the various cultures around the world.

The teaching of the Watchers is also found in the prophetic writing that contains the timeline to the Apocalypse. Dan 4:13 states that there were messengers/watchers, who were holy ones. These Watchers were sent to earth to instruct the human race. The recording in Daniel gives credence to the teaching that angels came to earth and instructed the human race.

These Watchers not only came to earth to teach the human race the secrets of heaven, but also took human women as wives.[105] An additional fact concerning the taking of human wives by Fallen Angels is that the human women were not simply the ones taken by the Fallen Angels, but were also active in the luring and enticing of the Watchers, the Fallen Angels.[106]

The Bible also teaches that angels came to earth and took human women as wives. The Biblical teaching that angels came to earth and took human wives is found in Gen 6:1-4. It is stated in Gen 6:1-2 that before the Flood the *sons of God* saw that the daughters of men were beautiful and the sons of God took human women as wives. The Hebrew for *sons of God* is also found in Job 1:6 where it is translated *angels.* Josephus states that the *sons of God* in Gen 6:1-2 were angels.[107]   What we see from the Bible and from all the extra-Biblical literature cited above is that the teaching that angels came to earth and took human women as wives was the view of the ancient world.[108]

A further fact to be included in this discussion of who were the *sons of God* is the description of the children who were produced from the union of the *Sons of God* and human women. The children of those unions were called

Nephilim (Gen 6:1-4). The Nephilim were giants (Num 13:31-33). The LXX[109] also translates Nephilim as giants; as does Josephus.[110] In addition, the book of Enoch also teaches that the Nephilim were giants (Enoch 7:1-6).

The word Nephilim is a plural noun from נפל which means to fall or to miscarriage.[111] Thus, the children of the union of the human women and *sons of God* were literally *Fallen Ones.* The understanding that the *sons of God* in Gen 6:1-4 were angels who transgressed by taking human women as wives would explain why there are some fallen angels who are bound in Tartarus awaiting the Day of Judgment (2 Pet 2:4) and why there are some fallen angels who are not bound in Tartarus but are free to serve Satan as demons. The angels bound in darkness and awaiting judgment were the angels who did not keep their positions (Jude 6). It can be stated that each and every angel who followed Satan did not keep the position assigned by God. Why then are there mentioned specific angels who did not keep their position and because of this are bound in darkness awaiting judgment while there are other fallen angels who did not keep their position as assigned by God and yet are free to serve Satan? The only explanation for this is that the fallen angels who are bound in Tartarus are the very angels who took human as wives as recorded in Gen 6:1-4. This is the teaching found in *Enoch* 10: 4-7 which states that after the Fallen Angels took human women and had children, God commanded that these Fallen Angels were to be bound in darkness to await the Day of

82

Judgment. The *Book of Jubilees* states that the reason that there are angels free to serve Satan while there are other angels bound in darkness is because Satan requested God to not imprison *all of the fallen angels who took human wives in darkness.* Satan requested that nine-tenths of the fallen angels be imprisoned in darkness, while a tenth of the fallen angels be allowed to serve Satan in freedom (*Jubilees* 10:8-10). What this implies is that it was all of the angels who followed Satan in rebellion against God which were involved in sexual activity with human women and not just a portion of the fallen angels.

The main objection to the understanding that the *sons of God* in Gen 6:1-4 were angels is the supposed idea that angels are not able to have sexual relations. Those who hold this idea base their position on Matt 22:30 which states that after the resurrection people will neither marry nor be given in marriage but will be like the angels. Jesus did say that angels neither marry nor are given in marriage. Jesus did not say that angels are incapable of sexual behavior. Angels, though spiritual beings, are capable of sexual behavior. The behavior of the Fallen Angels in marrying human women is described in this manner: *Though you were holy, spiritual, living the eternal life, you have defiled yourselves with women* (Enoch 15:3). Are angels capable of sexual behavior? The answer is found in the fact that there were angels who followed Satan in rebelling against God. If God created angels in such a way that they are not capable of sexual behavior, why did He not create them to not be able to rebel against Him? If angels, who were created pure, can rebel against God, these same angels would be able to engage in sexual behavior. The truth is that angels are just as capable of engaging in sexual behavior as they are of rebelling against God.

Those who disagree with the view that the sons of God in Gen 6:1-4 were fallen angels state that the phrase *"sons of God"* refers to the righteous sons of Seth who married the unrighteous daughters of Cain. Several questions are to be asked in reference to this view. The first question is: If the sons of Seth were so righteous, why did they marry unrighteous women? Does not the fact that the sons of Seth married unrighteous women prove that the sons of Seth were not righteous? The second question is: Why would the marriage between a believer (righteous person) and an unbeliever (unrighteous person) result in children who are giants? If the children of a marriage between a believer and an unbeliever are giants, wouldn't the world be full of giants today since there are many believers married to unbelievers. In addition, if the marriage between a believer and an unbeliever resulted in giants for children, would not the New Testament have mentioned something about giants as a result of marriage between a believer and an unbeliever? Since the New Testament does not state that one reason for a believer to not marry an unbeliever would be that giants would be born of this union, it leads to the conclusion that the marriage between a believer and an unbeliever does not lead to children who are giants.

It is more likely that those who hold the view that angels can not engage in sexual behavior base this view on the perspective that sexual activity is purely physical, which means that it is not spiritual and thus does not belong to the spiritual realm. The idea that sexual activity is purely physical and is not a spiritual activity is a clear denial of the teaching of God's Word which states that sexual activity between a husband and wife is very good (Gen 1:31) and that sexual activity is spiritual (1 Cor 6:15, 16). The teaching that matter or physical is evil and is to be separated from the so-called spiritual which is good is not a Biblical teaching. The distinction, therefore, that the spiritual can not engage in what is termed as a physical activity is based on a wrong assumption. The division which some hold to separating the physical from the spiritual has caused a tragedy in the Church. This tragedy is when Christians think that their so-called spiritual lives lived out on Sundays at church, and their physical lives lived out at work, play, school, and home during the rest of the week, are different and unrelated. The division between the physical and the spiritual has caused many to look at the lives and behavior of Christians and not like what they see.

However, there is more than ample evidence in the ancient documents that teach that it was angels who came to earth and took wives from human women and out of those relations had children that were giants.[112] The fact that there were some angels who by taking human women as wives passed a set limit or did not keep their positions (Jude 6) says that though angels are not supposed to marry and engage in sexual behavior, it is not impossible for them to do.

A further question is: Why would angels take human women as wives? One answer is to corrupt the seed of the woman. After the Fall of Adam and Eve in the Garden of Eden, God pronounced judgment on the Serpent, on Satan. God's judgment on Satan was that by the seed of the woman, Satan would be destroyed (Gen 3:15). Since the woman that God had in mind was not known by Satan; Satan had angels take wives from human women with the purpose of corrupting both the woman of God and the seed of the woman destined to destroy Satan. The taking of human wives by angels was then to disrupt God's plan and corrupt the seed of the woman and thus prevent the destruction of Satan by the seed of the woman. One of the purposes of the Flood was to destroy the children of the union between the angels and human women.[113] Since the aliens who came to earth were fallen angels;[114] we know that the aliens who came to earth will return. They will return in mass in the days of the rise of the Anti-Christ who will gather the world of unbelievers together in an attempt to prevent Christ from reclaiming the earth. Rev 9 tells that in the future there will be a demonic invasion of the earth. This demonic invasion is described in Rev 9: 2-11. The key to understanding that this is a demonic invasion of the earth is found in the place from which the so-called locusts come. Whether these are demonic locusts, demons[115] or whether locust are used as a symbol of destruction,[116] is not clear. What we do know is that these are demonic invaders of the earth. The locusts come from the Abyss (Rev 9:2-3). The Abyss is a place of confinement for evil spirits (Luke 8:31; Enoch 18:12-16; 21:1-10) and is the place out of which the beast will come (Rev 11:7). Because the *locusts* come out of the place where evil spirits are kept, it is clear that the locusts are demons and not some sort of natural insect. In addition, natural locusts devour vegetation; these demonic locusts are strictly forbidden to harm the vegetation of the earth (Rev 9:4). The objects of attack of these demonic locusts will be human beings who do not have the seal of God on their foreheads (Rev 9:5). The demonic locusts were not allowed to kill humans only to torment them (Rev 9:5). In other words, the first demonic wave rises out of the Abyss and will torment the Non-Christians who live on the earth. There is mentioned a second demonic wave coming to the earth. The first demonic wave is the demonic locusts that arise from the Abyss (Rev 9:1-11). This second demonic wave is described as two hundred million riders and horses (Rev 9: 16). A two hundred million member army rises and has the power to kill (Rev 9:18). It is not clear whether there will be exactly two hundred million members of this army or if the phrase two hundred million refers to an uncountable number.[117] What is clear is that this army will kill one third of the human population (Rev 9:18). The first demonic wave was only able to torment; this second wave of demons has the power to kill.

One view of this two hundred million army states that it refers to the army of Red China. A second view of this two hundred million member army is that this refers to a demonic cavalry.[118] There are two main reasons why the second view is preferred. The first reason is the context of Rev 9. The locusts which rise from the Abyss are clearly demons. The setting is thus set to describe demons. A second reason why the two hundred million member army is demons is their description. The horses are described as having mouths that shoot fire, sulfur and smoke. This may refer to tanks or other weapons of such nature. However, the difficulty is in the description of their tails. The horses have tails like snakes with which they inflict injury (Rev 9:19).

The Anti-Christ, who is the person who will lead the forces of darkness against God, will rise out of the fourth beast of Dan 7. As history has shown, the fourth beast, the kingdom which followed the Greek Empire, was the Roman Empire. The view that the Anti-Christ will come out of the Roman Empire means that the Roman Empire which has fallen, must be revived in some manner in the last days.

However, not all hold to the view that the Anti-Christ will come out of a revived Roman Empire.[119] Those who say that the Anti-Christ will not come out of a revived Roman Empire state that the kingdom of the Anti-Christ will include all the territory covered by all the prophetic empires[120] and will not be just a revived Roman Empire. It is a fact that the kingdom out of which the Anti-Christ comes and rules will be a kingdom that is located within Europe. All of Daniel's visions and prophecies concern the Gentile nations that are located within the area of the Mediterranean Sea, which is bordered by Europe. In addition, although the kingdom out of which the Anti-Christ comes may not be a revived Roman Empire, the area covered by the kingdom out of which the Anti-Christ comes is the same area covered by the Roman Empire. In 1993, the European Union covered the same geographical area as the former Roman Empire. What this means is that the Anti-Christ will be a citizen of the EU, or at least will be European.

In the beginning of the rise of the little horn, the kingdom is more visible. This explains the fact that when Daniel first saw the little horn, it was a little horn. However, after a period of time, the little horn, the ruler grew and the person becomes more and more visible.[121] The growth of the ruler over the kingdom is explained by the fact that the beast receives his kingdom from Satan (Rev 13:2). The fact that the beast from the sea receives his kingdom from Satan ties the identity of the beast from the sea to the Anti-Christ, for both are opposed to God. The Anti-Christ will be a powerful speaker and is able to persuade many (Dan 7:8). He will be a politician who will appear to have the answer to the world's problems. The *wisdom* that the Anti-Christ will have is because the Anti-Christ receives his power and spirit from the Devil. It is known that the Devil was originally created by God as angel who had access to not only the presence of God, but also the knowledge in the heavens; the Anti-Christ who would receive this knowledge from Satan, would be able to perform many signs and wonders that would convince the world to follow him (Rev 13:4). It is also possible that the Anti-Christ will acknowledge the so-called gifts that were given to the human race by the ancient aliens as coming from him.[122] The ability to perform signs and wonders is in part the reason that so many will follow him. The other reason that many follow him is that the Anti-Christ verbalizes and makes acceptable the disregarding of God. Many in the world today have already given up on God. God, to this majority is to blame for the world's ills. However, there is not yet a popular public figure who gives the world's people permission to loudly and passionately accuse and abuse God. When the Anti-Christ rises, part of his popularity will be his out-spoken antagonism against God. This antagonism resonates with many in the world. When the Anti-Christ rises to power and speaks against God, this will by itself draw people, who already hate God, to the support of the Anti-Christ.

When the world's masses are drawn to the Anti-Christ who verbalizes their feelings about God; they will also hear from the Anti-Christ that they will not need God. The Anti-Christ, who is one of them in their opposition to God, will claim to meet their needs. He will fully convince the world's masses by the so-called miracles and acts of power done in his name (Rev 13:13).

The identity of the beast from the sea is said by some to be a resurrected Nero who rises from the dead.[123] The reasoning for this idea is that the beast is said to rise from the sea (Rev 13:1). The reference to *sea* ties this beast to Daniel's four beasts of Dan 7, since Daniel saw the four beasts rising from the sea (Dan 7:3). The *sea* represents the world of nations, specifically the nations surrounding the Mediterranean Sea (Dan 7:17). The beast from the sea is said to come not only out of the world of nations (Rev 13:1) but is also said to come from the abyss (Rev 17:8). The Greek for abyss is ἄβυσσος. Ἄβυσσος means the deepest hole in the earth.[124] The abyss is said to be the place where Satan is kept (Rev 20:3). The abyss is the abode of the beast who is the Anti-Christ[125] (Rev 11:7) and it is the place of the dead (Rom 10:7). The fact that the beast from the beast from the sea is mortally wounded and comes to life again (Rev 13:3) and is said to rise from the abyss (Rev 17:8) has led some to the view that the beast is a resurrected Nero.

However, others say that the name of the Anti-Christ is not known[126] and the fact that the beast from the sea is mortally wounded, which means that he will die, and then rises out of the abyss does not necessarily lead to the conclusion that the beast from the sea is Nero resurrected. It is possible that several decades or more before the Second Coming of Christ, the beast from the sea is born, grows and reaches adulthood, as all humans do. Sometime during or near the time of the rise to power, the beast from the sea, who is the Anti-Christ, is killed. After the beast from the sea is killed, he will then go to the abyss, the place of the dead. Once the beast from the sea is in the abyss, after a period of time which no one knows, he will then rise from the abyss; that is from the dead.

Whoever the Anti-Christ is, he will indeed be the personification of evil and opposition to God, to Christ and to the Church. Trench has this to say concerning the Anti-Christ.

> The final Anti-Christ will be a false Christ as well as opposed to Christ. He will not call himself the Christ, for he will be filled with the deadliest hate against the name and spirit of Jesus of Nazareth, the exalted King of Glory. The Anti-Christ will assail and endeavor to utterly abolish the faith in Jesus the Christ. The final Anti-Christ will come as a savior; as one who will make the blessedness of as many as obey him, giving to them the full enjoyment of a present material earth, instead of a distant, shadowy and uncertain heaven. He will abolish the division between the Church and the world, the spirit and the flesh, between holiness and sin, between good and evil; those divisions which deny people of so many enjoyments. He will present himself to the world as the true center of its hopes, as the one who satisfies all its needs and the healer of all its hurts. The final Anti-Christ will take up and absorb into himself all names and forms of blasphemy.[127]

The Anti-Christ will be a charismatic political leader. He will be persuasive and appealing to the world's masses. He will claim to have the answer to the problems facing the world and the world will listen to him.[128]

However, the support of the Anti-Christ means that the time of the end is near.

92

The world's support of the Anti-Christ is the final sign that the Apocalypse has finally arrived. What the Bible teaches is that the Anti-Christ is not a savior but is the great adversary of both the human race and of God. The Anti-Christ rises in an attempt to wipe out righteousness, the people of God and to take God's throne.[129] The attempt by the Anti-Christ to take control of the earth ends with the Return of Christ. The rise of the Anti-Christ signals the end of the present age and the arrival of the Apocalypse. The Apocalypse is the return of Christ. The Apocalypse is not the world's destruction at the hands of human beings, but it is the return, the appearance of Jesus Christ. At the Second Coming of Jesus Christ, the Anti-Christ and his forces will be defeated by Jesus Christ and the armies that He brings (Rev 17:12-14).[130] Following the defeat of the Anti-Christ, Jesus Christ will establish the kingdom of God all over the earth.

CHAPTER 4

THE GAP

The Book of Daniel provides an historical timeline from the kingdom of Babylon until the Second Coming of Christ. The vision of the great statue in chapter 2 of Daniel is the parameters for this timeline. All of the other visions of Daniel add information that fits within the parameters outlined in chapter 2. As was seen earlier in this study, the visions of Daniel present the history of the Gentile nations that have a direct connection with the nation of Israel and the Church. The historical timeline begins with the kingdom of Babylon and ends with the Second Coming of Jesus Christ.

Within this history of the Gentile nations is found a prophecy concerning the nation of Israel which is called the prophecy of the seventy sevens (Dan 9:24-27). Because the visions of Daniel concern primarily the Gentile nations, the inclusion of a prophecy that concerns the nation of Israel interrupts the *flow* of the visions concerning the Gentile nations. The prophecy of the Seventy Sevens which interrupts the visions of the Gentile nations causes a *gap* in the visions concerning the Gentile nations. This *gap* or it could be called a parenthesis is a break in the flow of the visions concerning the Gentile nations. The *gap* in the flow of the prophecies concerning the Gentile nations is mentioned here as a basis for the subject matter of this chapter.

The existence of a *gap* in the flow of the prophecies concerning the

Gentile nations not only gives credence to the existence of a *gap* in the prophecy of the seventy sevens, but also gives legitimacy to the understanding of a *gap* in the seventy sevens. As has been stated before, the prophecy of the seventy sevens is located in Dan 9:24-27. The gap in this prophecy is found in Dan 9:26.

The end of the prophecy of the seventy sevens is seen in the finishing of transgression and sin which is done through atonement. Atonement then leads to righteousness, the end of vision and prophecy and the anointing of the most holy one (Dan 9:25). Found within the prophecy of the seventy sevens are also the main *steps* that lead to the conclusion of the prophecy which is found in Dan 9:25. The first main step is the decree to rebuild the temple and the city of Jerusalem (Dan 9:25). The second main step is the coming of the Anointed One (Dan 9:25) and the third main step is the setting up of the Abomination of Desolation (Dan 9:27).

The three main steps give a timeline to the prophecy. The time between the first main step until the second main step is 69 sevens (Dan 9:25); that is, the time between the decree to rebuild Jerusalem and the coming of the Anointed One. According to the prophecy, after the 69th seven, the Anointed One will be cut off, Jerusalem and the sanctuary will be destroyed and there will be a period of continuing war (Dan 9:26).

The final seven does not begin until Dan 9:27 with the discussion concerning the setting up of the Abomination of Desolation. Between the end of the 69th seven and the beginning of the 70th seven, there is a *gap* or it can also be called a parenthesis. What is to be understood is that Dan 9:26 does not belong to the first 69 sevens, nor does it belong to the 70th seven. Dan 9:26 is the *gap* between the 69th seven and the 70th seven. The period of the final seven ends with the death of the one who is the Abomination of Desolation (Dan 9:27). The Abomination of Desolation is the Anti-Christ (Rev 13:14, 15), who is defeated by the Lord Jesus Christ at His Second Coming (Rev 17:12-14).

The gap between the 69th seven and the 70th seven contain three main events which point to the beginning of the 70th seven. The first event is the cutting off of the Anointed One (Dan 9:26). This first event was fulfilled in the death of Jesus Christ.[131] The second event is the destruction of the temple (Dan 9:26). This event was fulfilled in 70 BCE when the Romans under Titus entered the city of Jerusalem and destroyed both the city of Jerusalem and the temple. The third event found between the 69th seven and the 70th seven will be the state of war that continues until the end (Dan 9:27). Jesus said that one of the signs of His return that precede the end will be the continuation of war (Matt 24:6).

What is interesting about the three events that are found in the gap between the 69th seven and the 70th seven is their order. The order is: the death of the Anointed One, the destruction of the Temple and the continuation of war to the end. These same events in the same order are found in the words and life of Jesus. Jesus was crucified, the temple was destroyed in 70 BCE and Jesus stated that war would continue until the end (Matt 24:1-6).

The subject of this chapter will be the *gap* that exists within the timeline of the prophecies of the seventy sevens. This *gap* covers the period of time from the death of Jesus Christ until the beginning of the seventy seven, which is seven years before the Second Coming of Jesus Christ. This period of time has been called the Church Age and the Age of Grace.

The phrase the Age of Grace is an unfortunate label given to this period of time. The reason for this is that the label the *Age of* Grace implies that there was/is a period of time when grace was not the means by which God relates to His creation. The truth, however, is that grace is the only means by which God relates to His entire creation. There is not, has not been nor will be a moment when God does not relate by grace to all of His creation. Thus, to designate a certain period of time within all eternity as the Age of Grace is by the mere label indicating that there are other periods of time when grace was not in existence or was not the means by which God related to creation.

The labeling of the *gap* in the timeline of the seventy sevens between the end of the 69th seven and the beginning of the 70th seven as the Age of Grace is based on the idea that throughout the history of the world, God works out His purpose by different means and in different stages.[132] For the purpose

97

of this study, the discussion of the different means of how God works out His purpose will be limited to what is called the Old Testament and the New Testament.

We begin this section with grace. Grace is kindness which is shown to someone who does not deserve such kindness.[133] According to the definition, grace is both the sentiment and the action towards someone. Grace is the reaching out to the helpless with the help that is needed.

In spite of this definition of grace, there are those who say that salvation for the believer in the Old Testament was by works and the animal sacrifices presented in the writings of the Old Testament. This position, however, is inaccurate. There has never been a time when salvation was by works or by the animal sacrifices listed in the Old Testament. Salvation in the Old Testament era was by faith in grace. If salvation in the Old Testament era was by the Law/works, then what did Adam, Eve, Abraham, Sarah do before the Law was given?

The fact that in the Old Testament era, God related to humanity through grace is seen firstly, in the first promise[134] of salvation which is found in Gen 3:15. After Adam and Eve had taken from the fruit of the Tree of the Knowledge of Good and Evil and sinned, in their meeting with God, God pronounced certain judgments or consequences of their actions. The first judgment spoken by God was to the Serpent (Gen 3:14, 15). There are several

98

points worth noting in this. The first point is that the Serpent after deceiving Eve was still hanging around. If the Serpent had left the Garden of Eden after deceiving Eve, God would not have been able to, at that moment and in the presence of Adam and Eve, have been able to speak with the Serpent. The second point worth noting is that after Adam and Eve had blamed someone else[135] for their sin; God judged the Serpent first (Gen 3:14, 15). Although the sin of Adam and Eve plunged the world into darkness and death (Rom 5:12-21), [136] God addressed the Serpent first in judgment. In God's pronouncement on the Serpent, God makes a promise that the damage done by the Serpent will not last forever, but will be undone by the seed of the woman (Gen 3:15). The damage done by the Serpent resulted in death to the race and destruction to creation itself. The fact is, God was under no obligation to undo the damage caused by sin. If God were to un-do the damage caused by sin, this choice and resulting action would be of grace and mercy. So the un-doing of the damage, that is death, is the gift of new life to those who have died.

When God breathed into Adam the breath of life (Gen 2:7) two gifts were given. The first gift was the very action of God breathing life into Adam. The second gift was what God gave, what He breathed into Adam and that was life itself. God was under no obligation to create the race or to give them life. What we are to see is that life is a gift of God. For God to undo the damage caused by sin, which is death, God must give again the gift of life. Since sin results in death, which is the loss of Paradise, which is to say, the loss of a personal relationship with God; the giving again of life is salvation, a re-entering of Paradise, a re-entering into a personal relationship with God.

The manner which God relates to the race, in the Old Testament era is of grace through faith. This fact was first seen in the first promise of salvation that Adam and Eve heard shortly after their sin. God's manner of relating by grace to the human race is seen secondly in Abraham. God promised to bless the world through Abraham and to make Abraham a great nation (Gen 12:1-3). After a time of struggle and self-attempts to have a son, Abraham finally *believed* God and because Abraham *believed* God, Abraham was reckoned[137] as righteous[138] by God (Gen 15:6). What is to be seen in this is the fact that for Abraham to have a right standing/to be righteous with God it was not because Abraham followed the Law or performed works, but because he believed God.

In the Old Testament era, God related to the human race through grace, as also seen by the words of David. David wrote that the one who is forgiven and blessed is the one whose sin is not counted against him or her (Psalm 32:1, 2). Paul understood David's words to mean that righteousness is given to the one who does not work but believes in God (Rom 4:4-8).

What is to be understood from the discussion regarding Abraham and David is that both Abraham and David understood that a right relationship with God was through faith and grace. The flip-side of their understanding was that a right relationship with God, also termed righteousness, was not through the Law. Both David and Abraham understood that the Law did not produce righteousness, a right relationship with God. The significance of mentioning Abraham and David in the discussion regarding righteousness that comes through faith is that David and Abraham were foundational patriarchs of the faith[139] who lived during the Old Testament era.

Although God gave the Law to the nation of Israel, the giving of the Law did not establish a relational basis of works between God and Israel. Paul states that the giving of the Law to Israel 400^{140} years after the giving of the promise of righteousness through faith pronounced to Abraham does not nullify the promise previously made by God (Gal 3:17). What is seen is that God established the basis of righteousness with Abraham. The established basis for righteousness and life was faith. There was never a time when God nullified the basis of life based on the promise given to Abraham and to the rest of the world.

The basis for righteousness by faith was given to Abraham, but was not meant only for Abraham. The promise of God to Abraham was that the whole world would be blessed through him (Gen 12:1-3). In addition, Paul writes that the basis of being reckoned as righteous by faith was not only for Abraham but was also for all people who believe in Christ (Rom 4:23, 24).

The Law was given for two main purposes. The first purpose was to define sin (Gal 3:19-23). The second purpose of the Law was to lead people to Jesus Christ (Gal 3:24). The meaning of the Law is fulfilled by Jesus Christ (Matt 17) and both the Law and the Prophets point toward Jesus Christ (Luke 24:25-28).

The Law was never given as a basis of righteousness before God. The Law could never give life or righteousness (Gal 3:21). If the Law was able to give life or impart righteousness, at any time, then both life and righteousness would be through the Law and there would not be a reason for faith, for the promise of God given to the world through Abraham. Furthermore, if the Law produced righteousness, the life, death, resurrection of Jesus Christ would be of no value. The fact that the Law was never given as a basis for righteousness is seen in the fact that the Law and the Old Testament sacrificial system was only copies of the heavenly reality (Heb 9:23). What this means is that the Law and the sacrificial system did not function on its own, nor did it have any true meaning on its own. The function and the meaning of the Law and the sacrificial system is found only in Jesus Christ.

It is true that the full content of faith was not made clear until the coming of Jesus Christ into the world (Gal 3:23). However, the fact that there were still mysteries concerning the faith does not mean that the Law was a basis for righteousness.

There is a question that must be asked and answered concerning the Law. This question is: If God gave the Law as a basis for righteousness; why would God give the Law and sacrifices for salvation only to condemn those who followed them? God would be very inconsistent and even a liar for giving the Law as a basis for righteousness and then condemning people for following the Law which God gave. If God gave the Law to Israel and then condemned them for following that Law, God would at best be inconsistent.

When history is looked at there can be seen periods of time when society transitioned from one period to another. However, these periods of transitions are not rigid, nor are they clearly delineated from the periods that precede or follow. There are periods of transition which contain within them emphasis from the previous period and the newly born emphasis from the period which is just beginning. However, what is to be seen is that there is an overlap between the two periods of history.

What the previous discussion means for salvation history is that there are not clear and enclosed periods of time separate and distinct from each other. The periods or ages which make up salvation history are periods which overlap other periods of time. Thus, there is not to be found a period of time separate and enclosed from other periods of time in which God can relate to the human race in one manner, which is distinct from how God relates to the human race in other periods of time.

The *gap* between the 69th seven and the 70th seven has also been called the Church Age. This label, while much more palatable than labeling this period of time The Age of Grace, still has much to be desired. The labeling of the gap between the 69th seven and the 70th seven as the Church Age, implies that the Church did/does not exist beyond the time limit delineated as the gap between the 69th seven and the 70th seven.

The question to be asked is: Is the Church a New Testament phenomenon? We begin to explore this question by defining the term *church*. The word *church* is from the Greek ἐκκλησία. Ἐκκλησία is defined as a congregation of Christians, implying interacting membership.[141] ἐκκλησία is used in reference to house churches, local churches and the church universal.[142] The previous definition of ἐκκλησία would seem to imply that the word was coined for use in the New Testament era to define God's people. However, the word ἐκκλησία is not only a New Testament term. ἐκκλησία was in use several hundred years before the New Testament era and was used to refer to an assembly of persons constituted by well-defined membership.[143] One understanding of ἐκκλησία is that ἐκκλησία means *called out ones*.[144] There is disagreement, however, over this understanding of ἐκκλησία. J. Louw and E. Nida state the understanding of ἐκκλησία as *called out ones* is not warranted by its use in the New Testament or its earlier use. They go on to say that the earlier use of ἐκκλησία is of a socio-political entity.[145] However, there is still room for discussion over the idea of *called out ones* for ἐκκλησία.

The understanding of ἐκκλησία as having well defined membership would lead to the understanding that those who belonged to the ἐκκλησία would understand that the membership vows they take leading to acceptance within the ἐκκλησία would separate them in some manner from those who did not belong to the ἐκκλησία. Whether there was an invitation to join the ἐκκλησία or not, there would still be some idea, some understanding that those who belonged to the ἐκκλησία were those who came out of the total population which surrounded the ἐκκλησία.

The point under discussion, however, is not if ἐκκλησία has implied within its definition a sense of being called out. The point under discussion is if the Church is a New Testament phenomenon. The fact that the word defined as *church*, that is ἐκκλησία, was used several hundred years before the New Testament era leads to the understanding that the *idea* of the Church as a group separate from society did not originate in the New Testament era.

For the purposes of this study, the meaning of ἐκκλησία, the Church, will be limited to the people who belong to God. The Church, as understood in this study, means the people of God. A question that arises from the study of theology is: How many people does God have? This question can be asked in the following manner: Does God have one people or two?

One answer to this question is that God has two people. These two groups are: Israel and the Church.[146] This view states that Israel is God's earthly people while the Church is God's heavenly people.[147] The further understanding of this view is that God has different and distinct plans for each of His people. The two people of God view is based in part on what is said to be the unfulfilled promises and prophecies of the Old Testament.[148] However, the fulfillment of the prophecies in the Old Testament and in the New Testament is Jesus Christ (Matt 5:17) and Him alone. It is Jesus who fulfills the Law and the *Prophets*. Because it is Jesus Christ who fulfills the Law and the Prophets; there will be no fulfillment to any prophecy apart from the person of Jesus Christ.

In disagreement to the view that God has two people is the view that God has only one people.[149] God's one people is represented by those who believed and were reckoned as righteous in the Old Testament era and by those who believe and are reckoned as righteous in the New Testament era. This view states that though separated by time and full content of the faith, there exists only one people of God. In the world today are many Christians. Some of the Christians who are living today have an extensive knowledge and understanding of the faith. Some Christians today, however, have a much more limited knowledge and understanding of the faith. The *amount* of the knowledge and understanding of the faith does not separate these Christians into two different peoples of God. Christians who have a limited knowledge and understanding of the faith are just as much the people of God as the Christians who have an extensive knowledge and understanding of the faith. In support of the view which states that God has one people, we will look again at some topics already discussed.

The first topic which leads support to God having one people is the promise that God made to Abraham. The promise of God to Abram (whose name was changed to Abraham (Gen 17:5)) was that God would bless the whole world through Abraham (Gen 12:1-3). God's promise to Abraham was to be a fulfillment of the original blessing on the human race (Gen 1:28). Abraham, called the Father of the Jewish people, is in truth the Father of *all* who believe in God and are reckoned as righteous (Rom 4:9-12). Abraham is the father of those who believe whether the one who believe is circumcised, that is belonged to the Jewish people and the father of the one who believes but is not circumcised, that is one who belonged to the Gentiles. What this means is that Abraham is the father of all who believe and are reckoned as righteous, whether the person is of Jewish or Gentile heritage.

A further statement to be made is that Abraham is not the father of either the Jewish people who do not believe but base their relationship to God on the Law (Rom 4:13) or the Gentiles who have not believed. Abraham is the father of the people of God; that is the father of those who believe and are reckoned as righteous. He is not the father of a people who are not righteous by faith. This is clearly seen in Gen 12:1-3 where the promise of God to Abraham is to bless the *whole world* through Abraham and Abraham's seed. From the promise of God to Abraham it is clearly seen that God's blessings are for all those who bless Abraham, whether they are from the people called Israel or from the people called the Gentiles. God's promise to Abraham is one. Because God's promise is one; the recipients of that one promise of God are also one. The oneness of God's people is seen fulfilled in Jesus Christ who came to make the two divisions[150] of humanity one (Eph 2:11-22). The promises God were to Abraham and his seed. However, Abraham's seed is one and not many (Gal 3:16). The one seed of Abraham is not the nation of Israel, either those who believe or those who do not believe. This one seed is Jesus Christ (Gal 3:16) and not the physical nation of Israel.

In addition, the time of the life of Christ is intrinsically important to salvation history, to the understanding that God has one people, and that the Law was not a means of righteousness. Paul wrote that when the time had fully come, Jesus came into this world (Gal 4:4). The word *fully* is from the Greek πλήπωμα. Πλήρωμα means the totality of a period of time, with the implication of proper completion, end.[151] Jesus not only lived in the fullness of time, He also lived in the transition period between the old and the new. Because Jesus is not only the fulfillment of the Law and the Prophets and He was also born in the fullness of time; what we are to see is that Jesus is also the transition between the old and the new, thus, there is no clear stop and start marks for an understanding of dispensations.[152]

In support of the view that God has only one people, it is to be seen that Paul the Apostle speaks of both Gentiles and Jews who believe in Christ being grafted into the same olive root (Rom 11:17-24). The olive root is to be understood as the promise of God given to the world through the Patriarchs (Rom 11:28) and is embodied in Jesus Christ (John 15:1). To be grafted into the olive root, Jesus Christ, is by faith (Rom 11:20) and not by the Law. When a person is grafted into Jesus Christ, that person becomes part of the Body of Christ. One of the names of the Body of Christ is the Church (Col 1:24). The Church, therefore is made up of all who are grafted into Christ by faith, whether that person comes out of the Jewish people or is a member of the Gentiles. Paul expands on this idea when he says that the descendents of Abraham are the children of the promise of faith (Rom 9:8-9). He makes a distinction between the Jew who is a descendent of Abraham and the Jew who is a Jew physically but who is not righteous by faith and thus does not belong to the promise of God. Jesus, in talking to the Jews made the same distinction as Paul, between the descendent of Abraham and those who were not the descendent of Abraham (John 8:31-47). Jesus' statements regarding the difference between those who were of physical Jewish heritage and those who belonged to God by faith express the same distinction as Paul's comments.

Jesus named those who were not of faith but who were physically of the Jewish people, as sons of the Devil (John 8:44).

There are those who state that the distinction between the physical nation of Israel and the promise of righteousness by faith is the means of belonging to God. This means that those who believe in Jesus as Lord and Savior constitute the true Israel.[153] The germ of this idea may have some truth to it. The germ being that Israel as an entity represents the people of God in the Old Testament era. However, there still exists in the Bible a distinction between Israel and the people of God.

The teaching that God has one people is found also in the one new person that Christ created in Himself (Eph 2:14, 15). This one new person is composed of Gentiles who were formerly excluded from the promises of God (Eph 2:11-13) and the Jews, those who were included in the promises (Eph 2:12). The promises are the promise made to Abraham that God would bless the world through him. The promises are of faith, not Law or physical heritage. Paul further states that physical heritage is of no value as a mark of belonging to or of entering the people of God (Gal 6:15).

Paul describes this one new person as fellow citizens with each other (Eph 2:19). All who belong to Christ's new people are one household (Eph 2:19). This one new people in Christ are all built on the foundation of the apostles and prophets (Eph 2:20). To be built on the foundation of the apostles and prophets means that the promises of God made through the prophets in the Old Testament era and the promises of God made through the apostles in the New Testament era all point to, are foundational to and belong to the one new people of God. What is to be understood in this is that neither the prophets in the Old Testament era, nor the apostles in the New Testament era taught that God had two people.

While it is true that the prophets in the Old Testament era did not fully understand the mystery of God which was only revealed to the apostles in the New Testament era. This mystery was that the Gentiles would be equal citizens in the one People of God (Eph 3:6). Because the prophets in the Old Testament era did not understand the mystery of God that the Gentiles would be one body with the believing Jews (Eph 3:6); their writings may have indicated that there are two people of God. However, the truth is that God has only one people made up of all who believe in Christ.

The next topic that leads support to the teaching that God has only one people is the promise of God to Abraham. God promised Abraham that the whole world would be blessed through him (Gen 12:3). The promise of God was that He would make Abraham into a great nation (Gen 12:1). God further promised that He would bless the nation that He would make out of Abraham. This nation had as its purpose to be the channel through which God would bless the world (Gen 12:1-3). This means that the promise to Abraham was

111

intended for the whole world and not just for a portion of the world. The teaching that God's promise to Abraham meant that God had one people is seen in the fact that there were many Non-Israelites who left Egypt with the sons of Abraham and were included within the promises of God (Joshua 8:35). The promise of God is experienced by faith; for it is only by faith that a person is reckoned as righteous (Gen 15:6).

Another topic or statement that God has one people is found in the statement of Jesus. Jesus said that He is the fulfillment of the Law and the Prophets (Matt 5:17). What this means is that all of the promises and messages of the prophets are fulfilled in Jesus Christ. As has been stated previously, Jesus Christ has as His purpose the creating of one people in Himself. We are to understand from this that since Jesus is the fulfillment of the Law and the Prophets; and Jesus' purpose is to create one people, therefore the message of the Law and the Prophets is also a message that teaches that God has one people. This one people of God, that began in the act of Creation, was re-established in promise of salvation[154] in the Garden of Eden after the Fall of Adam and Eve, was named in the promise to Abraham[155] and was fulfilled at the Day of Pentecost when the Holy Spirit[156] came to indwell everyone who believes in Christ Jesus. Pentecost is called the beginning of the Church.[157] It is not, however, the beginning of the people of God. Ladd recognizes this distinction when he calls the group of disciples before Pentecost the embryo church.[158] While it is to be recognized that there is a difference between the people of God in the Old Testament era and the people of God in the New Testament era; the fact remains that there were those who belonged to God in the Old Testament era as well as in the New Testament era.

There are differences between the Old Testament era and the New Testament era, for example: In the New Testament era, the name and person of the Messiah is known. In the Old Testament era, the name of the Messiah was still a mystery. In addition, in the New Testament era, the work of the Messiah is much more clearly expounded upon. In the New Testament era, beginning at Pentecost, the promise of the Holy Spirit being poured out upon all (Joel 2:28-29) would be realized.

The teaching that God has only one people and one means of making righteous the one who believes is seen in the fact that the sacrificial system of the Old Testament was only shadows, copies of the reality and not the reality themselves (Heb 8:5-6; 9:23). What this means is that the forgiveness offered and received by the people in the Old Testament era was hinged upon the ministry of Jesus Christ on the Cross. In fact, it could be stated that the sins of the people before Christ were forgiven only provisionally and that true and total forgiveness waited until the coming, death and resurrection of Jesus Christ (Rom 3:25).

Paul wrote that before Christ, God left sins unpunished (Rom 3:25).

What Paul meant when he wrote that *he left sins committed beforehand unpunished* is that the sins in the Old Testament era were punished symbolically in the animal sacrifices but would be fully punished in the sacrifice of Christ.[159] The sacrifice of Christ was a once for all experience. Christ came into the world and died once. His death was for all the sins of all people who have ever lived (Heb 9:24-28). The death of Jesus Christ, then, covered all time, from its beginning in Creation until the end of eternity. Not only did the death of Jesus cover all time; but the death of Jesus was for all sin. When Jesus died on the Cross, He bore on His body sin (1 Pet 2:24). The sins which Jesus bore was the sin of the whole world (John 1:29).

Though there are differences between the experience of the righteous in the Old Testament era and the New Testament era; we see from the above that those who belonged to God in the Old Testament era are included within the people of God. This fact is seen on the Mount of Transfiguration. Jesus takes three disciples with Him and they go up to the Mount to pray. While on the Mount, Jesus was transfigured[160] before the eyes of the three disciples. After Jesus was transfigured before the disciples, the disciples then saw three figures: Jesus, Moses and Elijah (Matt 17:1-3). Moses and Elijah with Jesus is very significant. Moses was given the Law and Elijah represents the Prophets. Moses, Elijah and Jesus were seen by the disciples having a discussion. We are told what Moses, Elijah and Jesus discussed that day on the mountain. The topic of discussion was how the Law and the Prophets would be fulfilled in the death of Jesus (Luke 9:30). With Moses and Elijah together with Jesus on the Mount talking about Jesus' upcoming death, it can be clearly seen that the Law and the Prophets are fulfilled in the life, death and resurrection of Jesus Christ. The whole Old Testament sacrificial system, Law and prophetic utterances all point toward and are fulfilled in Jesus. We see again in the fact of Moses and Elijah discussing with Jesus about His upcoming death that the Law and the Prophets were not given by God as a different means to salvation; that is as a means to be reckoned as righteous. The message of the Law and the Prophets is Jesus Christ and righteousness by faith. In addition, in the presence of Moses and Elijah on the Mount with Jesus, it is to be seen that God has but one people that span all of time from creation to eternity.

The teaching that God has only one people is found in the mystery of God that was revealed to the Apostles. This mystery is that God, in Christ, is including Gentiles as equal heirs with the Jewish believers in *one body* (Eph 3:5, 6; Col 1:26). What this tells us is that the Prophets and Patriarchs of the Old Testament were not as aware of God's plan and purpose as Believers in the New Testament era. However, because Believers in the Old Testament era were not as fully aware or were not given the whole knowledge, this does not mean that God has two peoples or two different ways of relating to people.

God has one people who are found *in Christ*. If God had two peoples, then the people of God in Christ would be two. However, Paul wrote that *in Christ* there is neither Jew nor Greek (Gal 3:28). The point here is to be emphasized that in Christ, there is neither Jew nor Greek. How can there be two peoples of God when *in* Christ there is neither Jew nor Greek? There cannot be two people of God. What Paul teaches here is that there is only one people of God. In fact, there is no clearer statement of the truth that God has only one people then the statement by Paul that in Christ there is neither Jew nor Greek. This one people is called by various names throughout the Bible. The fact that the one people of God have been called by various names, does not nullify the fact that there is and has been only one people of God. To unite this one people in a loving unit is the purpose of God. The purpose of God is to bring into *one body* in Christ all the peoples of the world (Eph 2:14-18).

The one people of God who are found from the beginning of Creation until the end of eternity are for the purpose of this study, discussed more fully in the *gap* in the prophecy of the seventy sevens (Dan 9:24-27). This discussion of the one people of God during the time period between the 69th seven and the 70th seven is found in summary form in Revelation 2, 3.

The vision of John called the Revelation of Jesus Christ is a letter containing many symbols. It is true that Revelation is highly symbolic. However, the meanings of the symbols are given as well as the symbols. The mistake that many make in reference to the book of Revelation is that they

116

give up on the book and its many symbols before they discover the meanings of the symbols written in the book itself. The symbols are given and then explained. For instance, John, in his vision sees seven golden lamp stands (Rev 1:12). The golden lamp stands are symbols for the seven churches (Rev 1:20). A second instance of a symbol and its definition are the seven stars that John saw in the hand of the One who walked amongst the seven golden lamp stands (Rev 1:16). The seven stars are the angels of the seven churches (Rev 1:20).

The book of Revelation, along with its many symbols is a document that does not always flow easily from one point to another.[161] John, in his vision, sees events in heaven and in the next chapter sees events on earth. There is structure to the vision of Revelation, however, and this structure is given in Rev 1:19. John is told to write what he has seen, what is now and what will take place later (Rev 1:19). Rev 1:19 is considered by many to be the outline of the vision given to John. One view of the outline of Rev 1:19 is that it is a three-fold division to Revelation.[162] The three divisions are: the things that you have seen, the things that are, and the things that will be. There is also an understanding of Rev 1:19 that is a two-fold division to the book of Revelation.[163] This view states that what John is told is: write the things that you are about to see, that is both what now is and what lies yet in the future.[164]

According to the three-fold division of Rev 1:19, the things that John

117

has seen are found in chapter 1. The second division is found in chapters 2 and 3 which are the things that are. The things that are refer to the present age.[165] According to the three-fold division view of Rev 1:19, chapters 4-22 are the things that will be.

According to Mounce, the two-fold division consists of the things that are and those things that lie in the future. The difference between a two-fold division and a three-fold division to the Revelation is very minimal. In both views, there is the command to write the things that are now and the things that are in the future. However, not all agree that chapters 4-22 of Revelation contain future events.[166] Sweet is of the opinion that Rev 1:19 is an adaptation of a common phrase and only expresses the mystery of the totality of existence.[167]

One needs to ask the question: is Sweet correct in his view? We know what John was told to write. John is told is to write on a scroll what he sees (Rev 1:11). John is then told that after he wrote what he saw, he was to send the scroll to the churches of Ephesus, Smyrna, Pergamum, Thyatira, Sardis, Philadelphia, and Laodicea (Rev 1:11). If one is to follow Sweet's thought, what John saw was the mystery of existence from creation unto eternity. What would be the purpose of sending a scroll containing what the churches already knew? Christians then, as well as today, understand that the mystery of existence is Jesus Christ (John 14:6). John did not see in his vision an

118

explanation of Christ as the mystery of existence. John saw coming events that would affect the seven churches. This we know from what John wrote to the churches. After John saw the totality of the vision and wrote what he saw; he wrote to the churches and said: *Look, he is coming with the clouds* (Rev 1:7). What John saw were the events that lead up to the Second Coming of Jesus Christ. John was not writing a mystical scroll concerning the mystery of existence. John saw in a vision and wrote on a scroll the events that lead to Christ's coming again to this world.

As it can be seen, both a two-fold division and a three-fold division are records of the present and the future. The major difference between a two-fold division and a three-fold division is that in a three-fold division, the things that John saw (chapter 1) are separate from the things that are. The separation from or the inclusion with of chapter 1 from chapters 2, 3 does not affect the fact that John saw a vision that included both the present and the future. The third division, according to a three-fold division begins with Rev 4:1 with the words *after this*. The phrase *after this* refers to after the period of time represented by Rev 2, 3.[168] As it has already been stated, chapters 2, 3 refer to the things that are, that is the present age. Thus, it would be understood that since Rev 4:1 refers to a period of time *after* the present age, Rev 4:1 refers to the future.

The phrase *after this* in Rev 4:1 is not the only indication that future events are being described in Rev 4:1. It can be seen that beginning with Rev 4:1, there is a change both in location and in content. The location of chapters 2, 3 of Revelation is on the earth. In Rev 4, there is a different location. John is called to heaven and what John sees beginning with Rev 4 and to the end of the vision occurs either in heaven or the event is seen by John from heaven. Beginning with Rev 4:1, John is in heaven; this is understood in the words of the command to *come up here* (Rev 4:1). The phrase *come up here* is also used in Rev 11:12 in reference to the two witnesses. The two witnesses will be witness for Jesus Christ during the period before Christ returns. These witnesses are killed and their bodies will lay in the street for 3½ days (Rev 11:7-9). After this 3½ day period, these two witnesses will receive again the breath of life from God, rise up and be seen by those who killed them (Rev 11:11). After being seen by those that killed them, these two witnesses will be called to heaven by the command *come up here.*

Rev 4:1 not only describes a different location from Rev 2, 3; the message of Rev 4:1 is different than Rev 2, 3. In Rev 2, 3 the conditions of the seven churches was described and how they needed to change to please God. Beginning with Rev 4, the message of the vision of John changes from a message of exhortation to holiness to a message that is called the Day of the Wrath of God (Rev 6:17). What we are to understand from the above discussion is that beginning with Rev 4:1, the events seen by John are not in the present age, but are in the future.

Rev 1:19, whether viewed as a three-fold division or a two-fold division does include the whole content of the vision of John.[169] For the purpose of this chapter, we want to look at the things that are, that is, the present age. This study will follow the thought that chapters 2, 3 of Revelation describes the things that are, that is the present age. The things that are, the present age, found in chapters 2, 3 are the seven letters to the seven churches. The present age is the *gap* between the 69th seven and the 70th seven in the prophecy of Dan 9:24-27.

We begin with the fact that the seven churches of Revelation 2, 3 were seven literal churches located in Asia Minor, what is today called Turkey. The seven churches do not exist today as organizations. However, there are in Turkey, Christians who are the descendants of those seven literal churches. In addition to being seven literal churches, when the seven letters to the seven churches are studied, what will be discovered is that the *conditions* found in the seven churches are *conditions* found in local churches throughout history.[170] For example, the church at Ephesus was a church that had lost its first love (Rev 2:4) and was in need of revival. There have been throughout history and there are local churches today that have lost their first love and are also in need of revival. The church at Smyrna was a church that existed in worldly poverty and stood strong in the face of attack by the society which surrounded her (Rev 2:9). There are churches found scattered throughout the world that though poor in worldly wealth are facing persecution and attack. These churches also are standing firm in their witness for Jesus Christ, in spite of these attacks. The church at Pergamum was a church that had stood firm in her faith for Jesus Christ, yet, in her was found teachers who were quietly teaching a compromise with the world (Rev 2:14). Throughout history and today, there are to be found churches that have stood strong in their faith, yet, there was a time when new teachers came in and began to teach the view that there were many things that could be taken from society, in essence to compromise the standards of the Gospel with worldly teaching. The church at Thyatira was a church that had been strong yet there came a time when the teaching of the church reflected tolerance toward society (Rev 2:20). There have been and are today churches that are compromising with the society in which they are found. The message of the Gospel is being diluted to reflect many of the teachings of society. The church at Sardis was a church that at one time was on fire for the Lord, yet, after time, became more and more a church of formality, one that lacked the passion for Christ, holiness, and missions. Many of the churches today can be described as churches that have lost their passion for Christ, holiness and missions. These churches meet regularly, but can be described as churches of mere formality. The church at Philadelphia was a local church that remained passionate for Christ, holiness and missions, in spite of the fact that she was a church tired and weak from remaining firm for Christ (Rev 3:8). There can be found churches throughout history and even today who have remained passionate for Christ, holiness and missions. Finally, the church at Laodicea was a church that had become rich and well established but spiritually was lukewarm (Rev 3:16, 17). Because of her condition, the church at Laodicea was not able to provide the healing message of the Gospel to any. On many street corners of the world, there are local churches that are well established, yet, have lost their reason for existence. These churches have no healing message from God to offer.

What is to be seen from the descriptions of the seven churches of Rev 2, 3, is that the messages in the seven letters to the seven churches are appropriate and applicable to local churches from the time of the writing down of John's vision to the Return of Jesus Christ. There have been throughout the history of the Church from the beginning of the period of time called the *gap* between the 69th seven and the 70th seven, local churches that can be described by one or more of the letters to the seven churches in Rev 2, 3. In addition, there are local churches today that fit the description found in each of the seven letters to the seven churches. What we are to understand from this is that though the seven churches were literal churches that existed in the days when John saw his vision; the churches are also examples of a type of local church that has, is and will exist until the Second Coming of Jesus Christ.

The seven churches of Revelation are thus, 7 literal churches and because of the conditions found with them, the churches are also types of churches that have existed throughout the whole period of time beginning from Pentecost and ending with Christ's Second Coming.

The seven churches of Revelation, in addition to being seven literal churches and seven types of churches, are also a timeline of the spiritual history of the Christian Church from Pentecost until Christ comes again.[171] The reasons that the 7 churches of Revelation make up a spiritual history of the Christian Church is that John in the beginning of his vision sees Jesus standing amongst the 7 lamp stands (Rev 1:12, 13). The symbolism of Jesus standing amongst the lamp stands is that Jesus, is personally involved and with the Christian Church. Jesus did not nor does He walk *just* amongst a certain number of Christian Churches. Jesus has been with the Church since the inception of the Church and will continue to be amongst the Church until the end of time.

The message of Revelation itself is another reason to understand that the 7 Churches of Revelation comprise a spiritual history of the Church. We saw above that the *conditions* described in the seven letters to the seven churches describe the *condition* of Christian churches throughout history. Thus, it is to be seen that the conditions of the churches described, leads to the understanding that the seven churches of Revelation comprise a spiritual history of the Christian Church from its inception to the end.

Another reason to understand that the seven letters to the seven churches is intended for the Church from its inception to the end is in the words of Jesus. The letters end with the phrase: *The one who has an ear, let it be heard what the Spirit says to the Churches.* Jesus told John to write the vision that he had seen (Rev 1:19). The vision consisted in part as 7 letters to 7 Churches. Each letter ends with the same phrase: to listen to what the Spirit says to the Churches. The point here is that each Church was to listen to what was said to all the churches, not just to that particular church. The individual letters themselves were intended for all the Churches.

The prophecy of the Seventy Sevens is primarily a prophecy that concerns the nation of Israel. However, found within the prophecy of the Seventy Sevens is a *gap* of time between the 69th Seven and the 70th Seven. This *gap* of time, for the purposes of this study, is called the Time of the Fullness of the Gentiles (Rom 11:25).

The Fullness of the Gentiles is a phrase that has several understandings amongst the commentaries. There are three main views for the Fullness of the Gentiles. The first view is the completing of the Gentile Mission. The second view is the complete blessing God intends for the Gentiles. Finally, the third view is the complete number of Gentiles saved.[172] To come to an understanding of this phrase we begin with the Greek. The

Greek πλήρωμα, depending upon its context, can be understood in three ways. The first meaning is a total quantity, with emphasis upon completeness, full number, or fullness.[173] The second meaning is a quantity which fills a space.[174] The third meaning of πλήρωμα is to come to an end of a period of time, with the implication of the completion of an implied purpose or plan.[175] As it can be seen, the three meanings for the word πλήρωμα correspond to the three views concerning the phrase the Fullness of the Gentiles.

The understanding of the phrase the Fullness of the Gentiles is found in the context of Rom 9-11. Within these chapters, Paul is describing the condition, the situation of the people of Israel in relationship to the Gentiles and the Gospel. Paul begins his discussion with the fact that not all those who are physically born into Israel are Abraham's children (Rom 9:7, 8). There are, according to Paul, two groups within Israel. There are those who are physically born into Israel and there are those who are Abraham's children. The two groups found within Israel are groups defined by the Law and faith. The Israelites that depend upon the Law are not Abraham's children because they are not righteous (Rom 9:3-32). Abraham's children, we remember, are those who, like Abraham, have believed and are reckoned as righteous (Rom 10:3-4).

After Paul has established the fact that within Israel are two groups with one group basing its righteousness on the Law, and the second group believing in Christ, he states another principle. This principle is that God uses the same basis for righteousness for Gentile and Jew (Rom 10:12). This principle of righteousness by faith is what separates the believer in Christ from the Non-believer. The principle of righteousness by faith is applicable to those outside of Israel and for those within Israel. In other words, whether a person has been born physically into Israel or not, is of no importance. What is important is faith in Christ. We see again that God has only one people and only one means to righteousness.

Paul goes on to state that the present situation with Israel, which is the fact that not many of Israel had believed in Christ, did not mean that God had rejected Israel (Rom 11:1-2). Paul states that the lack of faith is not a lack of the message. He says that all had heard the message of the Gospel (Rom 11:18). Paul uses himself as an example of an Israelite that had believed in Christ (Rom 11: 1). Paul then goes on to show that the Old Testament had long ago foretold that there would come a time when Israel would not respond to God in faith (Rom 10:19-11:6). While the vast majority of Israel did not respond to God in faith, there has been and is a remnant that did believe in Christ (Rom 11:5-6). Paul sums up his discussion regarding Israel with the statement that there exists within Israel, two groups of people. The first group is those who have believed in Christ and the second group is called by Paul as the hardened (Rom 11:7).[176]

After Paul has shown that the Old Testament had foretold Israel's rejection, he then goes on to say that the Gentiles who believed will arouse the envy of Israel and cause Israel to believe in Christ (Rom 11:11). This necessitates of course, that Christians are living examples of the message of the Gospel of Jesus Christ. The coming to faith of the Gentiles is in part an action to arouse Israel to faith. Paul states that after the fullness of the Gentiles has occurred, all Israel will be saved (Rom 11:25, 26). So there is to be seen in the phrase the Fullness of the Gentiles an understanding of the purpose of the Gentile mission.

Paul, in stating that after the fullness of the Gentiles has occurred, all Israel will be saved, is echoing the teaching of the prophets that at the end of history, there will be a revival in Israel. Paul quotes Isaiah 59: 20, 21 and Isaiah 27:9 in Rom 11:26, 27 to establish the fact of Israel's return to God, at the end of history. What we understand from this is that the period of time of Israel's hardening should not be a surprise, but was foretold by the prophets. In part, we turn to Daniel's prophecy of the Seventy Sevens to see that salvation history includes a time of Israel's return to God. This period of time is Daniel's 70th Seven. Daniel's 70th Seven will be discussed more fully in the chapter on the Final Seven. Suffice it to say, at this point, that Daniel's Seventy Sevens includes both the time of the Fullness of the Gentiles and a time of the revival of Israel.

A question to be asked at this point in reference to the meanings offered for the phrase the Fullness of the Gentiles is: Does the phrase the Fullness of the Gentiles also mean that the full number of Gentiles who will believe, have believed? The answer is no. We begin with the understanding that Paul, by his use of the word *all*, in Rom 11:26, meant the nation of Israel at the end of history.[177] He did not mean every single Israelite living at the end of history. We see here that in this case, the words *all* and *fullness* do not mean every single human person. The truth is God loves the world (John 3:16). The word world is from κόσμος. Κόσμος is the universe as an ordered system.[178] While there are times when the word κόσμος is used in a restrictive sense, the contexts where this occurs is when the word κόσμος is used for the world system and people that stand opposed to God (1 Cor 6:2).

In the case of John 3:16, the *world* includes all of the created order. This includes the material creation as well as every single human person. The teaching of the Word of God is that God desires that all people accept the Gospel and be saved (1 Tim 2:4). In 1 Tim 2:4 the Greek translated *all people* as πᾶς ανθρωπος. Πᾶς means the totality of any collective, that is all, every,[179] while ἄνθρωπος means a human being.[180] God *desires* the salvation of the human race. The word *desires* is from θέλω. Θέλω means to purpose based upon a preference or desire.[181] θέλω has the added meaning of the active willing, the will urging to action.[182] Because θέλω means desire, in the sense of the will urging to action, we ask: what action has God provided for the salvation of the world? The answer to this question is found in John 3:16 where it says that God gave His Son in order that all who believe might be saved. We see the action, the desire of God in 1 John 2:2 where it is stated that Christ is the atoning sacrifice for the sins of the *whole,* ὅλος, world. The word ὅλος means whole, complete, entire.[183] Jesus Christ, as the Lamb of God, took away the sins of the world (John 1:29).

Yet, we also know that there will be those who in rejecting Christ will spend eternity in punishment (Matt 25:46). The fact that God loves the world does not mean that everyone in the world loves God. This sad fact Paul has already established in Rom 1-5 in his discussion regarding the wrath of God and righteousness by faith. In Rom 1:16, Paul states that the Gospel is the power of God for the salvation of everyone who believes. The point is that the Gospel is God's power for salvation *to the ones who believe.* The offer of salvation is offered to all. Here is the basic reason for the continuation of missionaries, evangelists, witnessing and just plain sharing of the Gospel. The offer of salvation is to be offered to all. In fact, one of the signs of the Return of Christ is the world-wide spread of the Gospel (Matt 24:14).

The discussion of the desire of God and the offer of salvation raises the question of the love of God. There are many who question the truth of God's love for the whole world. This questioning of God's love is expressed in a view that limit's the love of God and the scope of the atonement, which is to say those for whom Christ died. Those who limit the love of God say that God, while, perhaps, loving everyone, has done nothing to provide salvation for everyone. This view states that the love of God and the death of Christ as the Lamb of God are separate actions. God may love everyone, but Christ did not die as the payment for everyone's sin. This view is answered in the above discussion.

There are others who question God's love. This group, this questioning is phrased differently. While the first group does believe that God loves some, interesting that the ones who hold this view always include themselves in the group of God's love; this second group dismisses entirely God's love. This second group says that if God loves, then why......? Why do bad things happen is their question. The fact that bad things happen is proof, to this group, that God is not love.

While this study is not the place to go into detail regarding the existence of evil; suffice it to say that the existence of evil is in part the result of human action and not the action of God. The basic reference to this statement is Gen 3 where it states that because of the choice of Adam and Eve, sin, evil, death, hate, blame enter the world and affected the whole human race. There are two basic views to Gen 3. The first view is that Gen 3 is the account of the Fall of the human race. The second view is that Gen 3 is a religious story that points to truth. Both views lead to the same conclusion. That conclusion is that sin, evil, death, etc. is the result of human action and not God's. In addition to human choice, evil, bad is the result of the work of Satan (Job 1:12-19). In summation, we are to understand that God does not cause all the bad things that happen in the world.

The question still remains of why does God, then, allow, bad, evil to happen? The answer to that is because of love. God loves the world, every human being. Love is not a warm-fuzzy feeling or the stirring of hormones. Love is both the desire and the action of allowing a person to choose. Choice, however, has consequences. Someone who, while ignoring the clear messages of healthy eating, still eats a diet that is not heart healthy and is loaded with fat, will eventually have dire consequences from this diet. God did not force the person to eat a diet that was unhealthy. God sent clear messages that change was necessary to that person. These messages came through the messages of healthy living and eating. This person is responsible for his or her own health issues.

The person who chooses to get behind the wheel of his or her car and drive while drunk, then crashes into another car, killing the occupants of that other car, has made a choice. That choice had consequences. The consequences were the death of the occupants of the other car.

Another example of the choice of one that affects others is seen in the financial world. While it is true that some people prefer not to work, it is not true that all of the poor fit that category. Many, if not most, of the poor do work hard. However, the economic system as such is set up to benefit a few and to impoverish the majority. Why does one person who works just as hard as another receive less for his or her effort? The answer to this question is varied and many will hide in the false idea that they deserve more because of their effort, training or position. For the Christian, however, the great divide in the economic world is a sin.

God did not set up the economic system which is followed and loved by so many. The economic system was set up by human beings. God did not cause the driver to drink too much. Nor did God cause the drunk driver to crash into the second vehicle killing the occupants of the second vehicle. God did allow the consequences of the choice of the drunk driver to happen. Why did God allow the consequences? The answer to that question is love. Love allows each and every human being to make choices. In the example of the drunk driver, God loves the drunk driver and will not interfere with the choice of the drunk driver. What we are to understand from this is that the choices of each and every human being have consequences. The consequences of our choices, of other people's choices effect and touch the lives of others. What I choose touches your life. What you choose touches the lives of countless others. No action, thought, lack of action occurs in a vacuum. What you and I do and what each and every human person does affects the lives of countless others. Our parents were right. Our choices do have consequences.

Why does God allow the choice of one to affect others? Again, the answer is love. God desires all to be saved. The experience of salvation is not simply the forgiveness of sins and the not going to hell. Salvation also means a new life. This new life is lived the way God intended life to be lived and that is in love. When a person is truly Christ-like, that person will live in love, which is to say, living life with the realization that what is done or not done, affects the entire universe. The choice of human beings affects not only other human beings, they affect the planet. Global warming, pollution is not God caused but is caused by humans. The resultant tragedies from global warming and pollution will and are affecting the entire human race. In addition, the choice of human beings affects heaven itself. This is the reason why the heavenly things had to be cleansed by the blood of Christ (Heb 9:23, 24).

There are still many people who ask the question of why God allows evil. This is an interesting phenomenon. These same people want the freedom and the ability to make their own choices, yet they do not want to accept the consequences of their own choices. People want to choose, but do not want to take responsibility for their choices. The love of God says that no one is independent, no one is autonomous. We are all inter-dependent. What we do or do not do touches the lives of others. Our choices do have consequences.

What the love of God does is elevate each person to a very high status. As human beings we are in the status of those who have choices that affect creation itself.

We return to the original discussion of God desiring all to be saved, yet, not all will be saved. The simple answer is that while God loves each person, not every person loves God. What is of utmost importance to understand is that God honors the choices people make.

We return to the phrase "the Fullness of the Gentiles." Does this phrase mean that all of the Gentiles who will believe have already believed? The answer is no. In the book of Revelation it is stated that both Jews and Gentiles will believe in Christ during the Tribulation and that some of that number will be martyred for their faith (Rev 6:9-11). Thus, we understand that the phrase "the Fullness of the Gentiles" does not mean that the total number of Gentiles during the period called *the gap*, have believed. There will be more Gentiles who will believe in Christ during the Tribulation period.

The time period covered by the seven churches is the period of time that is called the Fullness of the Gentiles. This period of time is also the *gap* of time between the 69th Seven and the 70th Seven of Daniel's prophecy of the Seventy Sevens. It is to this period of time that Jesus adds details to the history of the Church in Matthew 24.

The setting of Jesus' discourse concerning the history of the Church is just outside of the Temple in Jerusalem (Matt 24:1). Jesus and the disciples had just left the Temple and the disciples began to point out to Jesus how grand the Temple was (Matt 24:1). Jesus, knowing the course of history that not only the disciples themselves would face, but also the coming events that would affect the whole Church; began to tell the disciples concerning the history of the people of God.

The history that Jesus began to describe to the disciples begins a few short years after His death on the Cross, His resurrection and ascension to heaven. Jesus tied the account of the coming history of the people of God with the prophecy of the Seventy Sevens in Dan 9:24-27. In fact, Jesus, not only tied His account of the coming history of the Church to the prophecy of the Seventy Sevens, but Jesus also tied His words to the exact Seven in the prophecy of the Seventy Sevens.

According to the prophecy of the Seventy Sevens, there will pass 69 Sevens from the decree to rebuild the city of Jerusalem until the death of the Anointed One (Dan 9:25). The Anointed One, as has been discussed previously is Jesus. The next event in the prophecy of the Seventy Sevens is the destruction of the Temple (Dan 9:26). Dan 9:26, being after the 69th Seven and before the 70th Seven (Dan 9:27), is the *gap* of time between the 69th Seven and the 70th Seven. This time is the same period covered by the seven churches in Revelation. What we see from this is that Jesus, in His words to the disciples concerning the signs of His Return, begins exactly with Dan 9:26, the *gap* of time that exists between the 69th Seven and the 70th Seven.

Jesus, by beginning His discourse concerning the history of the Church with the destruction of the Temple (Matt 24:2) ties His discourse into the prophecy of the Seventy Sevens and in the *gap* of time between the 69th Seven and the 70th Seven. We see in this that not only did Jesus personally fulfill the Law and the Prophets (Matt 5:17), but Jesus did and said everything in order to fulfill the Law and the Prophets.

After Jesus had told the disciples that the Temple would be destroyed,[184] the disciples then asked Jesus what the signs of His return would be (Matt 24:3). What we are to understand from this point on in Jesus' discourse is that Jesus is talking about the history of the Church that ends with His Second Coming.

Jesus next mentions that there will be in the days after the destruction of the Temple a time when there will be many who come in the Name of Christ (Matt 24:5). Jesus has to be referring to a time that is past that of the disciples. The disciples who spent approximately 3 years living and walking with Jesus, would not be fooled by the claim of an imposter. Another way that we know that Jesus is referring to a time in the far future is that He again ties His discourse to the prophecy of the Seventy Sevens. Jesus states that the time when many false Christs would arise is a time associated with wars and rumors of war; a time when nations would rise up against nation (Matt 24:6, 7). The time of wars and rumors of war was not only a part of the prophecy of the *gap* of time found in the prophecy of the Seventy Sevens (Dan 9:26); but was also part of the salvation history that followed the destruction of the Temple (Dan 9:26). Here again, it is to be seen how Jesus in *His* discourse concerning the time leading up to His return is following exactly the prophecy of the Seventy Seven.

After Jesus stated that there would be wars and rumors of wars, He then said that there would be famines, earthquakes in various places around the world (Matt 24:7). These next events coincide exactly with the words found that describe what would happen during the *gap* between the 69th Seven and the 70th Seven in the prophecy of the Seventy Sevens. In the prophecy of the Seventy Sevens, after the prediction of war, there is the prediction of desolations (Dan 9:26). The Hebrew word translated *desolations* means desolations caused by some great disaster.[185] The words of Jesus and the words of the prophecy of the Seventy Sevens, again, are seen to be completely in agreement with one another.

The destruction of the Temple, the coming world condition described by the phrase *wars and rumors of wars*, the economic and ecological disasters that would have global impact, according to Jesus, are the not the end but are only the beginning of birth pangs (Matt 24:8). The period of time called by

Jesus as the *beginning of birth pangs*, as has been seen, corresponds exactly to the prophecy of the *gap* of time between the 69th Seven and the 70th Seven of the prophecy of the Seventy Sevens.

We have looked at the *time and who* of the people of God in the *gap* of time between the 69th Seven and the 70th Seven. Now, we will look briefly at the purpose of God's people during the present age.

Jesus, before He ascended to heaven, gave the disciples and through the disciples to the Church, a commission. This commission has been called the Great Commission and is found in Matthew 28: 18-20. In the Great Commission, Jesus commanded His followers to make disciples of all the earth (Matt 28:19). Why did Jesus command His followers to go into all the world for the sole purpose of making disciples? The answer to that question is that not all people belong to God spiritually, or are reckoned as righteous. To understand the statement that not all people belong to God spiritually, we must discuss salvation history from Creation through The Fall in the Garden of Eden up to the First Coming of Jesus Christ. In fact, the discussion that follows is not just of who belongs to God spiritually, but the discussion that follows tells how to belong to God spiritually. This discussion is both a definition of the Church, the ἐκκλησία, and is a description of the purpose of God's people during this period of time, the *gap*, between the 69th seven and the 70th seven.

To understand the purpose of the people of God in this present age, we begin with the fact of creation.[186] God created the human race to live in a personal relationship with Him. This personal relationship with God was to be experienced in living in perfect fellowship with each other and to be the stewards of God's creation (Gen 1:26-31). This was the purpose of God for the human race and for creation itself.

However, after God created the human race to live in fellowship with Him, there occurred a disruption of that relationship between God and the human race. The disruption of the relationship between God and the human race is termed "The Fall."[187] The fall of the human race occurred when Adam and Eve took from the Fruit of the Tree of the Knowledge of Good and Evil and which has been followed by every human being since that time (Rom 5:12). When the Fruit of the Tree of the Knowledge of Good and Evil was chosen, God was replaced with something else as the standard that determined right and wrong. In the act of replacing God with something other than God and His Word, the Fruit became that which determined the purpose of a person's life. In choosing the Fruit of the Tree of the Knowledge of Good and Evil, God was rejected and another god was followed. This act led the human race away from God, out of grace and finally, the loss of paradise.

Yet, The Fall was not the end of the story or the purpose of God. In the midst of rebellion, grace is offered to Adam and Eve (Gen 3:15). It is within rebellion and loss that God approached Adam and Eve and offered them hope.

This hope was that salvation, that rescue would come. This salvation, this rescue would be accomplished by the *seed of the woman* (Gen 3:15). Interesting phrase is this: "the seed of the woman." In most discussions concerning the male and female in connection to reproduction, the word seed is usually reserved for the male. It is the male that has the seed, the sperm.

In Gen 3:15, God makes the claim that the hope of the human race will be found in the seed of the woman. The fact that God makes this claim requires that the phrase be looked at and the question asked: What did God mean?

The message of Gen 3:15 was spoken by God to the serpent. Morris states that the curse was meant more for the malevolent spirit controlling the body of the serpent.[188] This spirit, Morris says is the Devil.[189] There is Biblical support for this statement as the Devil is called the ancient serpent (Rev 12:9). In light of Rev 12:9, the serpent in Gen 3:15 is either the malevolent spirit of Satan that inhabited the body of the serpent or the serpent is Satan, the Devil himself.

The identity of the seed of the woman is to be understood in the context of a cosmic battle between the seed of the Serpent and the seed of the woman (Gen 3:14-15). The seed of the woman, therefore, must be understood as one who battles and overcomes the seed of the Serpent. Paul, in Romans 16:20 writes that the God of peace will soon crush Satan under your feet. The God of peace will soon crush Satan under your feet; this phrase is seen as the fulfillment of the cosmic battle between the seed of the Serpent and the seed of the Woman. A further question is to be asked: How does the seed of the woman relate to God who is the one who will crush Satan, or the seed of the Serpent?

The answer to the above question is found in what is called the virgin birth of Jesus Christ (Matt 1:18-25). The virgin birth of Jesus is and has been debated for centuries. This study is not the place to delve into that debate. For the purpose of this study, the statements found within the Gospels will be the point of reference. Matthew's Gospel tells us that Mary, who was pledged to be married to Joseph (Matt 1:18) was found to be with child. It is understood by many that during the period of a Jewish betrothal, there were no sexual relations between the man and the woman. This is seen in the fact that when Joseph heard that Mary was with child, he determined to divorce her (Matt 1:18-19). Joseph, if he was truly a righteous man as he is called (Matt 1:19), he would not have made the decision to divorce Mary if the child was his; that is if he and Mary had sexual contact during their betrothal period. The fact that Joseph, upon hearing that Mary was with child, made the decision to divorce Mary, is evidence that Joseph thought that Mary had sexual contact with another man. This would be the only reason that Joseph would consider divorcing Mary.

Joseph, upon making the decision to divorce Mary, the Bible states, had a dream (Matt 1:20) and during this dream, an angel of the Lord appeared to Joseph and explained to him that the child that Mary was carrying was of the Holy Spirit (Matt 1:20). Upon this word, Joseph did as he was commanded and took Mary into his house as his wife (Matt 1:24).

The virgin birth of Jesus explains both how the seed of the woman will crush the seed of the Serpent and how the God of peace will crush the Serpent, Satan. Jesus Christ is both the seed of the woman and the God of peace (John 1:1, 2, 14; John 20:28). Because of this fact, Jesus Christ is the one who will rescue, bring salvation to the human race. In fact, this is what Luke has recorded Jesus as saying in reference to Himself (Luke 19:9, 10).

The person of Jesus Christ and how He fulfills the Law and the Prophets is the very essence of salvation history and the purpose of the people of God, not only in eternity but also in this life. We have seen that during the present age, the *gap* of time between the 69th Seven and the 70th Seven, the people of God are to make disciples of Jesus Christ throughout the whole world. God's people have no other purpose during this period of time.

Jesus after describing the events which will occur during the period of time called the *gap* between the 69th Seven and the 70th Seven, then with Matt 24:9 begins to describe a period of time that is past the *gap* of time between the 69th Seven and the 70th Seven. The events that Jesus begins to describe in Matt 24:9 belong to the time called the 70th Seven. This statement will be fully discussed in the chapter on the Final Seven.

CHAPTER 5

EVERLASTING RIGHTEOUSNESS

The prophecy of the Seventy Sevens is an historical timeline from the time of the rebuilding of the Temple to the Second Coming of Jesus Christ. The proclamation of this prophecy to Daniel by the angel, Gabriel (Dan 920, 21) contains within it the purpose of the people of God. This purpose is summed up in the phrase *to bring in everlasting righteousness*. It is a fact that only God can declare and make righteous. The purpose of God's people, however, is to love, proclaim, teach, and aid people to both experience righteousness in an initial aspect and to grow in an on-going experience of righteousness. The people of God, during the *gap* of time between the 69th Seven and the 70th Seven have but one purpose. The purpose of the people of God during this period of time is to proclaim the Gospel of Jesus Christ to the world. Although we have mentioned the Gospel in earlier chapters, the Gospel message is so important that I want to discuss the message of everlasting righteousness further.

The reception of the Gospel of Jesus Christ results in the experience called the new birth. The new birth is the initial experience of righteousness, while sanctification is the on-going experience of righteousness. The new birth is the beginning of the Christian experience.[190] At the moment of the new birth, justification happens.[191] Justification is the experience of God declaring the believing sinner as righteous in Christ Jesus. The new birth, then, can be seen as the foundational experience of the salvation experience.

Individuals, before the new birth, live lives that are in rebellion and in rejection of God (Rom 3:10-18). This life, the life lived in rebellion and alienation from God is more than simply an unethical or immoral life. The truth be known, there are many Non-Christian Believers who live lives of high ethical and moral character. This is seen in 1 Cor 13 where it is stated that the acts of love can be done, yet without love. The life lived in rebellion and alienation from God is a life lived according to a standard different than God and His Word; a life lived serving gods other than the Living God. The Bible describes this state as death (Eph 2:1, 2). This death that the letter to the Ephesians describes is not what is known as physical death or non-existence. This is seen in Eph 2:2 where it is stated that the ones who were dead in transgressions and sins used to live and this life was lived in following the ways of the world. The death that is described in Eph 2:1 is spiritual death.

Spiritual death is illustrated by what happened to Adam and Eve after they took from the Fruit of the Tree of the Knowledge of Good and Evil and ate. Gen 3 describes a change in their relationship with God. Before they ate the Fruit and rejected God, they walked and talked with God (Gen 2). After they took from the Fruit of the Tree of the Knowledge of Good and Evil and ate, their relationship with God changed. From walking and talking with God, they were now afraid of God (Gen 3:8). This change is also seen in Gen 3:9 where God called to the Adam and said: Where are you? (Gen 3:9). The change in the relationship with God resulted in Adam and Eve being kicked out of the Garden of Eden, out of Paradise. When Adam and Eve were kicked out of Paradise, this symbolized the loss of a personal relationship with God.

In addition to Adam and Eve's relationship with God changing after they took from the Fruit of the Tree of the Knowledge of Good and Evil, their personal relationship changed. Before they ate, they were seen as equals and helpers to one another (Gen 2:20-25). After eating the Fruit of the Tree of the Knowledge of Good and Evil, their relationship changed to the point where they now blamed each other (Gen 3:12, 13). Instead of being equals and helpers to one another, they became antagonistic towards and distant from each other.

A third change occurred in Adam and Eve after they took from the Fruit of the Tree of the Knowledge of Good and Evil and ate. This change reflects their relationship with God, with each other and with themselves. Before they ate from the Fruit of the Tree of the Knowledge of Good and Evil, they were naked and not ashamed (Gen 2:25). The description of being naked refers to having no clothes as well as being transparent, innocent, with no walls between God, others and self. Before Adam and Eve ate from the Fruit of the Tree of the Knowledge of Good and Evil, their image of God, each other

147

and their self-image was healthy and sound. After they ate from the Fruit of the Tree of the Knowledge of Good and Evil a change occurred. Before they ate from the Fruit of the Tree of the Knowledge of Good and Evil they were not ashamed, after they ate they were now ashamed (Gen 3:7-10).

Before a person is born again, experiences the new birth, the life they lived is one of rejection of God; it is a life lived hiding from God; it is also a life lived at a distance and with strained relationships with each other and it is a life lived with shame.

After Adam and Eve took from the Fruit of the Knowledge of Good and Evil; God banished them from the Garden of Eden (Gen 3:23). After Adam and Eve took from the Fruit of the Tree of the Knowledge of Good and Evil; they lost Paradise. They no longer had a personal relationship with God. They now lived lives where their relationship with each other became difficult. They were now ashamed. They were alive, yet they had no direct connection with God. This the Bible describes as death (Eph 2:1, 2).

A person is either alive by faith in Christ or is dead. These are the only two relations that an individual can have with God.[192] Biblical faith and the following of the Fruit of the Tree of the Knowledge of Good and Evil are both relationships; they are not mere acts or professions. This is seen in the fact that Adam and Eve either were in the Garden fellowshipping with God or they were living outside of the Garden, having lost their personal relationship with

God. In both relationships, in the Garden with a personal relationship with God or having been cast out of God's presence and not having a personal relationship with God but a relationship of following the Fruit, the relationship with God called Biblical faith and the relationship with the Fruit is seen. Every individual in the human race is either in a relationship of biblical faith or a relationship with the Fruit of the Tree of the Knowledge of Good and Evil, which is a relationship without God. What is further to be understood is that within these two relationships with God both true and what can be called untrue humanity is seen. True humanity is understood as individuals living in a loving relationship with God and others that God intended for the human race to live in. Untrue humanity is to be understood in life, living, existence apart from a loving relationship with God and others.

True humanity leads to wholeness with God, others and self; while untrue humanity leads to blame, anger, alienation, and murder (Gen 3: 11-Gen 4). True humanity is the individual becoming all that God intends for that individual; of that individual realizing his or her potential. While untrue humanity leaves a person in brokenness and failing to realize his or her potential. True humanity leads to wholeness; while untrue humanity is decayed[193] humanity.

The act of creation by God of the human race in His image and likeness constitutes the true human being. True human beings live in a personal relationship with God which is expressed in a heart desire to please God by living according to His standard as revealed in His Word. The act of choosing another standard, of rejecting God causes the human being to fall from true humanity into inhumanity.[194] As inhuman human beings, people are not what God created them to be. They are rebels; those who have rejected God and are attempting to live their lives apart from both God and their true selves.

The new birth is the experience where a person living in death is given spiritual life by God. The life given by God in the new birth is not primarily an ethical life.[195] Paul is an example of the life of the new birth not being primarily ethical or moral. Paul, before his new birth experience, was a Pharisee and according to the accepted standard, he was faultless (Phil 3:6). Although Paul was faultless, according to the standard of the day; he was dead according to God (Phil 3:10).

The life given by God in the new birth is the life of the Spirit (Rom 8:9, 10). The Holy Spirit both is the life given by God and brings the life given by God. The life given in the new birth, while not being primarily an ethical or moral life in the world's terms is a holy life, for God is holy (Rev 4:8).

The life given by God in the new birth is a life that has God and His Word as the standard which the believing sinner base his or her living. In the new birth experience, the believing sinner receives a new nature (2 Pet 1:4). This new nature longs after God in Christ.[196] This new life that longs after God

150

in Christ is a holy life, because this new life is the Holy Spirit. The new birth, as a life-giving experience, gives a life that has God as its source, origin, direction, passion and goal (2 Cor 5:9). This life given by God is the life of His own Spirit.

The new birth is the act by which God makes alive spiritually the sinner who was dead in his or her transgressions and sins.[197] The act by which a person is made alive is the indwelling, the giving of God's own Holy Spirit to be the life of the believer. The giving of the Holy Spirit into the life and heart of the believing sinner makes that person a Christian, for without the Holy Spirit indwelling a person, that person does not belong to God (Rom 8: 9, 10). The Holy Spirit is the life of God by which we become God's children (Rom 8:16). To be a child of God is to be accepted by Christ and God (Rom 15:7). A Christian is therefore, an accepted child of God who has been declared righteous and by the new birth has become righteous before God.

The new birth is seen also in the experience of righteousness is reconciliation. Reconciliation means to restore a relationship, to renew a friendship.[198] The word reconciliation talks about the present relationship between two parties and assumes that there was a previous relationship between the two parties; a relationship that at one time or another was disrupted and discontinued. Reconciliation, therefore is the restoring of a relationship that at one time existed but is now broken.

The relationship that is restored in reconciliation is the relationship between God and the human race that was broken by the Fall, the act of Adam and Eve choosing the Fruit of the Tree of the Knowledge of Good and Evil in the Garden of Eden.

The choice of Adam and Eve to take from the Fruit of the Tree of the Knowledge of Good and Evil and thus to reject God was both an individual choice and a corporate choice. There are those who hold the position that Adam and Eve were individuals. There are those who hold that Adam and Eve represented the human race. These two positions are found in Rom 5:12-21). Adam is called the one man through which sin entered the world (Rom 5:12). The result of sin entering the world was death (Rom 5:12). The death that entered the world was not simply the death of Adam and Eve, as two individuals. The death that entered the world affected the whole human race (Rom 5:12). The death that the human race died was caused by the choice of one man, Adam (Rom 5:15, 17). In addition, not only did the whole human race die because of Adam's sin, Adam's sin brought condemnation on all human race (Rom 5:18). The choice of Adam, the sin of Adam in taking the fruit and eating it, not only brought condemnation on the whole human race but it also means that the whole the human race are sinners before God (Rom 5:19).

Adam and Eve were also individuals who made personal choices to choose something other than God to follow and in that choice they rejected God. So, Adam and Eve were both individuals and represented the human race.

Reconciliation, the restoring of a broken relationship, is the act of God whereby He restores, renews the relationship that was broken by the choosing of the Fruit of the Tree of the Knowledge of Good and Evil by Adam and Eve, both as individuals and as representatives of the human race. This means that the act, the work of God called reconciliation concerns and is directed towards the whole human race. God loves the world (John 3:16) and sent His son to be the sacrifice for the sins of the world (John 1:29; 1 John 2:2).

Jesus, as the sacrifice for the sins of the world, died to bring reconciliation to a broken relationship (2 Cor 5:11-21). As has been stated, reconciliation means the restoration of a broken relationship. A relationship has two parties in it. When a relationship is broken, both parties are estranged to each other; both parties are no longer friends. If the relationship is to be restored, that means that both parties must be reconciled to each other; both parties must be restored to one another. This bringing together of the two parties of a relationship is what the death of Jesus has done. Jesus' death first of all reconciles God to us, to the human race (2 Cor 5:18, 19). Because God loves the world, it is God's desire that all would come to repentance and reconciled (1 Tim 2: 3, 4). The death of Jesus has reconciled God to the human race. God is no longer at odds with the human race because of their sin.

The second party in a broken relationship that reconciliation restores is the human race. As it has been shown, God is now reconciled to us (2 Cor 5:18, 19). This does not mean, however, that the whole human race has been saved or reconciled. Although God is reconciled to each and every person; each and every person, every individual must personally accept God's reconciliation and be reconciled to God (2 Cor 5:20).

Reconciliation is accomplished, not by God overlooking sin, but because Jesus died as the sacrifice that paid for sin (2 Cor 5:21; John 1:29; 1 John 2:2). Sin is no longer blocking the relationship with God. The way back home is open from God's perspective. Yet, as has been said, individually, we must make the choice to come to our senses and return to the Father.

The result of reconciliation is a restored relationship between God and individuals. This restored relationship is also called righteousness (2 Cor 5:21). Reconciliation is accomplished when Jesus took our sin and died. Jesus died as the sacrifice, the offering for sin (2 Cor 5:21). The results of reconciliation is righteousness (2 Cor 5:15-19). Those who are reconciled to God are in a right relationship with God, which is the basic meaning of justification and righteousness.

Because God is reconciled to the human race, the way is now open for each and every individual to be reconciled to God. This is the choice that lies before each and everyone. Will they continue to belong to the Fruit Group, that is those who have chosen the Fruit of the Tree of the Knowledge of Good and Evil and thereby be rejecters of God or will they accept the death of Jesus as that which paid for their sins and freed them so that they might be righteous in Christ (2 Cor 5:21).

There is an intertwining of the images, aspects of salvation. As it was seen, justification, the declaring and the becoming righteous of the believing sinner, at the moment of the new birth, when the life of the Holy Spirit is implanted within the believing sinner. At the same moment of the new birth, the believing sinner is reconciled to God and is now at peace with God (Rom 5:1). This is seen in the fact that reconciliation leads to being righteous (2 Cor 5:21). Brunner, who represents those whose emphasis is on God's declaration in justification states that in Christ a person is reckoned as righteous[199] and that Christ's righteousness takes the place of our missing righteousness.[200] Further he states that justification is the restoration of the Creation, the restoration of the image of God.[201] He also says that in justification the person is declared right with God as a totality.[202] He further states that in Jesus Christ, the guilt of sin is blotted out. [203] To sum up Brunner's position it would seem that in essence, Brunner understands that in justification the person is new, i.e. the restoration of the Creation. This would agree with Wesley who states that in justification God both declares the believing sinner righteous and makes the

155

believing sinner righteous by the impartation, the giving to the believing sinner the righteousness of Christ in the moment of the new birth.

The initial experience of righteousness is experienced in conversion. Conversion is the change of heart, the turning from the previous way of life of one's own choosing and a turning to the will and way of God. [204] In conversion, the believing sinner changes their mind and turns from following the Fruit of the Tree of the Knowledge of Good and Evil and a re-turning to following God and His Word. Conversion is the end of rebellion, the rejecting of rejection. Conversion occurs within repentance.

Conversion is the beginning of the new person in Christ. This means that the initial act of conversion occurs during the new birth, the moment when a believing sinner is both declared and becomes righteous. This is also the moment when a person accepts the reconciliation of God and is now personally reconciled to God.

Forgiveness is experience of the new birth. Forgiveness means that sin and guilt no longer exist (Jer. 50:20) and that the Christian stands before God without accusation (Col. 1:22). Paul writes that it is *before Him,* that is before Christ, who is the Judge (Acts 10:42) that the Christian stands without accusation (Col. 1:22). This means that on the Day of Judgment, Christians stand before the Judge, who is Jesus Christ, without accusation. When Christians stand before Jesus Christ there will be no list of sins to be accounted for. Further, when Christians stand before Jesus Christ there will be no recounting of their sins followed by the proclamation of *forgiven.*

A Christian stands before God without accusation. Without accusation does not mean acquittal, but that no accusation against Christians even exists.[205] The meaning of without accusation is further clarified when Louw and Nida state that without accusation pertains to one who cannot be accused of anything wrong.[206] Trench says that without accusation means: not acquittal, but the absence of so much as a charge or accusation brought against him of whom it is affirmed.[207]

The Christian stands before God, the Judge of the Universe without accusation. The reason for this is that Christ has forgiven the Christian for his or her sins. Forgiveness means that sin is gone and that God will no longer remember the sins of the forgiven (Heb 8:12; 10:17). Because sin is gone, no one is able to bring any accusation against the one who has been forgiven. To state the case more plainly is to state that there exists no accusation against the one who has been forgiven. Forgiveness means the removal of sin, punishment and even the record of sin's existence.

In both Hebrews 8:12 and 10:17 it is stated that when God forgives sin, wickedness and lawlessness, sin, wickedness and lawlessness are no longer remembered. In forgiveness, God puts our sin out of sight (Is. 38:17). When God forgives, sin is put out of reach (Ps. 103:12; Micah 7:19). As far as the east is from the west, God has removed our sins from us when He forgives us. East and west on a compass are two opposite ends of the spectrum. Forgiveness means that sin is put out of God's mind (Jer 31:34; Heb 8:12; Heb 10:17). When God puts sin out of His mind, this means that God no longer remembers sin. God being God remembers all things. This is not a contradiction to what has been said. The word in Heb 10:17 for *remember* means to remember for the purpose of making mention of and responding to in an appropriate manner.[208] The remembering does not imply that what is remembered has actually been forgotten.[209] The *remembering* is to remember for the purpose of responding to. The response in this case is contextual. The context may be positive or negative. The remembering and responding may be to aid the needy, to help those who need help (Gal 2:10) or it may be to punish (Rev 18:5). The word remember also has the added meaning of make mention of.[210] In the act of forgiveness, sin and the sinner have been separated. The sin is no longer *part of* the sinner. In the words of John 1:29, sin has been taken away. Taken away means from the sinner, this is the meaning of the Scapegoat in Lev 16. The Scapegoat was one of two goats chosen as sacrifices during the Day of Atonement. The first goat was slain and its blood sprinkled on the altar. Upon the second goat, the Scapegoat, the High Priest, by the symbolic act of laying his hands upon the head of this goat, took the sins of the people from the people and transferred the sins of the people and placed them upon the

Scapegoat. The sins of the people were thus taken away from the people. The people and their sins were thus separated. The Day of Atonement and the two goats was fulfilled in the death of Jesus Christ upon the Cross (John 1:29).

When God forgives the believing sinner, God separates the believing sinner from his or her sins. The sin of the world was placed taken by Jesus and He bore them on His body on the Cross (1 Pet 2:24). In addition, when God forgives sin, He no longer remembers them, but He no longer will respond to them. The response that God now makes toward the believing sinner is one of acceptance, grace, mercy and love.

There is one other aspect of the word remember that is to be made clear. The word 'remember' means to recall with the purpose of responding in an appropriate manner. As it is clear, the only appropriate manner in which God will respond to sin is punishment. When God no longer remembers sin, God no longer makes mention of those sins.[211] When the Christian stands before God at the Day of Judgment and gives an account of his or her life; that Christian will stand before God forgiven. To be forgiven means that the sin and the Christian have been separated. The sin of the Christian was born by Jesus Christ on the Cross of Calvary. The Christian will not stand before God carrying his or her sins, for they have been taken by Jesus; the sins of the Christian are no longer his or hers. For the forgiven, God will no longer remember with the purpose of responding appropriately. The only appropriate response by God to sin is to punish. For the Christian, there is no longer punishment (1 John 4:18). Furthermore, when the Christian stands before God at the Day of Judgment, God will no longer make mention of his or her sins.

What is to be seen in the understanding of the word *remember* is that the Day of Judgment for Christians will not be a day when their sins are recounted and then the proclamation of *forgiven* is made. In forgiveness, God will no longer make mention of the sins of the forgiven. If God no longer makes mention of sins, now then can there be a recounting of sins? To recount sins is to make mention of them. It is stated clearly that God in forgiveness will no longer remember sins and transgression. As it has been stated before, this remembering carries with it the meaning of to make mention of. For the forgiven, the Christian, the Day of Judgment will not be a day of fear for the hearing again of their sins. The Christian's sin will not be made mention of or recounted.

The statement that God no longer remembers sin in forgiveness is the very heart of the Gospel message that Christians are to be spreading during this period of time, that period of time which is called *the gap* between the 69th seven and the 70th seven. In forgiveness, God no longer remembers sin because when forgiven, sin does not exist (Jer 50:20; Is 43:25; Acts 3:19). How can that which no longer exists be made mention of? It cannot.

The Blood of Christ has not only cleansed the believing sinner from sin, but has also cleansed heaven from sin (9:23-28). Sin no longer is in nor will be in heaven. The believing sinner will not bring sin into heaven again, for heaven has been cleansed once for all by the Blood of Jesus (Heb 9:25-26). If at the Day of Judgment for the Christian, the sins of the Christian were recounted, this would then be a bringing into the Holy Place, of heaven of sin. This will not happen for the Blood of Jesus has once for all cleansed heaven, the Holy Place of sin. There will not be a second cleansing of heaven, of the Holy Place.

Forgiveness is also the means whereby the record of a Christian's sin has been wiped away (Col 2:13, 14). Paul, in the letter to the Colossians, describes the experience that surrounds forgiveness. He begins his discussion with the statement that at one time the Colossian Believers were dead in their sin and trespasses (Col 2:13). Paul then says that God made the Colossians alive spiritually (Col 2:13). Paul goes on to state that God also forgave their sins and trespasses and also to wipe away the record of their sins (Col 2:14). The word for *record of their sins* is χειρόγραφον. Χειρόγραφον means: record of debts.[212] The record of debts is a record that contains the debts/sins of the sinner. In forgiveness, the record of the believing sinner has been wiped clean. The meaning behind the phrase wiped clean is to cause something to cease by obliterating any evidence, to eliminate, to do away with, to wipe out.[213] The record of the debts after forgiveness simply no longer exists. This

161

record has been completely wiped clean so that there is no longer any evidence that what was once on the list was even on the list.

Forgiveness means that the record of one's sins, wickedness and lawlessness is no longer remembered by God. In addition, in forgiveness the record of one's sins, lawlessness and wickedness no longer exists, but has been wiped clean, which is to say that in forgiveness the stain of sin, the imprint on the list no longer exists.

The Christian believer, the one who is forgiven by God because of his or her faith in the Lord and Savior Jesus Christ has both his or her sins taken away (John 1:29) and also the record of his or her sins is wiped clean which is to say that even the evidence of their sins has been wiped away, that it no longer exists.

Forgiveness, the putting away of the debt and guilt of sin along with the wiping clean of the record of our debts occurs at the moment of the new birth. Paul wrote: When you were dead in your transgressions, you were made alive with Christ. He forgave us all our sins and wiped clean the record of our debts (Col 2:13, 14). What is to be understood is that the being made alive with Christ is the new birth. The Holy Spirit, who is the Spirit of God and of Christ, is the active agent in causing the new birth (John 3:3-8).

In Col 2:13, 14 the verb form for both forgave and canceled the written code is an aorist participle. One of the characteristics of the aorist participle is the time of action described by the participle itself. In the case of the aorist

participle, the time of action described occurs before the time of the action of

the main verb.[214] In Col 2:13, 14, the main verb is *made alive with*. The

meaning then of the participles forgave and canceled is that the action of these

two aorist participles occurs before the action of the main verb made alive

with. What this means in practical terms is that when a sinner believes the

Gospel and accepts Jesus Christ as Lord and Savior, at that moment, that

believing sinner is made alive with Christ. Yet, because of the specific nature

of the time element in the aorist participle, before the believing sinner was

made alive with Christ, or born again, the believing sinner was forgiven of all

his or her sins and the record of his or her debts was wiped clean. There is no

discussion in the aorist participle of how long before the action of the aorist

participle occurs before the action of the main verb. The action of being

forgiven of all transgressions and of the record of one's debts being wiped

clean occurs, mille-seconds before the sinner is born-again. This means that

forgiveness and the wiping clean of the record of one's debts does not occur in

any measurable time frame before the new birth occurs. It can be said that

forgiveness, the wiping clean of the record of debts and the new birth are

simultaneous actions.

What is important to draw out of the above discussion of the time

element of the aorist participle and its relationship to the main verb is seen is

163

this: the evidence that one is forgiven and that the record of one's sins has been wiped clean and no longer exists is the new birth, the being made alive with Christ. In addition, because the new birth occurs at the same time as justification, the evidence that one is justified, that is in right relationship with God, is the new birth, the being made alive with Christ. Furthermore, because reconciliation and conversion also occur simultaneously with the new birth, it can be seen that the evidence that one is reconciled with God and has experienced conversion is the new birth, the being made alive with Christ. Righteousness, a right relationship with God is only through forgiveness which is experienced when one accepts Jesus Christ as Lord and Savior, is then born again through the Blood of Christ which cleanses the believing sinner from guilt and sin (Heb 10:22).

Thus it can be seen that the new birth, justification, reconciliation, conversion, the forgiveness of sin and the wiping clean of the record of one's debts are all simultaneous actions when a sinner believes the Gospel and accepts Jesus Christ as Lord and Savior. The experiences that are simultaneous with the new birth are all included in the phrase the initial experience of righteousness. This means that one can not be in right relationship with God unless one is born again. One birth is not enough; one must be born twice. There must be the first birth, which is physical birth and there must be the second birth, the new birth, if one is to be right with God.

This discussion can be included to say that one cannot do good works, works that come out of love which are the only works acceptable to God without the new birth. Without the new birth, a person is still in their sin; this person is not a spiritual child of God. This person is not righteous, that is in a right relationship with God.

The record of one's debts that is wiped clean in the act of forgiveness and evidenced by the new birth for the Christian believer is the very record that the Non-Christian Believers will have opened before them at the Day of Judgment (Rev 20:11-15). The record of our debts is the record of our lives as human beings. This record contains the listing of all our sins, transgressions, trespasses and failures to conform to the standard of God as found in both His Word and His holiness. What is to be remembered is that for the Non-Christian believer all their righteousness is but filthy rags before God (Isa. 64:6). In other words, all of the actions, the whole life experience of the Non-Christian believer is considered by God as unrighteousness (Rom 3:9-18). For the Non-Christian believer, there will be no hope based on their own life's record. There is simply nothing one can do while serving the Fruit, which is rejection of God, that God finds acceptable. God does not, nor will not, accept rejection of Himself and His Word as acceptable, as righteousness. This record at the moment of the new birth is wiped clean for the Christian believer. For the Non-Christian believer it is the very record that the

Non-Christian believer will have to give an account for and thus it can be seen why the Non-Christian believer will be cast into the Lake of Fire, the Second Death.

In the previous discussion it was stated that Christians stand before God as forgiven. It was also stated that forgiveness means that sin is no longer remembered and that the record of the Christian's sins no longer exists. Because the record of the Christian no longer exists, the Christian stands before God without accusation. In this section a further look at the phrase *without accusation* will be conducted.

In the act of forgiveness, one's sins are taken away (John 1:29), which means they no longer exist and the record of one's debts, sins, and wickedness is wiped clean so that there is no longer a record that one's sins existed. The result of forgiveness and the wiping clean of the record of one's debts is that the Christian believer stands before God without accusation (Col 1:22). There are two main views of without accusation. One view is that the Christian believer will stand before the Judgment Seat of God and their sins will become known and proclaimed.[215] The purpose of the proclaiming of the sins of the Christian is so that the guilt of all will be known to God.[216] After the proclaiming of the Christian believer's sins, then the announcement will be made by God that the Christian believer is forgiven, the punishment paid.

The view mentioned above teaches that although forgiven, the Christian believer will still stand before God as guilty. As guilty people, this guilt must be at least proclaimed so that the Blood of Christ will then be seen as the ground for forgiveness and the removal of punishment (1 John 4:18). There is in this view a concern that justice will not be served if there is no recounting of the forgiven sins of the Christian.

The view under discussion has a number of areas that are of concern. The first area is that justice is seen apart from the Cross of Christ. This view teaches that although the Blood of Christ forgives and cleanses, there is still a need for justice. Justice in this view is seen as the Christian receiving what is due him or her. This receiving is not punishment for sin, for that has been taken by Christ. Yet, there is still an understanding within this view that justice must be served. Because Christ has endured the punishment for the Christian and thus there is no punishment remaining for the Christian; there is in this view, still the re-counting of the sins of the Christian so that all will know how sinful each and every Christian is or was.

According to Brunner, his position on judgment is that it is a complete revealing of the depth of our sin. There are a couple of observations that are to be looked at in light of this. The first observation comes out of Brunner's own understanding of justification and righteousness. First of all it is to be understood that a Christian is new, a new person. This new person is righteous. The righteousness of the Christian is Christ Himself (1 Cor. 1:30). When one is united to Christ, one has the whole of Christ and not simply a part of Christ. It is the total person who is declared right with God at the moment of justification.

The whole person is declared right with God and has received the whole Christ, who is righteousness. It is perhaps well understood, but it must be stated that there is no sin in Christ. Since a Christian is a new person, one created in righteousness and if judgment is a revealing of the depth of one's sin, how then can a new person who in Christ's righteousness have sin?

The purpose of the death of Jesus Christ as a substitute for the sinner was also to give spiritual life to the sinner who was dead in his or her sin (Eph 2:1-5). The Bible teaches that not only are Christian believers given spiritual life but they have also been cleansed from guilt by the sprinkling, the spiritual application of the Blood of Jesus Christ (Heb 10:19-22).

The Bible is clear in teaching that the one who trusts in Jesus Christ will never be put to shame (Rom 9:23; 10:11). The reason for this is that Christ endured the Christian's shame on the Cross (Heb 12:2). Jesus not only bore sin on the Cross (1 Pet 2:24); Christ also took the shame upon Himself that was at one time the Christian's. A Christian is without shame. The understanding of without shame refers both to now and to the future, especially in the Day of Judgment. If it is true, as some hold that the Day of Judgment for the Christian is a day when all the sins of the Christian are listed and afterwards a proclamation is made of forgiven, is there not to be seen, to be experienced in the recounting of one's sins, shame?

How can one stand before not only God but all other Christians and hear one's sins without a tremendous amount of shame? The Blood of Christ not only removes the penalty of sin, but also the shame of that same sin. Christ endured the shame on the Cross. For the Christian, there will be no shame, even, or should it be said especially, in the Day of Judgment.

The second view of without accusation is that the Christian believer not only stands before God free from punishment but also free from accusation (Col 1:22). "Without accusation" is the translation of the Greek ἀνέγκλητος. This word pertains to one who cannot be accused of anything wrong.[217] G. Berry goes even further when he defines ἀνέγκλητος as: that which designates one against whom there is no accusation, implying not acquittal of a charge, but that no charge has been made.[218]

How can there be no accusation made against those who have sinned? The answer is that Christ by His death on the Cross bore not only sin (1 Pet 2:24) and its punishment (1 John 4:18) but also the total curse of the law (Gal 3:13). The Blood of Christ has so cleansed both heaven and the Christian believer from sin and its effects that there remains nothing left of sin to accuse the Christian believer of.

The initial experience of righteousness is also the beginning of the on-going experience of righteousness. The one who experiences the new birth also begins the experience of sanctification. Sanctification is both instantaneous and an on-going process. The instantaneous aspect of sanctification is seen in 1 Cor 6:11 where it is written that when a person is justified, that is born again by faith in Jesus Christ as Lord and Savior, one is also sanctified.

A definition of sanctification at this point is necessary. Sanctification means to be made holy.[219] To be made holy is in the name of the Lord Jesus Christ (1 Cor 6:11). Holiness, sanctification, then is only in Christ and is a description of what happens to Christian believers. Sanctification is by the Holy Spirit (1 Cor 6:11). This means that part of the Holy Spirit's work in the life of the Christian believer is to sanctify that believer; to make the believer holy.

1 Cor 6:11 elucidates that the one who is justified is also sanctified. What we see here is that the one who has been born again has also been made holy. When a believing sinner accepts Jesus as Lord and Savior, the Holy Spirit indwells that person. When the Holy Spirit indwells a believing sinner, the Holy Spirit, being the Spirit of God and of Christ, brings to the believing sinner the righteousness and holiness of Jesus. The indwelling Christ is the sanctification that is imparted, given to the believer (1 Cor 1:30). When Christ indwells, through the Holy Spirit, the believing sinner, then

righteousness and holiness is also given to the believer. This is the instantaneous aspect of sanctification.

Sanctification is also an on-going process. It is a process of becoming more and more, in experience, Christ-like. Paul exhorts the Ephesians to put on the new self that has been created in the likeness of God (Eph 4:24). This *putting on* is the process of sanctification. After Paul has exhorted the Ephesians to put on the new self; he then exhorts them to put off the old (Eph 4:25-32). What is to be seen in this is that the Christian believer, at the moment of justification, at the new birth, is made holy in Christ. Yet, the Christian believer is then exhorted to put on the new self. This is detailed further in Col 3:1-17.

In Col 3:1-17 can be seen the two aspects of sanctification. The first aspect of sanctification is found in Col 3:1-10 where the description of the present experience of the Christian believer is seen. In the Greek the verb tenses used in Col 3:1-10 is primarily indicative. The indicative is the declarative mood, which denotes a simple assertion or statement.[220] In other words, in Col 3:1-10, Paul is writing and stating the facts of who the Christian believer is. These statements, these facts are certainties. They are facts that are true at the new birth. Paul states in Eph 2:4-6 that the new birth, being made alive (Eph 2:5) results in being made alive in Christ (Eph 2:5) and the fact of being raised up with Christ and seated with Christ in the heavenly realm (Eph

2:6).

The facts of a Christian believer is that the Christian believer has been raised with Christ (Col 3:1); they have died with Christ (Col 3:3), they are with Christ in heaven, it is described as hidden with Christ in God (Col 3:3); they have taken off the old self (Col 3:9) and they have put on the new self (Col 3:10). These are all true at the moment of the new birth, the being made alive with Christ (Eph 2:5). These are irrefutable truths; truths that every Christian believer is to hold onto. These facts are true regardless of the Christian believer's life struggles, doubts or even miss-step. Here again is seen the instantaneous aspect of sanctification.

The on-going process of sanctification is also stated in Col 3:1-10). The on-going process of sanctification is based on the reality, the fact of the instantaneous aspect of sanctification. Because a Christian believer is in Christ; has been raised up with Christ; has been made alive with Christ and has been seated in the heavenly realm with Christ; the Christian believer is then to set their hearts and minds on the things above (Col 3:1, 2); Christian believers are to put to death the practices that belong to their earthly nature (Col 3:5); and they are to rid themselves of practices that are characteristic of the old self, the rebel, the self, the person who had chosen the Fruit of the Tree of the Knowledge of Good and Evil (Col 3:8). These verses use the imperative mood. The imperative mood is the mood of command.[221]

172

What is to be seen from Col 3:1-10 is that Paul describes the fact of who

the Christian believer is and then exhorts, encourages the Christian believer to

become in practice, in experience what they are in Christ. The facts of who the

Christian believer is are true because of who the believer is in Christ. This is

the result of the instantaneous aspect of sanctification. The becoming in

experience who you are in Christ is the on-going aspect of sanctification.

Christians have been declared righteous by God at the moment of the

new birth and have been sanctified by God, in their heart, at the same time.

The sanctification of the Christian is seen in the heart desire to obey Jesus

Christ in all things (2 Cor 5:9). Sanctified Christians are not perfect human

beings, however. The believing sinner can be said to be holy and not holy at

the same time (2 Cor 4:7). In this passage, Paul writes that Christians have the

treasure of the Gospel in earthen vessels. What is seen in this passage is that

God has placed a treasure in frail, broken bodies, (earthen vessels). The

vessels that hold the treasure is of a different *kind* than the treasure itself.

There is that which is holy within that which is not holy. 2 Cor 4:7 is a

description of an imperfect Christian; one who is righteous and yet at the same

time not perfect, in the sense of sinless perfection. This being righteous but not

yet, tells very clearly the truth that Christians are in the process of being

transformed into the image of Christ, that is from glory to glory (2 Cor 3:18).

The imperfect Christian is still in process to become in experience what they are in Christ. This process is on-going and will take a life-time. This process is at times easy and at times difficult. This on-going process of sanctification causes the Christian believer to examine who they are, what they think, how they act and re-act and to evaluate these in the light of Christ's holiness. Christ's holiness, as revealed in the Word of God, is the standard by which the Christian believer desires to live his or her life.

At times, during this process, Christian believers will not measure up to what they desire (Rom 7:21-15). There are times in the life of the Christian when the Christian believer will live as his/her heart desires, in a manner which is pleasing to Christ Jesus. Paul in Romans 7 refers to a mature Christian believer. This is seen in the fact that it is only a Christian who desires to please God (Rom 7:22). Paul is not referring to a Non-Christian here. He has already stated in Rom 3:10-18 that there is no one who truly seeks God (Rom 3:11). Paul goes on to emphasize that there is not even one who does good (Rom 3:12). In describing the sinner, Paul furthermore states that there is no fear of God before their eyes (Rom 3:18). The word fear means reverence, awe, respect. [222] When it is seen how Paul has already described a Non-Christian in Rom 3:10-18, it then is to be understood that it is only a Christian who delights in God (Rom 7:22).

Paul, in Rom 7 describes the inner struggle of a Christian believer. Paul the Apostle lists several elements in Rom 7:25 that can only describe a

Christian believer. This elements are the fact that the person in Rom 7 gives thanks to God for Jesus Christ (Rom 7:25). A Non-Christian does not give God thanks for Jesus Christ. Why would a Non-Christian be thankful to God for Jesus Christ? It is only in the realization of acceptance of the Gospel of the forgiveness of sins through the Blood of Jesus Christ that a person is thankful to God for Jesus Christ. The acceptance of forgiveness through the Blood of Jesus Christ would then make a Non-Christian a Christian.

Another element that Paul lists in Rom 7:25 that can only describe a Christian is the connection, the relationship between God and Jesus Christ. It is only Christians who see the eternal connection of God and Jesus. This eternal connection for Paul is that Jesus Christ is the fact that Jesus Christ is the image of the invisible God (Col 1:15) and that in Christ the fullness of God dwelt in bodily form (Col 1:19; 2:9). In essence, for Paul, the eternal connection between God and Jesus Christ is that Jesus is the Second Person of the Trinity. Paul, in Rom 7:25 is stating the truth of the Trinity.

Non-Christians do not believe in the doctrine of the Trinity. Because Paul in Rom 7:25 is stating his belief in the relationship of Jesus Christ to God within the teaching of the Trinity, it is to be seen that the person Paul is describing in Rom 7 must be a Christian believer.

A third element that Paul has stated in Rom 7:25 that makes clear that Paul is referring to a Christian is that Paul states that the way to God is through

Jesus Christ. Paul thanks God *through* Jesus Christ. Jesus Himself said that no one goes to the Father but through Christ (John 14:6). The belief that Jesus is the way to the Father is a particularly Christian belief. It is true that[223] there are some hold to the view that Jesus is one way amongst many ways to God. Jesus refutes this belief when He stated that no one comes to the Father *except* through Jesus Himself (John 14:6). The vast majority of Non-Christians do not believe that Jesus Christ is the way to God. There are a few that hold to the belief that Jesus is one way amongst many to God. Yet, the claim that Jesus is the only way to the Father is purely a Christian claim.

A final element that Paul mentions in Rom 7:25 that can only be made by a Christian is the Lordship of Jesus Christ. Paul calls Jesus our Lord (Rom 7:25). The word Lord means one who exercises supernatural authority over. A Non-Christian would not call Jesus his or her Lord. A Non-Christian does not recognize Christ's Lordship over him or her. The recognizing and confessing that Jesus is Lord, according to Paul is part of the salvation experience (Rom 10:9). Thus, for Paul, only a Christian would call Jesus Lord.

In Rom 7, Paul is describing the inner struggle of a Christian believer. This inner struggle is of an intense nature for Paul calls himself *wretched* (Rom 7:24). For Paul to call himself wretched is not the confession of a person with a poor self-image but the confession of a person that understands that sin has tainted every part of his or her being. The cry of wretched is the cry of one who truly desires to live for God in Christ, yet, finds that sin has affected his or her mind, actions, will, his or her very being. The cry of wretched in Rom 7 is the cry of not only a Christian believer but of a mature Christian believer.[224]

The inner struggle of a Christian believer is also seen in Gal 5:17. In this passage, the Christian believer is exhorted to live by means of the Spirit (Gal 5:16). It is to be understood that only a Christian believer can live by means of the Spirit. The believer who lives by the Spirit will not fulfill the desires of the flesh (Gal 5:16). The flesh here is the earthen vessel that Paul says holds the treasure of the Gospel. It is to be seen in this statement that the believer who lives by the Spirit will not fulfill the desires of the flesh, that Christian believer is faced with the desires of the flesh. Within the Christian believer, the flesh and the Spirit are in conflict with each other (Gal 5:17). This conflict, at times leads the Christian believer to not do what they desire to do (Gal 5:17; Rom 7).

The Christian has been set free from sin (Rom 6:18). To be freed from sin is not to become sinless, but it means to be freed from sin's hostile enslaving power.[225] The Christian has been freed from the realm of sin.[226] Sin in this context is to be understood as a power[227] that has subdued the person. This power is considered a master; a master that has control over the person.[228] Sin no longer rules over the Christian as a master (Rom 6:14). When Adam and Eve chose the Fruit of the Tree of the Knowledge of Good

177

and Evil, they not only rejected God as the authority over their lives, but they rejected God as their Lord. When Adam and Eve chose the Fruit over God, the Fruit became their lord; their master. The Fruit of the Tree of the Knowledge of Good and Evil does not lead to independence, to autonomy as the Serpent said to Eve (Gen 3:4-5). One of the biggest lies of the Serpent is the lie that apart from God there is independence; there is autonomy; there is freedom. Choosing the Fruit of the Tree of the Knowledge of Good and Evil does not lead to independence, to freedom. The choice of the Fruit of the Tree of the Knowledge of Good and Evil which is the rejection of God, leads not to freedom but to slavery. The idea of the autonomous person is an illusion, a lie.[229]

The choice of the Fruit of the Tree of the Knowledge of Good and Evil is the rejection of one master and the choosing of another master. The choice to follow the Fruit of the Tree of the Knowledge of Good and Evil leads to the rejection of God. To reject God is the essence of sin, so the master that is chosen in the choice of the Fruit of the Knowledge of Good and Evil is sin. In repentance, the believing sinner rejects sin, autonomy, the Fruit of the Tree of the Knowledge of Good and Evil and returns to God in Christ as Lord. Jesus Christ is now Lord of the Christian and sin is no longer the master, the Lord. When a believing sinner is set free from sin as master over his or her life, that believing sinner is made a slave of righteousness (Rom 6:18). To be freed from sin is to be a slave of righteousness. There is only slavery to sin or slavery to righteousness. Sin is either the master of the person or Jesus Christ is the master of the person. There is no middle ground; there are no autonomous individuals.

The Christian has been set free from the ruling power of sin because the Christian is no longer under the law (Rom 6:14). When a person believes the Gospel and accepts Jesus Christ as Lord and Savior, that person is released, transferred from the kingdom of darkness into the kingdom of God's Son (Col 1:13).

While it is true that a Christian is a new person in Christ it is also true that Christians still struggle with the old person (Rom 6:11-14). Paul has stated that in Christ a person is no longer a slave of sin (Rom 6:6-7). This is the declaration of righteousness for the Christian. The Christian is right with God, which means freed from sin. The declaration of righteousness is not the end of the story, however. Paul further encourages the Christian, the one freed from sin, to not let sin reign in his or her mortal body (Rom 6:12). Here can be seen the present experience of the Christian. The Christian is freed from sin, yet, at the same time most not let sin reign. There is no discrepancy here. Paul has stated that the Christian has been freed from sin as a master, has been transferred from sin's kingdom. In the being set free from sin as a master, the Christian has returned to his or her rightful master, Jesus Christ and is now in the kingdom of Christ. Sin no longer is the master of the Christian; the Christian has rejected the Fruit of the Tree of the Knowledge of Good and Evil and has returned to God and His Word as the ultimate authority over his or her life. Although the Christian is now in the Kingdom of God and Christ is his or her Lord, there is still the struggle with sin in the life of the Christian (Rom 7; Gal 5:17). The struggle with the old person still leads the Christian to acts, thoughts, and behaviors that are not in agreement with Christ's righteousness. The Christian is thus exhorted to not let sin rule at all in any part of his or her life.[230]

A Christian lives in the present but has also experienced the future. To be in Christ is both a present experience where the believing sinner is freed from his or her sins, that is released from the bondage of sin, set free from the punishment for sin, reconciled to God, declared and made righteous, sanctified and made holy. These are all experienced the moment when a believing sinner accepts Jesus Christ as Lord and Savior, asking for forgiveness and wholeness. They are all vital and life-changing events in the present.

All the above mentioned experiences are to be understood in the fact that the above mentioned experiences are both present and future. The Christian believer, although righteous by both imputation and impartation, is not perfect. The Christian believer, living at the present time, is living in the now and in the not yet of the eschatological age.[231] What this means is that the

180

Christian's present experience in Christ is not yet the full experience which is called glorification.[232] Christians are told that when Christ returns, they will be like Him (1 John 3:2-3). It is when Christ returns that Christians will be fully like Him. Now, in the present, Christians are growing from glory to glory (2 Cor 3:18). In the present, Christians are not yet glorified, and they have not experienced in full what Christ is doing in and through them. While in the present, Christians are to grow from glory to glory, knowing that they are in partially fixed and partially broken bodies (Rom 8:23).

When the fullness of time came, God sent His Son, born of a woman, to redeem those who were under the law, that we might receive the full rights of God's children (Gal 4:4,5). The fullness of time is seen as both a present moment and an eschatological claim.[233] This means that the fullness of time was not simply the moment in which Christ came into the world. It does refer to the time when Christ was born of a virgin and grew into adulthood. Yet, it refers to more than the mere ticking of the clock. The coming of Christ into the world, the fullness of time, is also the coming of a new age.[234] This age is the Kingdom of God. In addition, there is the understanding that the Kingdom of God is the end of history.[235] The end of history is both the temporal aspect—that is the passing of time--and the aim, the goal of history.[236]

Included within this understanding of the coming of the Kingdom of God in the fullness of time is also the understanding that with the coming of

Christ into the world, Jesus Christ brought the future into the present.[237] The future brought by Christ into the present is called the Kingdom of God. The Kingdom of God is both the place where God reigns and the reign of God itself. There is in Christ an overlapping, if you will, of the future and the present. The present is now the place where the future, the Kingdom of God is breaking into. The fact that the full Kingdom of God is not yet present in the world means that the full experience of the Kingdom of God is still future. Yet, because the Kingdom of God is present, God is indeed ruling the hearts of His people, there is the now, the present of the Kingdom of God. The future is present in the hearts of the people of God now, in the present.

The future that Jesus Christ brought into the now, the present is not only the Kingdom of God as understood as the rule, the reign of God over creation, but also includes the new humanity.[238] The new humanity is composed of Jews and Gentiles (Eph 2:15). These who make up the new humanity are those who live under God's rule, God's authority which is God's kingdom.

The new humanity is included in Christ, because Jesus Christ is the Second Adam, here called the Last Adam (1 Cor 15:45-47). The word *second* used in reference to Jesus Christ is intentional. Adam, the one created by God and placed in the Garden of Eden, the one who ate from the Tree of the Knowledge of Good and Evil was a pattern of the one who to come (Rom

5:14). Thus, Adam was the *first* Adam. It is stated that Adam was a pattern of the one who was to come. The one who was to come is Christ (Rom 5:12-21; 1 Cor 15:45-49). Adam was a pattern of Christ in that through the sin of Adam, Adam affected all people. Adam affected all people in that he brought condemnation to all people (Rom 5:18). The theological term for the sin of Adam which brought condemnation to all people is original sin. While it is debated amongst the theologians whether the guilt of Adam's sin is reckoned or imputed to all people, the Word of God simply states that the one sin of Adam brought condemnation to all people and that through the disobedience of Adam people were made sinners (Rom 5:19). The question to be asked is: If the guilt of Adam's sin is not imputed to all people; how then did Adam's sin bring condemnation to all people?

Adam was a type of Christ, in that Adam's act, his sin affected the whole human race, called all people (Rom 5:18). As Adam's sin affected the whole human race, so the obedience of Jesus Christ affected the whole human race (Rom 5:18). The death of Jesus Christ on the Cross of Calvary was for the sin of the whole world (John 3:16: 1 John 2:2). The fact that Jesus Christ died for the whole human race does not mean that all people will eventually live in what is called heaven, the new world that God is preparing for those who love Him. Paul writes that those who benefit from the death of Christ are those who receive God's grace and gift of righteousness (Rom 5:17). Though Christ died for the entire human race, only those who accept Jesus Christ as Lord and Savior and thus are born-again will become righteous and become a child of God.

Christians, in the now, the present are living in bodies not yet fully redeemed (Rom 8:23) also belong to the new age, for they are in Christ. While living in bodies not yet redeemed, Christian believers groan waiting for full redemption, fully experiencing all that Christ has and is doing for them (Rom 8:18-39). The coming of Christ, the coming of God's kingdom means that the Christian now, in the present lives in the old age and the new age at the same time. This living simultaneously in both the old age and the new age is seen in that the Christian still has an ongoing struggle with that part of their nature that is influenced by sin.[239] There is much debate within the Christian world of whether the sin nature remains in a Christian or not. This study will not enter that discussion.[240] The position that this study takes is that the Christian is not yet sinless, that there remains *something* within the Christian which is still influenced by and at times under the control of temptation and sin. Many if not all of those in the discussion on whether the sin nature remains or not, agree on this point, that is that there is *something* within the Christian that is still influenced by sin. What one calls this *something* is in essence the point of the discussion.

There is seen in Gal 4: 4, 5 both a present reality and a future experience. God sent His Son who was born of a woman in time, at a specific moment in the life of the human race. It is also stated that God sent His Son to redeem those who were under the law that we might receive the full rights of God's children. Here is the present experience of salvation, which includes forgiveness, reconciliation, redemption, justification, sanctification, new birth and eventually glorification.

The believing sinner experiences the moment of faith salvation, according to this passage, the full rights of God's children (Gal 4:5). Yet, at the same time as the present experience of the full rights of being God's children, there is also the fact that the experience which the believing sinner experiences in the present is only the first fruits of the full rights that belongs to the Christian (Rom 8:23). The experience of the first fruits of the Spirit is the guarantee of the receiving of the full rights (Rom 8:23; Eph 1:13, 14). The Holy Spirit is God's guarantee that the believing sinner is both now, in the present a Child of God and will receive in full the inheritance, which is the experience of the full rights of being God's child (Eph 1:13, 14).

A guarantee is given both for the present and the future. If the fullness is received now, in the present, there is no need for a guarantee for the rest. God has given to the believing sinner a guarantee, embodied in the Holy Spirit, that the present experience of forgiveness, reconciliation, justification, redemption, new birth, is both a reality in the now and will be fully experienced in the future.

The new humanity which is in Christ is a people that are righteous. To be in Christ is to be righteous (Rom 5:1). To be righteous means to have a right relationship and standing with God. While being righteous, the Christian is still in jars of clay (2 Cor 4:7), that is in bodies that are still broken and affected by sin. The righteous standing and relationship of Christians is to be seen as a present experience that reflects the future reality, the not yet of the Kingdom of God. When a believing sinner accepts Jesus Christ as Lord and Savior that believing sinner is forgiven and that experience is a present experience. Yet, the present experience, as wonderful as it is a foretaste of what God has both given in the present and will give in the future (1 Cor 2:9).

The purpose of the Church in the present age is to proclaim, love, teach and aid others so that they might experience righteousness, both in its initial experience and in the on-going experience of sanctification. The truth of the matter is, as has been stated before many times and in a number of ways is that though God loves the world, the whole world does not love God and does not belong to God spiritually.

The Church is to live and preach the Good News so that all might hear and believe. God loves the world and gave His Son that the world might believe (John 3:16). The Bible is very clear that God desires all to be saved and to come to the knowledge of the truth (1 Tim 2: 3,4). Jesus Christ is the Lamb of God who takes away the sin of the world (John 1:29). Jesus did not die *just for those who believe*. Jesus died for every individual who has lived, is living or will live (1 John 2:2). The *whole* world is from the Greek ὄλος. ὄλος is a word that expresses totality.[241] Christ is the sacrifice for sin, not just for those who believe (our sins in 1 John 2:2) but for the sins of the whole, complete, entire world.

This fact does not lead to the teaching of universalism. Universalism is the thought that all people will eventually be in heaven. The Bible is clear that not all people will be in the new world, called heaven that God is preparing. Jesus divided the human race into two groups, those who endure eternal punishment and those who will experience eternal life, which is to say, life in the new world that God is preparing (Matt 25:46). The new world, what in Matt 25:46 is called eternal life is a world that God is preparing for those who love Him (1 Cor 2:9). The line that divides the human race is Jesus Christ, if He is loved by the individual or not.

The Lamb's Book of Life is a register of those who are in the kingdom. The kingdom is referring to the kingdom of God. To be a member of the kingdom of God is to love God in Jesus Christ. There are individuals whose names are not in the Lamb's Book of Life (Rev 20:11-15). The individual whose name is not found in the Book of Life will be cast into the Lake of Fire (Rev 20:15) to endure eternal punishment (Matt 25:46).

Jesus Christ has finished the work (John 19:30) of fulfilling the Scriptures (John 19:28) and, from God's side, the work is understood as the work that all might enter and live in the new world. God is indeed reconciled to the world (2 Cor 5:19), yet, that is only one side of the equation. The world, individuals must be reconciled to God in Christ and through Christ (2 Cor 5:20). God is reconciled to all people. This reconciliation from God's side opens the door, so to speak, gives the opportunity for people to be reconciled to God. God does not force anyone to accept the message of reconciliation. God is the father waiting for the wayward child to return, watching every day for His children to come home. Though God is reconciled to all, He allows each and everyone to choose for him or herself. The choice of each and everyone will determine where he or she spends eternity. Jesus Christ's blood has reconciled God to each and everyone and is the basis for all to be reconciled to God, if they accept the message of reconciliation.

A question at this point is to be asked: Since Christ died for the world, does this include those who spend eternity in the Lake of Fire? The answer to that question is yes. Those who spend eternity in the Lake of Fire are of the human race, the world that Christ died for. It is then to be asked: if Christ died for the sins of those who spend eternity in the Lake of Fire, why are they to be cast into the Lake of Fire? The answer to that question is found in the desire of those who will be cast into the Lake of Fire. They did not "desire" Jesus

Christ. They did not love Him. It can also be said that the Lake of Fire is not a place for sinners; if that were the case, all would spend eternity there. The Lake of Fire is a place for unbelievers; those who are not born-again; those who do not love Jesus Christ.

God gives to each individual what he or she desires. Those who spend eternity in the new world that God is preparing want Jesus; those who spend eternity in the Lake of Fire do not want Jesus. Each individual will receive what he or she wanted in this world. The experience of receiving what is wanted is borne out through heaven or hell.

Although Jesus Christ died for all, not all will be members of the kingdom of God and spend eternity in God's world. What this means is that the teaching of universalism is not true (1 John 2:2; Matt 25:26).

A second error to be avoided is the error of lawlessness. This error simply states that once a person accepts Jesus Christ and is forgiven; that person can live anyway that he or she determines. Another way of saying the same is that because Jesus Christ has fulfilled the law, the Christian is free to determine what he or she wants to do.

Christ has set us free from the law (Rom 8:2). The law that Christians are set free from is the law of sin and of death. This law is indeed a law of rules (Gal 3:10). The basic understanding of this law is that to be accepted by God, one must follow the law. Acceptance by God is by faith (Eph 2:8-10) and not

189

by following a certain set of rules.

We are indeed free in Christ; yet, this freedom does not give the choice to live anyway one decides. The freedom in Christ does not lead to lawlessness (Gal 5:13). Freedom from sin means that one has become a slave to righteousness (Rom 6:18). The person set free in Christ will no longer live as the world lives but will live according to God's principles (Eph 4:17-32). Freedom in Christ will not be expressed as the Christian choosing anything and everything. Freedom in Christ is expressed in love (Gal 5:14). Love is to be understood as loving the Lord your God with all that you are and all that you have and your neighbor as yourself. To love God with all that you are and all that you have means that you are a disciple, a follower of Christ (Matt 28: 19, 20) and includes obedience (Matt 28:20) to the commands of God. True freedom in Christ is seen and expressed in a heart desire to live life that is pleasing to God (2 Cor 5:9). It is by faith that God is pleased (Heb 11:6). Faith is not the mere intellectual holding of certain facts, but is found in a life that is lived according to God's principles, God's heart (James 2:14-26).

To be set free from the law of sin and of death, of finding acceptance by God in rules, is by the law of the Spirit (Rom 8:2). Christians are set free from one law by another law. The law of life sets a person free from the law of sin and of death. The evidence that one is set free from the law of sin and of death is that one follows the law of the Spirit of life. The law of life, the law of the

Spirit, is experienced in a heart that follows the Holy Spirit (Rom 8:5). To be set free from the law of sin and of death is to desire what the Holy Spirit desires (Rom 8:5). To desire what the Holy Spirit desires is to desire what God desires.

To be set free from the law means that at the Day of Judgment, the law will not be used to judge a Christian's life. The Christian has not only been set free from the law but is no longer under the law (Rom 6:14). The law was not given to be the standard which people were to follow and thus be judged. The law is not the standard by which God declares that a person is righteous or not (Rom 3:20). No one will be declared righteous by God by observing the law (Rom 3:20). The law was never intended to be obeyed as a way of being right with God. The purpose of the law is to make clear what sin is (Rom 3:20; 5:20). Once a person is aware of what sin is, the law has a further purpose of leading a person to Jesus Christ so that in Christ that person might be justified, to be in a right relationship with God through faith (Gal 3:24). No one can be right with God by the law. The law brings only God's wrath (Rom 4:15) and is not able to bring a right relationship with God (Rom 8:3). Because the law brings only wrath, the Christian will not be judged according to the law. In fact, the one who is attempting to be right with God by the law, the one who holds to the teaching that the Day of Judgment will be a day that reveals how one has kept the law is alienated from Christ (Gal 5:4). Those who hold to the teaching that only those who have kept the law faithfully will be allowed into heaven have fallen from grace[242] (Gal 5:4). In addition, those who say that once a person has been born-again that person will stand before the judgment throne of God to be judged on how he or she has kept the law does not know grace. Grace is the only basis for which a person can be saved (Eph 2:8). So, when a person has fallen from grace, this person is both alienated from Christ and is not in a saved relationship with God. In essence, the person who seeks to be right with God by the law is a Non-Christian. A Christian is one who is saved and salvation is by grace through faith (Eph 2:8, 9). The Christian, the one who has believed in Jesus Christ as Lord and Savior is righteous. The Christian is righteous not because the Christian has or will fulfill the law, but because Jesus Christ has fulfilled the law (Rom 10:4) and the one who is in Christ has become righteous in Christ.

To be freed from the law does not lead to chaos or to living in any manner whatsoever. The Christian having been freed from the law is now a servant of righteousness, of Christ. The heart of the Christian is set on following the royal law of love (James 2:8). When the Christian loves, that Christian is fulfilling the law, because love is the meaning, the fulfillment of the law (Rom 13:8-10). Jesus Himself stated that the law and prophets were fulfilled by love (Matt 22:34-40). Thus, when a Christian loves, that Christian will do no harm to his or her neighbor (Rom 13:10). In love, no one will steal,

192

covet, commit adultery or murder (Rom 13:8-10). Love is the care, the concern for the neighbor that goes beyond mere rules and regulations (Matt 22:34-40) for love is the concern for the neighbor that clothes the naked, feeds the hungry, visit's the lonely, the shut-in, the prisoner. Love is the giving of not only the tithe, but of all to God for the spread of the Gospel, that those who are still in darkness might receive the light. Love, not rules gives one's sons and daughters as missionaries. Only love will enable a Christian to stand for Christ during persecution. Rule and law will not comfort the broken heart in the loss of a loved one; only love will bring both comfort and hope. Law will not bring assurance of salvation, of being accepted by God, this is a gift of love, of grace. The law does not free one to love, but enslaves one by fear. The law will never be satisfied in its demands of not enough. A person who lives by law is afraid that one has not done enough to meet the law's requirements and thus to be allowed into God's presence. The law is a standard that can never be reached; it is only love that steps down to the sinner and lifts him or her up to the throne of God in Christ and proclaims accepted (Col 3:1-4). Law does not free anyone to be concerned about others; the concern of the law following the law is themselves and the attempt of doing enough so that they themselves are allowed into God's presence. It is only love that sets the heart free to be able to love the neighbor and God. Jesus has finished the work of salvation (John 19:30). The finished work of Jesus refers to God's side of salvation. God is now reconciled to the world (2 Cor 5:19). There is still the imperative of believing in Christ for salvation. Individuals must accept Jesus Christ as Lord and Savior; they must be born-again. The finished work of salvation also does not include the keeping one's heart right with God. Christians have entered into the finished work of Christ when they accepted Jesus Christ as Lord and Savior and were born-again. However, there is still the need, the imperative for Christians to live in righteousness, to maintain a right relationship with God.

Jesus said that in Him we are clean (John 15:3), yet, we, who are in Christ, are to remain in Him (John 15:3). To remain in Christ is evidenced by bearing fruit for the Kingdom of God (John 15:4, 5). One can only remain in Christ when one remains in love with Jesus (John 15:9). To be in love with Jesus is to obey Him (John 15:10). Obedience to God, the living of one's life to please God in Christ is the evidence of love for Jesus Christ. In John 15:1-17, Jesus said that Christians are to remain in Him. It is only when Christians remain in Christ that they will bear fruit for the Kingdom of God. To remain in Christ is to love Christ. To love Christ is evidenced by obedience to the will and commands of God.

It is imperative that Christians remain in Christ. To remain in Christ is evidenced by obedience to Christ in all things. There is the possibility of not remaining in Christ (John 15:6). The phrase not remaining in Christ can be understood as apostasy, the living of life as a Christian in an unworthy manner of God's love or possibly as both is an understanding that is open to all.[243] However, one has to understand that there is a remaining in Christ and a possibility of not remaining in Christ. The basic understanding of Jesus' words here is that it is possible for someone in Christ to live in such a way as to not remain in Christ. If the not remaining in Christ is the lack of fruit for the kingdom of God, the living of life in disobedience; then to not remain in Christ is the Christian living life in whatever manner the Christian chooses. The Christian is to live life in obedience to Christ; that is love for Him. For the Christian to choose what he or she wants as to the values and actions of his or her life is to choose the Fruit of the Tree of the Knowledge of Good and Evil, which is to reject God.

Although Jesus finished the work of salvation, this refers to God's side of salvation. There still remains the human response to accept Jesus Christ as Lord and Savior and for the Christian there is still the remaining in Christ through a life of obedience to Jesus Christ as Lord.

Lawlessness is thus excluded in Christ. It is not possible to live at the same time according to God's principles and opposing principles. This is found clearly in the choice of the Fruit of the Tree of the Knowledge of Good and Evil. If a person chooses the Fruit, being self-determination of what is right and wrong, then that person has rejected God.

The preaching and spread of the Gospel of Jesus Christ which is the bringing in of everlasting righteousness, is a sign that the world is moving toward the Apocalypse (Matt 24:14). Perhaps that is one reason why there is a call for a moratorium on sending missionaries by some within Christian organizations. It is a sad truth that not all who claim to be Christian are truly Christian. Jesus Himself said that in the Day of Judgment there will be many who claim the name of Christ, but are unknown to Christ (Matt 7:21-23). The truth that the spread of the Gospel of Jesus Christ is a sign that the world is moving towards the Apocalypse maybe the reason that others within Christian organizations who say that they believe Christ and the Gospel are no longer passionate about the sending and supporting of missionaries. The thought is: if the spread of the Gospel is moving the world closer toward the Apocalypse, and the Apocalypse is an event that will turn the world upside down, then, the individual Christian's lifestyle will be affected and that is not acceptable to many who claim the name of Christ. Perhaps the subconscious fear of the loss of a certain lifestyle is the reason that so many within the Christian world have lost their passion for the spread of the Gospel and the sending and supporting of missionaries.

Whatever the reason so many within the Christian world have lost their passion for the Gospel and sending of missionaries, the fact is that the spread of the Gospel is a sign that the world is moving toward the Apocalypse. The

Apocalypse will change the world as we know it. Some of the changes that the Apocalypse will bring will be discussed in the remaining chapters of this book.

CHAPTER 6

THE RAPTURE

Included within any and every discussion regarding the Apocalypse is the topic of the rapture. The rapture is a point of discussion that either one holds to dearly or rejects altogether. In this chapter we will attempt to answer two questions regarding the rapture, one being the validity of the rapture and the second being the timing of the rapture, if it does exist.

In an attempt to answer the first question, we must first begin with a short history of the word *rapture*. The word *rapture* is the English transliteration of the Latin translation of the Greek ἁρπάζω found in 1 Thess 4:17. In 382 CE, Pope Damasus I commissioned Jerome to update the existing Latin Bible. Jerome, for the most part completed his work in 384 CE, but continued to make different revisions over the years. The completed work of Jerome became known as the Latin Vulgate. The Latin Vulgate, considered by some to be the most influential work in Western Europe from 400 to 1530 CE, is also said to have influenced the translation of the King James translation of the Bible. The Greek ἁρπάζω, translated into Latin and from which we get the English transliteration of *rapture*, means to grab or seize by force, with the purpose of removing, to seize, to snatch away.[244] We learn from this that the word *rapture* has been in the Church since at least 384 CE and more likely before the completion of the Latin Vulgate. We are to understand from this

198

that the word *rapture* has a long history and use in the Western Church.[245]

We now want to look at the event which is termed the *rapture.* We are not as concerned about the name of the event which is called the rapture, but with the event itself. If the event that is termed the rapture was named instead *the snatching up,* there would be a clear teaching of the *event.* As it has already been stated, the name rapture is simply the English transliteration of the Latin translation of the Greek ἁρπάζω. What we must remember is that the name of the event is not as important as the event itself.

Paul wrote concerning the coming, the παρουσία of the Lord that when the Lord comes again, there will be a *snatching up,* ἁρπάζω, of both the dead in Christ and those Christians who are alive at that time. The corporate body of Christians will then rise to meet the Lord in the air (1 Thess 4:13-17). Since 1 Thess 4:17 is the main passage of Scripture that teaches of a snatching up, of the rapture, of Christians: we will take a little closer at this passage.

In 1 Thess 4:13-17 there are several events that occur. The first event is the descent of the Lord (1 Thess 4:16). The second event is the resurrection of the dead in Christ (1 Thess 4:16). The third event is the *snatching up* of both the dead in Christ and the Christians who are alive at that time to meet the Lord in the air (1 Thess 4:17).

We will look at each of the three events and discover their meaning. First of all we notice that there is a day when the Lord will return. Many in the world do not believe that the Lord will return. They live their lives as if there is either no Lord Jesus or as if He will never return. However, the clear teaching of the Word of God is that this life as we know it will end and a new life will begin. The ending of this life and the beginning of a new world is with the return of the Lord Jesus Christ.

The second point that we notice about the Lord's παρουσία is that He does not come to the earth, but remains in the air (1 Thess 4:17). The word air is from ἀήρ. Ἀήρ refers to the space immediately above the earth's surface.[246] In this passage it is not said that Jesus returns to the earth itself, but that in His παρουσία He meets the Christians in the air. This fact is important to remember because at the Second Coming of Jesus Christ, He returns to the earth itself (Rev 19:11-21, esp. 19 which says that the beast and the armies of the earth gather to make war against Christ and His army).

We are told of another distinction between the παρουσία of Jesus and the Second Coming of Jesus. At the παρουσία of Jesus, the Christian meets the Lord in the air. Nowhere is there any indication that we will meet anyone else, besides other Christian believers. However, at the Second Coming of Jesus, we are told that He does not come alone. When Christ returns to the earth at His Second Coming, Christ comes with the armies of heaven (Rev 19:14).

What is interesting is that when Jesus returns at His Second Coming,

He comes with the *armies* of heaven. We are told that when Jesus returns, He returns with more than one army. One of the armies of heaven is the angelic host (Matt 26:53; Psalm 68:17). The other army that makes up the *armies of heaven* is that of the Christian believers (Rev 17:14). What we are to understand from this is at Jesus' παρουσία, He comes *for* His people. At the Second Coming, Christ comes *with* His people.

The second event that Paul wrote concerning is the resurrection of the dead in Christ (1 Thess 4:16). The teaching of the resurrection of the dead in Christ is a great comfort to all Christian believers. The great cloud of witnesses that have gone before includes many of whom we know and love. Their death is not the end. We will see them again at the resurrection of the dead in Christ.

The teaching of the resurrection of the dead in Christ at Christ's παρουσία raises a question. Before Christ's παρουσία and the resurrection of the dead in Christ, in what condition are the dead in Christ? Another way to ask the question is: at the death of a Christian, does that Christian's soul go to sleep or is the Christian's soul awake and aware?

The teaching of Scripture is clear on this subject. We begin with the Old Testament teaching found in 1 Sam 28. We are told that at one point in the life of Saul, while he was still king of Israel and after the death of Samuel the prophet, that the army of the Philistines was encamped against the Israelites.

201

As Saul the king saw the Philistines, he was overcome with fear. Saul inquired and was told that there was a witch who lived at Endor (1 Sam 28:7). Upon hearing this news, Saul changes his clothes and goes to consult with the witch (1 Sam 28:8). At the meeting of Saul and the witch, Saul asked the witch to bring up Samuel the prophet (1 Sam 28:11). We must remember at this point that Samuel was dead and already buried (1 Sam 28:3). So, when the witch wanted to know whom she was to bring up (1 Sam 28:11), what the witch meant was who to bring up from the dead. In answer to the witch's question, Saul asked for Samuel the prophet to be brought up (1 Sam 28:11). Saul then asks the witch what she sees (1 Sam 28:13). The witch replies that she sees a spirit[247] coming up from the ground. Saul then asks the witch what the spirit looked like and she answered that the spirit looks like an old man wearing a robe (1 Sam 28:14). Upon hearing this Saul knew that the spirit was Samuel (1 Sam 28:14).

What we are to understand from this passage is that after death, the righteous are still awake and aware. The righteous after death still have a form, a shape; one can say a body which can be recognized, for Saul knew that it was Samuel. After death, Samuel could speak for he asked Saul why Saul had disturbed him (1 Sam 28:15). Samuel, as well as being able to speak after death, was also able to hear for he heard what Saul said to him (1 Sam 28:15, 16). In addition, after death, Samuel was still very cognizant of what was happening in the life of Saul (1 Sam 28:16-19).

We continue our discussion regarding the dead in Christ with the words of Jesus Himself. Jesus tells the disciples about a rich man and Lazarus (Luke 16:19-31). Lazarus was a poor man who stayed near the gate of the rich man (Luke 16:19, 20). One day, Jesus, said, both the rich man and Lazarus died (Luke 16:22). After death, the rich man, being in torment (Luke 1623) looked up and saw Abraham with Lazarus by the side of Abraham (Luke 16:23). The rich man called out to Abraham and asked Abraham to send Lazarus to dip his finger in water to cool the tongue of the rich man (Luke 16:24). Abraham replied to the rich man that that was not possible to do (Luke 16:25). The rich man then asks Abraham to send Lazarus to his father's house to warn the rich man's brothers so that they will not come to this place of torment (Luke 16:28).

We see in this passage the same teachings that we saw in the passage concerning Samuel. In this passage, Jesus, tells us that after death, the dead are able to see, for the rich man saw Abraham and Lazarus. The dead are also able to speak, for the rich man and Abraham engaged in a conversation with each other. Included with speaking is the ability to hear and understand the words that are spoken to them. We see this in the fact that the rich man heard and understood what Abraham said to him. In addition, the dead are able to remember for the rich man remembered that he had brothers who were still

203

living. Finally, we see that after death, the dead are able to not only see but to recognize who and what they see. The rich man not only saw Abraham and Lazarus, but he recognized who they were.

The final point to understand from this passage is that the soul after death is able to experience various sensations. The rich man after death experienced torment, fire and agony (Luke 16: 23, 24). In addition, the rich man must have been able to experience refreshment and comfort for he asked Abraham to send Lazarus to dip his finger in cool water to cool the tongue of the rich man (Luke 16:24).

The words of Jesus in Luke 16 are not to be seen as a parable, for if it was a parable, it would be the only parable in which Jesus gave a name to the characters. A second reason to not see this as a parable is that the teaching here corresponds exactly with the teaching in 1 Sam 28.

A third passage that describes the righteous after death is the experience on the Mount of Transfiguration (Matt 17:1-8). In this passage, we are told that Jesus took with Him three disciples: Peter, James and John up the mountain by themselves (Matt 17:1). While on the mountain, Jesus was transfigured before their eyes. After Jesus was transfigured, Moses and Elijah appeared and began speaking with Jesus (Matt 17:3). Although Elijah was taken to heaven in a whirlwind (2 Kings 2:1); Moses had died many years before this time (Joshua 1:1). Both Moses and Elijah appeared with Jesus.

Again, we are to understand that Moses after death had a form, a shape, a body for the disciples saw Moses (Matt 17:3, 4). In addition, Moses had ears to hear with and a voice to speak with for he spoke with Jesus (Matt 17: 3). We can state from implication that Moses had eyes to see with for he did not look wildly around for the person with whom he was speaking. He had a mind that remembered and understood for in his conversation with Jesus it is not stated that he rambled and spoke incoherently. In fact, we are told of what Moses and Elijah spoke with Jesus about. They spoke with Jesus of His upcoming death (Luke 9:30).

A fourth passage that describes the condition of the dead is found in the vision of John called the Revelation. John had a vision and was told to write what he saw for the words were true (Rev 22:6). This point is important to remember. John was told that what he saw and heard was trustworthy and true.

John, in writing down all that he saw and heard, sees the Lamb who is Jesus Christ open the seven seals (Rev 6:1). After Jesus opened each seal, an event was seen and recorded by John. At the opening of the 5th seal, John records that he saw under the altar the souls[248] of those who had been slain because of their standing firm for Christ (Rev 6:9). John is describing those who had been killed; they were not alive as we would describe it. The first point that we are to understand is that a soul can be seen. The second point to understand is that the soul after death has a shape, form or body. We see this in the fact that the souls under the altar were given white robes (Rev 6:11). If the soul after death did not have some sort of shape, form or body, why were they then given a white robe? It is possible that they were given a white robe to place in their *hope chest* waiting for the day of resurrection when they would then be embodied. However, it is much more consistent with the teaching of the Old Testament, Jesus and the vision of John to understand that after death, the soul does have some sort of shape, form or body. What that body is made of, we do not know. The plain teaching of Scripture, however, is that after death the soul does have a shape, form or body. If not, then Saul would not have recognized Samuel, the rich man would not have recognized Abraham and Lazarus and the disciples would not have recognized Moses.

The third point to understand form John's vision of the soul after death is that the souls under the altar had a voice for they cried out to the Lord (Rev 6:10). This is consistent with the teaching in 1 Sam 28 concerning Samuel and Luke 16 concerning the rich man and Abraham. We are told that Samuel after death was able to engage in a conversation with Saul and that the rich man after death was able to converse with Abraham. This means of course, that they had a vocal apparatus that functioned, a mind to remember what words to speak and working ears that heard what was told them.

John writes and tells us that the souls under the altar asked for the

Lord to avenge their death (Rev 6:10). The point we are to understand from this is that the souls under the altar were able to remember what happened to them. This, also is consistent with the teaching concerning Samuel and the rich man. Samuel was able to remember Saul and what Saul had done; while the rich man was able to remember that he had brothers still in this world.

The Bible teaches that after death, the soul does not fall asleep in the sense that it is not aware. Nor, after death does the soul become a misty, translucent, fog like substance. After death, the soul retains some sort of shape, form or body, which is recognizable by others. The soul after death is able to speak, hear, remember and experience different feelings.

The condition of the soul after death is seen in the experience of Jesus Christ. Jesus, after death, went to the spirits in prison and preached to them (1 Pet 3:18-20). This means that Jesus must have had a shape, form or body and an ability to speak and communicate with others. From this, it is to be seen that the experience of Jesus is consistent with the teaching found throughout the Scriptures.

The next question to be explored concerning the resurrection of the righteous at the παρουσία of Jesus is from where do the dead in Christ come? Paul wrote that at Christ's παρουσία that the dead in Christ will rise first (1 Thess 4:16). The word *rise* is from ἀνίστημι, which means to cause someone to live again after having once died.[249] To cause someone to live again after death does not mean that at death the soul ceases to exist. This fact has already been established for us by the Biblical teaching above and is seen clearly in the death and resurrection of Jesus.

We begin our study of the resurrection from the dead with the word for resurrection. The word ἀνίστημι used by Paul to describe the dead in Christ (1 Thess 4:16) is the same word used to describe the resurrection of Jesus from the dead (John 20:9). This means that resurrection from the dead or to cause to live again after death does not mean that at death the soul ceases to live. Resurrection from the dead then must mean that the soul, which at death is separated from the body, is re-united with the body at the time of resurrection.

At death, where then does the soul go? We have seen from the Biblical teaching that after death the soul still retains form/shape/body and is able to hear, see, speak, remember and experience. Another point we must understand is that *all* souls after death experience the same conditions. What I mean is that it is not just the souls of the righteous that maintain some body and are able to experience life; the souls of the unrighteous also share the same condition as the souls of the righteous. We know this because in Luke 16, the discussion is concerning the rich man, who was certainly not righteous. We know that the rich man was not righteous because we are told that after death he went to hell (Luke 16:23). We learn from this that the souls of every person, after death shares the same experience. The souls of the righteous and unrighteous maintain some sort of body, are able to hear, speak, experience, remember and recognize others.

We continue our discussion of the destiny of the soul after death with the situation before the death and resurrection of Jesus. The death and resurrection of Jesus has changed everything, especially concerning the destination of the righteous soul after death.

Before the death and resurrection of Jesus, when a person died, that person's soul went to a place called Hades. This is in fact the destination of the rich man in Luke 16:23. While it is translated as hell, the word in Greek is ᾅδης.[250] ᾅδης is the place or abode of the dead.[251] As the abode of the dead, Hades is the place or abode of both the righteous and the unrighteous.[252] What this means is that after death, both the righteous and the unrighteous go to Hades.

Hades as the destination of the dead is separated into two different locations. Within Hades is a place for the unrighteous and a different place for the righteous (Luke 16:22-26). These two places are separated by a great chasm which no one is able to cross (Luke 16:26). Apparently, however, although separated by a great chasm, the two distinct places in Hades are visible to each other. In Hades, the rich man looked up and saw Abraham and Lazarus (Luke 16:23). Also, in return, Abraham was able to see and speak to the rich man across the great divide (Luke 16:25). While the souls of the righteous and the unrighteous, after death, share the same experience of maintaining a shape, form or body and are able to speak, hear, experience an remember, the experiences of the righteous souls are different than the unrighteous souls. In Hades, the place that is reserved for the unrighteous is a place of torment (Luke 16:23); while the place reserved for the righteous is a place of blessedness and peace.

The death and resurrection of Jesus has changed the destination where the righteous dead go. The reason that Jesus has changed the location of where the righteous dead go is because the death, resurrection and ascension to heaven of Jesus has opened heaven to the righteous. This is symbolized by the tearing of the curtain in the temple at the death of Jesus (Mark 15:38). The curtain in the temple separated the holy place, where the priests were to minister, from the most holy place, where the Ark of the Covenant was located. The Ark of the Covenant symbolized God's presence (Ex 26:31-35). The death of Jesus has opened heaven to the believer (Heb 10:19, 20). Because heaven is now open to the believer in Christ, the righteous, Paul is able to say that when a person in Christ dies, that person does not go to Hades but goes to be with the Lord (2 Cor 5:6-8).

In 2 Cor 5:6-8 we see the two life situations of the Christian believer. The first life situation is to be at home in the body (2 Cor 5:6). When a

Christian believer is at home in the body, what Paul meant is living in this life, that Christian believer is away from the Lord (2 Cor 5:6). Paul, here is not referring to the spiritual presence of the Lord, for the Lord, through the Holy Spirit who indwells the Christian believer (Rom 8: 9, 10). When Paul wrote that to be alive in this world means absent from the Lord, he meant physically absent.

The second life situation that Paul describes for the Christian is to be absent from the body and at home with the Lord (2 Cor 5:8). To be absent from the body means one is to die. For Paul, then, death was a departing from the physical body and a going to be with the Lord. This same teaching Paul expressed when he was in the jail in Philippi facing the possibility of martyrdom.

Paul, when facing the possibility of death wrote that for him to live is Christ and to die is gain (Phil 1:21). How can death be gaining? Paul answers this question when he says that to die is to depart from the body and to depart from the body is to be with the Lord (Phil 1:23).

The third event that Paul wrote that would occur at Jesus' παρουσία is the *snatching up*, ἁρπάζω, of both the resurrected Christian dead and the Christians who were still alive at the time of the παρουσία (1 Thess 4:17). At this third event, Christ is said to be in the air (1 Thess 4:17) where He waits for the Christians to meet Him. Before, however, the Christians meet the Lord in the air, two changes will occur. The first change is that the Christian dead are resurrected (1 Thess 4:16). When the Christian dead are resurrected, they will be changed by the putting on of that which is imperishable (1 Cor 15:52). By imperishable, Paul meant the opposite of perishable. By perishable he meant that which was mortal, that which was bound to die and disintegrate.[253] The Christian dead will put on that which is imperishable (1 Cor 15:52). The word imperishable means not subject to decay and death.[254] When referring to the dead, it is their physical bodies which have disintegrated. At the παρουσία of the Lord, the Christian dead will be raised from the tombs and will be clothed with immortal bodies.

The second change is of the Christians who are still alive at the moment of Christ's παρουσία. The change of the Christians who are still living will be from perishable to imperishable (1 Cor 15:52). That which is bound to die is the physical body in which Christians now live. In other words, the living Christians will be given imperishable bodies.

Paul writes that at the παρουσία of the Lord Jesus, all the Christian dead will be raised and given immortal bodies and those Christians who are still alive will be changed by the putting on of immortal bodies. This means that the Christian living and the Christian dead will be the same; that is, in immortal bodies. The point here is that Paul mentions two groups who will be changed. The first group is the dead in Christ and the second group consists of

212

the Christians who are living in this world at that time. There will be no one

who is a Christian at that moment, at the moment of the παρουσία of the Lord

who will not be changed and who will not rise to meet the Lord in the air. After

the Christian dead are raised and given immortal bodies; the Christian living

will be changed by the putting on of immortal bodies. Together, the Christian

dead and the Christian living will stand together as one immortal, living body

and will rise to meet the Lord in the air.

After the dead in Christ are raised and changed and the Christian

living are changed, both groups, the whole mass of individuals who are

Christian at that particular moment, will rise to meet the Lord in the air. At the

παρουσία there will not be *one Christian* remaining on the earth. All

Christians, those who are called the dead in Christ and those who are called the

living Christians, will be changed and will rise together to meet the Lord in the

air. The world at that moment will be void of any and all Christians. Every

Christian will have been changed and will have risen to meet the Lord in the

air.

The event in which the earth is emptied of every Christian is called the

snatching up. *Snatched up* is, as we have noted above, from the Greek

ἁρπάζω. ἁπράζω means to grab or seize by force with the purpose of

removing someone or something from a situation.[255] A further meaning of

ἁπράζω is that of a taking away suddenly.[256] As has already been stated

213

before, the Latin translation of ἁπράζω is transliterated into English as rapture.

The word ἁρπάζω is used to describe the act of being taken from one location to another. In 2 Cor 12:2, Paul states that he was *caught up,* ἁρπάζω, *to heaven.* In Rev 12:5, ἁρπάζω is used to describe the son of the woman being *snatched up* to the throne of God. Acts 8:39 tells us that Philip was *suddenly taken away,* ἁρπάζω, from the desert where the Ethiopian Eunuch was to another location—a location where the Eunuch could no longer see Philip. Jesus gave the promise that once a person believes in Him, no one would be able to *snatch,* ἁρπάζω, *them out of His hand* (John 1:28).

The event that we are calling the *snatching up,* ἁρπάζω, removes the Christian believer from the earth and unites the Christian believer with the Lord (1 Thess 5:17). After the *snatching up* of the Christians, all Christians will no longer be on the earth, but will be with the Lord.

At the Second Coming of the Lord, the Lord will bring with Him the armies of heaven. One of those armies is the angelic host. The other army that will accompany the Lord at His Second Coming is the army of Christians who were changed and who rose to meet the Lord in the air at the Lord's παρουσία. What we are to understand is that at the Second Coming of Christ, Christians will return to the earth. This distinction must be kept in clearly in mind. The snatching up of the Christian empties the earth of Christians; while

214

the Second Coming of the Lord fills the earth with Christians. Another point to notice is that the snatching up of the Christians, which we have already stated, empties the earth of Christians and the Second Coming of the Lord which fills the earth with Christians are two different events in the timeline to the Apocalypse. The Second Coming of Christ is when He returns to establish His kingdom on earth and will occur when Christ returns to engage the forces of the Anti-Christ in battle (Rev 19).

Why would the Lord empty the earth of Christians? Paul answers this question in his discussion regarding the Lord's παρουσία when he reminds the Thessalonian Christians that the Day of the Lord would come like a thief in the night (1 Thess 5:2) and that they were not to worry for God had not appointed the Christian to suffer wrath (1 Thess 5:9). The Lord empties the earth of Christians because the Day of the Lord has arrived.

The Day of the Lord is a topic that is taught in both the Old Testament and in the New Testament. The Day of the Lord will be a day of darkness wrote the prophet Amos (Amos 5:18). The darkness of the Day of the Lord will be total, completely devoid of any and all light (Amos 5:20). Jesus called the Christian the light of the world (Matt 5:14). As the light of the world, we Christians, are to live our lives so that the light might shine before all (Matt 5:16). A day completely devoid of any light at all, says Amos concerning the Day of the Lord. How can the Day of the Lord be empty of all light? The answer is that the earth must be emptied of the light before the Day of the Lord. At the snatching up, rapture, the earth is emptied of not only Christians, but also, because Christians are the light of the world, the earth is emptied of the light of the world as well. When the snatching up, rapture occurs and everyone who is a Christian at that moment rises to meet the Lord in the air, the earth will be completely devoid of the light of Christ and the earth will be dark.

The Day of the Lord will also be a day of destruction from God (Joel 1:15). The prophet Joel echoes the message of Amos that the Day of the Lord is a day of darkness and gloom (Joel 2:1-2). Included within the message of the Day of the Lord is a warning of a great army that spreads destruction across the land (Joel 2:2, 3). Ezekiel says that The Day of the Lord is a day of battle (Ezekiel 13:5) and doom for the nations of the world (Ezekiel 30:3). Along with the ideas of gloom, darkness and battle is the idea that the Day of the Lord is a day of God's judgment on the nations of the world (Obadiah 15; Zephaniah 1:14-23) and on the nation of Israel (Zephaniah 1:4-13). Tied intimately to the idea of judgment is the idea that the Day of the Lord is a day of punishment (Zephaniah 1:14-18). The Day of the Lord is called the day of wrath (Isaiah 13:9). The New Testament also teaches that the Day of the Lord is a day of wrath (1 Thess 5:1-9). The day of God's wrath is also when God's righteous judgment is revealed (Rom 2:5).

The Day of the Lord, according to the prophet Zephaniah is a day when God will bring a sudden end to all who live on the earth (Zephaniah 1:18). In the Septuagint, which is the Greek translation of the Hebrew Bible, the phrase *all who live on the earth* is πάντας τοὺς κατοικοῦντας τὴν γῆν. Literally the phrase means all the ones who live on the earth.

The phrase *"all who live on the earth"* is a phrase that describes the scope of the wrath of God on the Day of the Lord. As we have seen above, the Day of the Lord is the day of God's wrath and judgment. God, according to the prophets and the apostles, has stated that He will pour His wrath at the Day of the Lord on all who live on the earth. The question we ask now is: how does the pouring out of God's wrath on all the ones who live on the earth affect the Christians?

We begin our exploration of this question by stating that this same phrase, *all who live on the earth,* is found in Rev 3:10 to describe the ones who will experience the Tribulation. We begin with Rev 3:10 because this verse is in the center of the discussion on whether the rapture is or is not. The first point to understand is that the Tribulation is the Day of the wrath of God (Rev 6:16, 17). As the Day of God's wrath, the Tribulation is also connected to the Day of the Lord. So, when we compare the phrase *all those who dwell on the earth* in the context of the Day of the Lord and in reference to the Tribulation, we will be discussing the same day. Secondly, because the Day of God's wrath and the Tribulation are the same day, the phrase, *all who dwell on the earth*, refers to the same people.

Who are *all who dwell on the earth?* One understanding of the phrase, *all who dwell on the earth*, is that the phrase refers only to the faithless, the heathen.[257] According to this view, the phrase *"all who dwell on the earth"* does not mean every single human being living on the earth at that time. The phrase, according to this view, means only the Non-Christian segment of the world's population. This understanding is based in part on the statement found in Rev 11:10 which says that the inhabitants of the earth will rejoice over the death of God's Two Witnesses. The thought behind this is that God's people would not rejoice over the death of His Witnesses. We know that there will be some of God's people on the earth at that time. There will be the Two Witnesses (Rev 11) and there will be at least the 144,000 from the tribes of Israel, who are God's servants (Rev 7:1-8). The ones who rejoice over the death of God's Two Witnesses will not of course come from the servants of God. Therefore, according to this view, the phrase, *the inhabitants of the earth*, must refer only to those who would rejoice over the death of God's witnesses, that is Non-Christians or the enemies of the Church.[258]

We will look further at how the phrase, *all who dwell on the earth*, is used in the book of Revelation, the vision of John. The phrase, *all who dwell on the earth*, is used in Rev 6:10 to describe the ones who killed those who

218

remained steadfast in their faith in God. It is used in Rev 8:13 to describe the ones on which the Fifth Trumpet plague would fall. The phrase, *all who dwell on the earth*, refers to all those whose name is not found written in the Book of Life (Rev 13:8). The Book of Life is the record of all who are members of the kingdom of God and who will live with God forever; that is Christians (Rev 20:15). In Rev 13:12, the phrase, *all who dwell on the earth*, refers to all who have taken the mark of the beast and in so doing have worshipped the beast, that is sworn allegiance to the beast. The phrase is used in Rev 17:2 to describe all who entered into spiritual adultery with the city that during the last days becomes the economic and political center of the world (Rev 17:18). Finally, the phrase *all who dwell on the earth*, is used to describe those who are deceived by the Anti-Christ (Rev 17:8).

Rev 3:10 says that *all the ones who dwell on the earth* refers to ones who dwell on τῆς οἰκουμένης ὅλης. Οἰκουμένης can be understood in several ways. The first meaning is the surface of the earth as the dwelling place of the human race and thus does not mean the heavens above or the world below the surface of the earth.[259] The second meaning of οἰκουμένης is all people who dwell on the earth, all of the human race.[260] There is a limited use to οἰκουμένης where it means the Roman Empire.[261] This last understanding can be excluded, because the Tribulation will affect the whole earth and not just the area covered by the former Roman Empire. The reason that we know the Tribulation will affect the whole earth and that ὀικουμένης does not mean a limited area is because in Matt 24:14, Jesus said that the Gospel of the kingdom will be preached in the whole world, ὄλῃ τῇ οἰκουμένῃ. Jesus made clear what He meant by the whole world in His final words to the disciples before He ascended and returned to heaven. He told them that the Gospel is to be preached to all nations,[262] that is to the whole world (Matt 28:18-10). We can also exclude the meaning of the earth's surface as the target of the Tribulation. The reason for this is that the Tribulation is the day of God's wrath (Rev 6:15-17) and the day of God's wrath is the day when He destroys sinners (Isaiah 13:9). The meaning of οἰκουμένη that remains is that οἰκκουμένη means the total population of the earth.

Thus we are to understand that οἰκκουμένη means the total population of the earth. This is seen when we notice in Rev 3:10 that the Tribulation, the hour of testing, will affect not just the οἰκουμένη, but the οἰκουμένης ὅλης. Ὅλος means whole [263] with the understanding of totality.[264]

The phrase *all who dwell on the earth* is used in Luke 21:35. Luke 21:35 states that the Day of Wrath will affect all who dwell on the earth, ἐπὶ πάντας τοὺς καθημένους ἐπὶ πρόσωπον πάσης τῆς γῆς. The Day will come upon *all who live on the face of the whole earth.* We notice first of all that the Greek word in Luke 21:35 for all who dwell on the earth,

καθημένους, is different than the word used in Rev 3:10, κατοικοῦντας.

Καθημένους is from κάθημαι which means to remain, to reside, to inhabit.[265]

Secondly, the phrase *on the face of the whole earth,* where the word *face* is

from πρόσωπον, which means surface, face.[266] The word *earth* is γῆ, which

carries the meaning of the surface of the earth.[267] Finally, the word *all* is πᾶς

which means entire, whole.[268] The Greek, thus, means everyone who dwells

on the surface of the earth.

There is another use of the phrase *all who dwell on the earth* and is

found in Luke 4:5. In this verse, we are told that the Devil takes Jesus to a

high place and showed Him in an instant all the kingdoms of the world, τῆς

οἰκουμένης. τῆς οἰκουμένης in this case cannot be limited to those who

oppose God, because in Matt 4:8 it says all the kingdoms of the earth, κόσμος,

with κόσμος meaning the surface of the earth.[269]

There is also the use of the phrase "*all who dwell on the earth*" in Rev

8:13 where *woe* is proclaimed to the ones who dwell on the earth. Even if all

who dwell on the earth is limited to the ones who oppose God, the coming

Tribulation will affect everyone on the earth. There will be righteous ones

killed during the Tribulation (Rev 6:9-11) and the Anti-Christ will control the

economic system in such a way that no one without the mark of the beast will

be able to buy or sell (Rev 13:16). If one is the subject of not only persecution by the Anti-Christ and if one is not able to buy or sell, how will that person go unaffected by the Tribulation?

In our quest to understand who will be affected by the Tribulation, we will now look at the many ways in which the Tribulation is described. The Tribulation is called a time of testing (Rev 3:10). A time of testing that will affect the entire world. Jesus described the Tribulation as a time of great distress, unequaled from the beginning of the world until now and never to be repeated (Matt 24:21). In other words, Jesus said that the Tribulation is a one-time event in all eternity. He went on to say that the Tribulation will be so severe, that if it went beyond a certain limited time frame, no one would survive (Matt 24:22). The Tribulation is described as a time when the people affected by this period seek to hide and they wonder if they will survive (Rev 6:16, 17). Daniel the prophet describes the Tribulation as a time of great distress that has not happened before (Dan 12:1). Jeremiah the prophet describes the Tribulation as a time like no other (Jer 30:7). Joel describes the Tribulation, that is the Day of the Lord as a day such as never was of old, nor ever will be in ages to come (Joel 2:2).

The above verses not only describe the Tribulation as a time of great distress; but also describe who will be affected. Jer 30:7 says that the Tribulation, the Day of the Lord, will be a time of trouble for Jacob; that is, Israel. So, we see from this verse that the nation of Israel will experience the

Tribulation. The kings of the earth, the princes, generals, the rich, the mighty, every slave and free person living on the earth will experience the Tribulation, the Day of God's wrath (Rev 6:15, 17). The phrase in Rev 6:15, *every slave and person,* is from πᾶς δοῦλος[270] καὶ ἐλεύθερος.[271] The most important word in this phrase is πᾶς. πᾶς means the totality of any mass, all.[272] All slaves and all free persons will be affected by the Tribulation. When the whole verse is looked at, and the kings, princes, generals, rich, mighty and every slave and free person are included, what must be understood is that every person on the earth will be affected by the Tribulation. The Tribulation, the Day of God's wrath, then will be a one-time event in all eternity and will be a time of testing which will affect the entire earth and the entire population of the earth.

Since Rev 3:10[273] is in the midst of the discussion regarding whether the rapture is or is not, we return to Rev 3:10 in an effort to understand the promise the Lord made to the Church at Philadelphia.[274] The NIV[275] states Christ's promise in this manner: Since you have kept my command to endure patiently, I will also keep you from the hour of trial that is going to come upon the whole world to test those who live on the earth. One view of Christ's promise is that Rev 3:10 is God's promise to faithful Christians that they will be taken out of the coming Tribulation.[276] While others hold the view that Rev 3:10 is not God's promise to take Christians out of the Tribulation, but this verse is God's promise that He will protect Christians in the midst of Tribulation.[277]

In Rev 3:10, the phrase in question is: I will also keep you from the hour of trial. What the discussion regarding this phrase centers on is: *from the hour*. The Greek is: ἐκ τῆς ὥρας. The two understandings of this Greek phrase is: out of the hour and from the hour. The first understanding means that God has promised faithful Christians that they will be kept out of the hour of trial, the Tribulation. This meaning states that since the Tribulation will affect the entire world, and since faithful Christians are to be kept out of the hour of trial, the faithful Christians must not be in the world. The second meaning of ἐκ τῆς ὥρας is that God has promised to protect the faithful Christians from the hour of trial, but does not mean that they will be taken out of the hour of trial to come. This view states that the thrust of Rev 3:10 is God's protection in the midst of the time of trial[278] but does not mean that God will take the Christian out of the time of trial.

This second view is based in part on John 17:15 where Jesus prayed that His followers would not be taken out of the world, but that they would be kept *from* the evil one, ἐκ τοῦ πονηροῦ. While Christians remain in the world, they are to be protected from the evil one. However, in response to this second view and the use of ἐκ to mean *from* in the promise of Christ in Rev 3:10, the same phrase is used in Acts 8:39. The context of this passage is that Philip met an Ethiopian Eunuch who was reading from Scriptures. After Philip explained

the Scriptural reading to the Ethiopian Eunuch, the Eunuch requested to be

baptized. Both the Eunuch and Philip went *into* the water (Acts 8:38). After

Philip baptized the Eunuch, they both came up out of the water.[279] The phrase

came up out of the water is: ἐκ τοῦ ὕδατος. The obvious meaning in this

verse is not that Philip and the Ethiopian Eunuch were protected *from* the

water while they were in the water at the baptism of the Eunuch; but after

Philip had baptized the Eunuch, they both came *out of* the water. The phrase

means that at one time they were in the water but now they were no longer in

the water, they had left the water. What we see in this verse is that ἐκ means

out of and not from.

At issue in this discussion is the preposition ἐκ. Ἐκ, has the root

meaning of *out of, from within,*[280] but depending upon its context has a

number of meanings.[281] The various meanings of ἐκ are sometimes a shade of

meaning to the root meaning and sometimes is a meaning that is loosely

connected to the root meaning.[282] What will help determine the meaning of ἐκ

in each case is the context in which ἐκ is found, both the immediate context

and the larger context which includes the total teaching of the Bible on a

particular topic.

So we ask what is the context of Rev 3:10 and the promise of Christ to

faithful Christians? The immediate context of the promise of God in Rev 3:10

is that the church at Philadelphia had come in contact with a Jewish synagogue and that this contact had resulted in a time of trial for the church at Philadelphia. We know that this was a time of difficulty for the Christians at Philadelphia in relation to the Jewish synagogue because of what Christ said He would cause the so-called Jews to do. Christ said that He would cause the members of the synagogue to fall down at the feet of the Christians at Philadelphia (Rev 3:9) and to acknowledge that God loves the Christians and not the members of the Jewish synagogue (Rev 3;9). We recognize that there is a difference between God loving the world, which means everyone and God having a special relationship of love with His followers. It is this special relationship that the members of the Jewish synagogue will first of all have to admit that God has with the Christians and then the members of the Jewish synagogue will have to acknowledge to the Christians. Many groups, including the Jewish community, think that they are the only ones to have a special relationship with God. By the fact that Christ will cause the members of the synagogue to acknowledge that God loves the Christians at Philadelphia, must mean that the Jewish community had in their contact with the Christians at Philadelphia stated that to have a special relationship with God, one had to be Jewish. This, Christ denies by what He will cause the synagogue members to do. He will cause the members of the Jewish synagogue to admit to themselves and then to the Christians at Philadelphia, that the Christians at Philadelphia had the special relationship with God and not the Jews.

While it does not say directly, but we can derive from the broader teaching of Scriptures, is that the Jewish community was hostile and violent towards the Christians at Philadelphia. We see the hostility of the Jewish community against Christians in the account of the stoning of Stephen. Stephen was brought before the Sanhedrin and the Jewish high priest to give an account of his actions and his preaching about Jesus (Acts 6:14). The defense of Stephen so angered the Jewish leaders that they took up stones and killed him (Acts 7:54-60). The hostility of the Jewish community against the early Christians is seen also in the early life of Paul, while he was still called Saul. Saul, we are told watched and gave his approval to the death of Stephen (Acts 8:1). After the stoning of Stephen, Saul gained approval from the Jewish leaders to hunt down the Christians and destroy them (Acts 9:1-2). Saul, himself admitted that at this point of his life, his purpose was to destroy the Church of God (Gal 1:13).

The context of Rev 3:10 is that the Church at Philadelphia had already gone through a time of suffering and trial caused by the Jewish synagogue. What are we to draw from the message of Jesus to the church at Philadelphia? Are we to understand that since they had already kept Christ's command to endure (Rev 3:10) and they had already gone through a time of persecution

227

and suffering, that Christ's promise, their reward for standing strong, to them is another time of suffering? This would seem to be the case if the promise of Christ is to strengthen the Christians at Philadelphia while they were going through a time of suffering that was yet to come. That truly does not seem to be much of a promise, much of a thank you. They had already remained steadfast in the time of suffering that they just endured. If the promise of Christ in Rev 3:10 is that He will keep them in the midst of a time of suffering that will be unlike any other, what is the message we are to understand? What seems to be the message is that if you endure one time of suffering, your reward is to undergo another time of suffering that is so great that the earth is at stake.

While it is true that in this world, we Christians will face trials and persecution. That is not the point at issue here. The point is Christ's promise to, His reward for their faithful obedience in a time of trial already endured is that they will face a time of suffering so great that will affect the very core of the earth itself.

If the promise of Christ in Rev 3:10 is that He will keep them in the midst of the suffering that was to come, then why did He not say it in the way He said it to the Church at Smyrna? To the Church at Smyrna, Jesus said plainly: Do not be afraid of the persecution that you are about to suffer (Rev 2:10). Jesus told them plainly that persecution was on their horizon. Along

228

with the coming persecution, Jesus told the Church at Smyrna that some of them would be cast into prison. We are happy to notice that our friend ἐκ is in Rev 2:10 as well. The phrase is ἐκ ὑμῶν, some of you. Literally, the phrase would be *out of you.* The idea is that there is coming a time when some of the Christians at Smyrna would be taken from, out of the church and cast into prison. The Christians cast into prison were at one time *in* the church and then all of a sudden they were no longer in the church but in prison.[283] The point is that Jesus clearly and plainly warned them that they would undergo persecution. Because of the context of Rev 3:10 and the fact that ἐκ does mean *out of*, the message to the Church at Philadelphia does not seem to be as clear a message of their undergoing future persecution as the message to the Church at Smyrna.

The broader context of Rev 3:10 is the Day of the Lord and upon whom the wrath of God will fall. As we have seen above, the Day of the Lord, the Tribulation is the Day of the wrath of God (Rev 6:17). The word for wrath is ὀργή. Ὀργή means anger, fury.[284] However, this fury is not an anger that quickly flairs up and is gone, it is more of a state of mind.[285] What is meant by ὀργή being a state of mind is that ὀργή is God's opposition and reaction toward evil.[286] Closely aligned with the idea of fury is the concept of punishment, in this case, God's punishment of those He is angry with.[287] A further point to be made concerning the wrath of God is that although God has

229

in the past demonstrated His opposition toward evil, for example in the Flood, (Gen 6), and in some way His wrath is being revealed in the present (Rom 1:18); the teaching of the Scripture is that the wrath of God, for the most part is stored up and will be fully revealed in the future, in the coming Day of Wrath (Col 3:6; 1 Thess 1:10).

The question we will now explore concerning the wrath of God is "upon whom will the wrath of God fall?" To answer this question, we will mention again some of the verses that were mentioned above regarding the Day of the Lord. The wrath of God will fall upon the nation of Israel (Zephaniah 1:4-13) and upon the nations of the world (Obadiah 15; Ezekiel 30:3). The prophet Zephaniah sums up in one verse upon whom the wrath of God is coming when he says that at the Day of the Lord, the wrath of God will consume the whole world (Zephaniah 1:18) and God will make a sudden end to all who live on the earth (Zephaniah 1:18).

When the coming Day of Wrath arrives, the teaching of the Scriptures is that the whole world will be consumed.[288] When Zephaniah states that the whole world will be consumed, he does not mean the planet itself. Zephaniah makes clear that it is the people of the earth who will be consumed on the Day of the Lord when he says that God will make a sudden end of all who live on the earth (Zephaniah 1:18).

We return to the meaning of the phrase *"all who live on the earth,"* as the subject of the wrath of God and the objects destroyed on the Day of the Lord. Zephaniah teaches that there is a comprehensiveness or totality of destruction on the Day of the Lord. This comprehensiveness, this totality, is seen in the fact that the *whole* world will be consumed. The whole world, not a part of the world will be destroyed when God pours out His wrath. Again, we are to remember that Zephaniah means all the ones who dwell on the earth when he says the whole world.

On the Day of the Lord, when God pours out His wrath on the world, we are told that all the ones who dwell on the earth will be brought to a sudden end. The objects of God's wrath are more clearly spelled out in the New Testament.

The wrath of God will be poured out on those who are disobedient, ἀπείθεια (Eph 5:6). Ἀπείθεια in it's general meaning is an unwillingness or refusal to comply with the demands of some authority.[289] When ἀπείθεια is used in a specifically Biblical context, ἀπείθεια has the understanding of a refusal to believe the Christian message.[290] The meaning, then, of those who are disobedient are those who reject not only the Gospel message, but the Lord Jesus Himself as the one who has authority over their lives. When a person rejects the Gospel message and the Lord Jesus, this rejection is not necessarily seen in a life of chaos and anarchy. Adam and Eve rejected the authority of the Word of God and in rejecting the Word of God, they also rejected God as having authority over their lives. Because they rejected God, they lost Paradise. Adam and Eve did not begin to live a life of chaos and anarchy after they were kicked out of Eden. It is possible that Adam and Eve lived a more ethical life than is lived by the vast majority of the world's population today, including Christian believers. What Adam and Eve lost was a personal relationship with God. To be disobedient to the Lord Jesus Christ and to the Gospel message is seen not in an unethical life, but in a life that lacks the Spirit of God (Rom 8:9) and thus that person is unknown on a personal level to Christ (Matt 7:21-23).

Many of the disobedient people who live in the world are religious. This is known by the truth that the wrath of God will be poured out on the nation of Israel (Luke 21:23; Rom 2:9). The category of religious, however, is not confined to the religious, yet Christ-rejecting Jewish persons. The religious, who are disobedient, are found within many religions. I will focus only, however, on the Christian religion.

Within the Christian religion are those who, while thinking that they are obedient, are in fact disobedient. There are those who do the right things, but without the right motive. Paul says that it is possible to do the right things, yet, without love (1 Cor 13). While 1 Cor 13 is commonly known as the Love Chapter, 1 Cor 13 is also a message that clearly states that the Christian act can be performed without Christ. It is possible to speak in the tongues of men of angels, to speak prophetically, to understand all mysteries, to move mountains, to given all to the poor and to surrender one's body to the flame (suffer a martyr's death) all *without* love. We are told that God is love (1 John 4:16). To do all the Christian activities without love is then to perform them without God.

Those who are disobedient are those who live out of a selfish motive (Rom 2:8). Many within the Christian world live outwardly Christian lives, say the right things, yet, do not tithe, give to the poor, nor visit the widow or the orphan. These also see their view of Christianity as that which perpetuates a certain lifestyle. This lifestyle maybe seen belonging to the Left and it may be seen belonging to the Right. When Christians think, live, act, vote in a way as to preserve their particular lifestyle and not in a manner that shares the love of God to all equally, this is seen as living out of a selfish motive.

The wrath of God is destined for each and every person, whether Jew or Gentile who has rejected the Lord Jesus Christ (John 3:36). In fact, whoever rejects the Son of God, God's wrath is said to *remain* on that person. Remain is from μένω which means to continue to exist, to remain.[291] The meaning of this is that the wrath of God is already on those who have rejected Jesus Christ. Those who at this moment in time have not accepted Jesus Christ are already living with God's wrath on them. In summary, then, we see that the wrath of God is destined for those who are disobedient to the Gospel and who have not

233

accepted Jesus Christ.

The Day of the Lord does not just have negative connotations, however. The Day of the Lord is also the day when the Lord returns (1 Cor 1:7, 8) and thus will be the day when the full salvation of the Christian is revealed and experienced (Eph 4:30). Because the Day of the Lord has both negative connotations, the punishment of the wicked and those who have rejected Jesus Christ and has positive connotations, that is it is the Day when the Christian will experience fully the salvation which they have only in a first fruit and promise (Eph 1:13, 14); what we are to understand is that the wrath of God is only for a particular part of the human race and not for everyone.

According to the Bible, both in the Old Testament and in the New Testament, there will be people who will not experience God's wrath. Jeremiah states that the Day of the Lord, which he calls Jacob's Trouble (Jer 30:7); will be a day that Jacob will be saved out of (Jer 30:7). The prophet Jeremiah defines who he means by Jacob. Jacob is the nation of Israel (Jer 30:10). However, Jeremiah is not stating that the nation of Israel will not experience the Day of God's Wrath. Jeremiah is stating that the members of the nation of Israel whose God is the Lord will be saved out of the Day of Wrath (Jer 31: 1). Those who will be saved out of the Day of Wrath will be the ones restored to God (Jer 30:1). Whether we are to understand the words of the prophet Jeremiah as referring to the True Israel, that is those who are righteous by faith, which would include Gentiles and Jews, or if Jeremiah is referring only to the Jews who are physically part of Israel who repent and believe in Jesus Christ as Lord and Savior; the promise of salvation out of the Day of Wrath is only for those of Israel who have repented and are restored to God by faith.

The teaching that not all of Israel will be saved out of the Day of the Lord is seen in the prophet Isaiah. Isaiah states that the Lord Almighty has a day coming; a day of tumult, trampling down and of terror (Isaiah 22:5). At the onset of this Day, the Lord called Israel to repent and put on sackcloth (Isaiah 22:12). Israel as a whole, however, did not repent, but tried to prevent the coming Day by building up the walls of the city and made other plans that did not include God (Isaiah 22:9-11). Israel, after convincing herself that she was secure in her own position, did not repent but continued to live a self-centered life (Isaiah 22:13). Because Israel did not repent, nor return to God, God has promised that Israel will die in an unforgiven state (Isaiah 22:14-19). In addition to dying in an unforgiven state, Israel will also lose what she has and it will be given to others (Isaiah 22:20-25). When the teaching of Jeremiah and Isaiah are integrated, what we see is that there will be some in Israel who do repent and turn to God and will be saved out of the Day of God's wrath. In other words, not everyone who is of Israel will suffer the wrath of God, there will be some who are spared from the wrath of God on that Day.

235

The New Testament also teaches that not every single human being will experience the Day of God's wrath and that some will be spared from it. Paul wrote that faithful Christians (1 Thess 1:6-10) will be rescued from, ἐκ, out of the coming wrath (1 Thess 1:10). The understanding of ἐκ as *out of* is clarified by Paul when he said that God has not appointed the faithful Christian to suffer wrath (1 Thess 5:9). The word *appointed* is τίθημι. Τίθημι means appointed, designated, assigned.[292] τίθημι has a further meaning of subjecting someone to a particular experience.[293] This understanding of τίθημι is also stated by Arndt and Gingrich.[294] τίθημι has also been used in the sense of to appoint, to designate something by the use of a will.[295] A will in this case is a last will and testament where someone is designated, given something from someone else.

Paul has stated that God has *not* appointed, τίθημι, designated, assigned, Christians to experience a particular event and that event is God's wrath (1 Thess 5:9). The Christian is not the subject of God's wrath (1 Thess 5:9). Christians, however, are appointed, designated to receive salvation through Jesus Christ (1 Thess 5:9). In this verse, Paul is comparing and contrasting two groups of people. Both groups are facing a particular future. The future of the first group—those who live in darkness (1 Thess 5:4)—has already been set, assigned, appointed by God. That future is to suffer wrath. The description of those in the darkness as referring to Non-Christians is seen in the words of Jesus when He said that Light has come into the world, but human beings loved greater the darkness and would not come to the Light. Darkness is a term that describes those who have not accepted the Light of the World, Jesus Christ (John 3:19-21).

The future of the second group has already been set, assigned by God. The second group's future is to *not* suffer wrath, but to receive salvation (1 Thess 5:9). Salvation, in part, means to share in God's glory (1 Thess 2:12; 2 Thess 2:13, 14). In addition to sharing in God's glory, salvation for Christians means that Christians will be saved from ἀπό, οp wrath (Rom 5:9). After a person has received Jesus Christ and is born-again, that person is made righteous by faith. The phrase to be made righteous is also called justified. After a person has been justified, that person will be saved from ἀπό, οp wrath. The word ἀπό has the meaning of away from a person or event.[296] Another example of the use of the word ἀπό is Rom 9:3. In Rom 9:3, Paul writes that his grief for those in Israel who had not believed in Jesus Christ, caused Paul to say that if possible, he would be cut off from, ἀπό, Christ so that they might be saved (Rom 9:3). We see in this use of ἀπό the idea of *from* in the sense of being separated from. Paul wrote that if possible, he would be separated from Christ if that would be salvation for Israel.

In Rom 5:9, Paul wrote that when a person believes in Jesus Christ and is born-again, that is when a person is made righteous by faith, that person is saved from, ἀπό, wrath. By the use of the word ἀπό, saved from God's wrath means to be delivered, separated from all the effects of God's wrath.[297]

Christians are to be saved from the wrath of God (Rom 5:9). The word *saved* is from the Greek σῴζω. Σῴζω means to be rescued from danger and to be restored to a former state of safety.[298] Peter, when walking on the water towards Jesus, began to sink. He cried out to Jesus "σῶσόν,i ※save me." Jesus, in response to Peter's cry, reached out His hand and rescued him (Matt 14:30, 31). We see in this use of the word σῴζω deliverance from danger and restoration to safety. σῴζω is also used in reference to the salvation which the person experiences when he or she accepts Jesus as Lord and Savior. Paul wrote that it is by grace through faith that we are saved, σῴζω. Salvation in Christ then has the meaning of being rescued from, taken out of danger and restored to a safe place; that is, in Christ.

When Christians are looked at, it will be seen that there is not even one Christian who is perfect. This statement, unfortunately, has been used by countless Christians to justify their lack of growth in holiness and their continuation as mere infants in Christ. However, that being said and recognized: Why are Christians *not* appointed to suffer God's wrath?

We begin with the fact that Christians are a new creation in Christ (2 Cor 5:17). The phrase *in Christ* means united with Christ by faith in Him which is expressed in a commitment to obey Jesus Christ as Lord. A Christian

238

is a new, καινός, creation, κτίσις. Καινός is new in the sense of that which has been in existence for only a short time; that which has not existed before.[299] Paul elaborates on what he means by new when he says that being new in Christ means that the old, ἀρχαῖος, things have passed away (2 Cor 5:17). ἀρχαῖος has the meaning of that which has existed for a long time or from the beginning.[300] The old things have passed away in the sense of no longer existing.[301] When a person believes in Jesus Christ and is born-again, that person, at the same time dies and begins a new life (Rom 6:2, 3). The death of the old person is the death of the person whose center is him or herself.[302] The new life, the new creation is the beginning of the God-created person. This newly, God created person has a new moral stance and new priorities which are summed up in the purpose of living to please Christ (2 Cor 5:9) and living not for the things of this world.[303] This new creation in Christ is a person that fulfills God's intention for the human race which God had at creation (2 Cor 4:6). We know that the new creation is the fulfillment of God's intention at creation because Paul connects the light shining in the darkness at creation, (Gen 1:2-4), with the giving by God of His light to shine in our hearts which occurs at the new birth (2 Cor 4:6). There is a darkness residing in the hearts and souls of people which can only be driven out by the light of Christ.

The new birth is when the Holy Spirit comes to indwell the believing sinner and gives to that person a new life. This new life, ζωή, of the Christian is hidden is Christ (Col 3:4). The meaning of ζωή is best understood in a comparison/contrast with another word, βίος, that is also translated as *life.* Βίος has the connotation of the *means of life,* which is to say the living out of life. ζωή is the essence, the principle of life itself. Without ζωή, βίος cannot happen. Βίος can be understood as the expression of that which animates the body itself. That which gives life to the body is ζωή.[304] Jesus Christ is the animating principle of the Christian. Jesus Christ is righteous (1 John 2:1) and since the life of the Christian is Christ, the life of the Christian is righteous.

As new creations in Christ, Christians are forgiven. When a person believes in Jesus Christ as Savior and commits him or herself to obey Christ as Lord, and that new person is given new life in Christ, at that moment, God also forgives that person's sins (Col 2:13). When forgiveness occurs, God no longer remembers the wickedness, sins of the person who is forgiven (Heb 10:17, 18). The reason that God no longer remembers is because when forgiven, sins no longer exist (Jer 50:20).

When a person is forgiven at the new birth, not only does the Blood of Christ cause that person's sins to no longer exist, the Blood of Christ also wipes clean the record of that person's sins (Col 2:13, 14). Forgiveness, then means that when forgiven a person's sins no longer exist and even the record, the stain of their existence has been wiped away by the Blood of Christ.[305]

As a forgiven, new person in Christ, the Christian no longer has the specter of future punishment to face (1 John 4:18). There is no fear in love, we are told, because fear has to do with punishment. To be made complete in love, therefore, is in part to arrive at the understanding that the death of Christ was the Christian's punishment and the Christian him or herself will not face punishment for his or her sins. Another reason why the one in Christ will not face punishment is because in Christ there is no condemnation (Rom 8:1). Condemnation is from κατάκριμα. Κατάκριμα means to judge someone guilty and thus subject to punishment.[306] There is no condemnation, no sentence of guilty and thus no punishment for the one who is in Christ Jesus. The new humanity in Christ is righteous (1 Cor 1:30). Christ indwelling the Christian makes the Christian righteous. The righteous will not face wrath and thus will not be punished. The wrath of God is poured out on the godless and wicked, not on the righteous (Rom 1:18).

Since there is no condemnation for those who are in Christ, this means that those in Christ will not face the day of wrath and punishment. The day of wrath and punishment is only for the unrighteous (2 Pet 2:9). The word unrighteous from ἄδικος, means a person who is not a member of the Christian community and by implication is unjust and not in a right relationship with God.[307] The Christian, however, will be rescued from trials. The verb form of the noun translated trials in 2 Pet 2:9, is used in Rev 3:10 to describe the coming day of Tribulation.

The Tribulation is the day of God's punishment of the unrighteous.[308] Since Christians are righteous, they are not subject to punishment. Since the Tribulation will affect the entire world (Rev 3:10) and Christians are not subject to punishment, how will Christians not experience God's punishment of the unrighteous? Peter tells us that Christians will be rescued by the Lord Himself from the punishment which God is going to pour out on the entire world (2 Pet 2:9).

How will the Lord rescue the Christian from God's punishment of the unrighteous? The view that says the promise of Christ in Rev 3:10 is that Jesus will keep the Christian strong in the midst of the Tribulation states that the Tribulation will affect only the enemies of the Church and of Christ.[309] However, when the Tribulation arrives and is affecting the entire, ὅλος, with ὅλος meaning whole, entire, complete,[310] world, how will Christians be kept safe from it?

The promise of Jesus, according to one view, is that He will keep the Christian safe during the Tribulation. The means by which the Lord will accomplish this is to seal the Christians who are on the earth (Rev 7:1-8). In Rev 7, the 144, 000 from all the tribes of Israel are said to be sealed (Rev 7:7). The view that says Christ will seal the Christian so that he/she will be kept safe during the Tribulation states that the number 144, 000 in Rev 7 is symbolic and is not a definite number, but means totality.[311] This view also states that

242

the 144,000 from all the tribes of Israel refers to not literal Israel, but to Spiritual Israel and really means Christians from every language, nation and group.[312]

If we are to follow this line of reasoning, then it would be appear that every time *Israel* is mentioned, at least in the New Testament, we are to understand that to mean the Church. There is no warrant, however, to make the connection that Israel in Rev 7 refers to Spiritual Israel and not literal Israel. In fact, because the tribes of Israel are all mentioned, the meaning is the literal 12 Tribes of Israel. Paul, when discussing the righteousness of Christ and lists all that he has given up to be clothed with Christ's righteousness, mentions that Paul himself was of the people of Israel and of the Tribe of Benjamin (Phil 3:5). There is no way that Paul, when mentioning *Israel* meant Spiritual Israel. His reference was clearly to literal Israel. Also, in Rom 9-11, Paul is grieving over the fact that Israel has not believed in Jesus as the Christ, Messiah. Paul, again, here, can not mean the Church, for the Church, Spiritual Israel, are the ones who have believed in Jesus the Christ.

While it is true that in one place the Church is called the Israel of God or the true Israel in Gal 6:16,[313] it is not true that every time the word Israel is mentioned it refers to the Church.[314] It is also true that Revelation is a document filled with symbolism, however, as we have discussed earlier in this book, when a symbol is given, the meaning is also given. In the case of the

243

144, 000 of all the tribes of Israel mentioned, there is no indication that the 144, 000 is symbolic. When there is no clear statement made that something is a symbol, the best method is to understand it literally.

Another reason to understand the 144, 000 from all the tribes of Israel as literal Israel is the fact that there will be a revival in Israel before the Day of the Lord (Mal 4:5, 6). Paul also states that there is coming a revival amongst the Jews in Rom 11:25, 26. Who will be the evangelists to the Jewish nation? Most likely it will not be Gentile Christians. The 144, 000 sealed in Rev 7 will be the godly remnant of Israel on earth.[315]

A third reason to understand that the 144, 000 are not symbolic for all Christians is the description of the 144, 000 as those who did not defile themselves with women (Rev 14:4). One way of understanding the phrase not defiling oneself with women is to keep oneself from relationships with the world system. Paul in 2 Cor 11:2 prays that the Corinthian Christians would remain pure in their devotion to their true husband, Christ. In addition, the symbol for the world system in Revelation is a prostitute (Rev 17:1).

However, it seems more in context to see the 144, 000 as those who did not defile themselves with women is to understand that the 144, 000 did not marry so they could devote themselves entirely to the Lord's service. The Bible, here is not teaching that sexual relations between a man and a woman in a marriage relationship is bad. There is the Biblical teaching which says that if a person remains single, that person will be able to devote everything to serve Christ (1 Cor 7:32-35). It is this understanding of not defiling oneself from women that is more fitting in the context of the description of the 144, 000.

Another question regarding the view which states that the 144, 000 symbolizes the Church is: why is the Church limited to 144, 000 when in other places in the Bible, when the Church as a whole is described, words such as myriads, thousands upon thousands, a multitude that no one could count is used? Why limit the Church here and not in all other places that describe the Church corporate?

If the sealing of the 144, 000 is to protect them from death, then the sealing does not work, because there will be those who are martyred for their faith during the Tribulation (Rev 6:11). It is a fact that during the Tribulation, there will be those who are righteous that will die. They will be killed both directly and indirectly by the Anti-Christ. Because the Anti-Christ will be the ultimate cause of the death of the righteous in the Tribulation, whether the Anti-Christ pulls the trigger or gives the command to kill the righteous, then, the righteous during the Tribulation were not kept from the evil one. In addition, the Two Witnesses will be killed (Rev 11:7) and their bodies will lie in the street for 3 ½ days (Rev 11:9). In addition to the Two Witnesses there will be those who are martyred for their faith, during the Tribulation (Rev 6:9-11). If a Christian is killed during the Tribulation, how, then is the promise of Christ to keep that Christian safe during the Tribulation fulfilled? Are we to understand that the death of Christians before the sealing of His people as recorded in Rev 7 is somehow acceptable to God but that the death of Christians after the sealing is not acceptable? If that is the case, there still is a problem and that problem is the death of the Two Witnesses which occurs after the sealing of the 144, 000 (Rev 11).

There is another factor that speaks against the view that Rev 3:10 is Christ's promise is to keep the Christian safe during the Tribulation and that is the mark of the beast. During the Tribulation, the Anti-Christ will institute a mark which everyone, small, great, rich, poor, free, slave must receive (Rev 13:16). Without this mark, no one will be able to buy or sell anything (Rev 13:17). In other words, without the mark of the beast, no one will be able to go to the store and buy a gallon of milk or a loaf of bread. How will Christ's promise to rescue the godly from wrath be fulfilled when they are not able to buy food to eat?

If the sealing of the 144, 000 is to preserve and protect them from physical evil and harm, the sealing of the 144, 000 should have occurred before the opening of the 1st seal. At the opening of the 1st seal, death, famine, sickness, great earthquakes and other catastrophes occur (Rev 6:1-17). The sealing of the 144, 000 in the midst of the cosmic catastrophes of the 6th seal, certainly does not protect the 144, 000 from all that which occurred at the opening of seals 1-5. John himself, in his vision, hears the cries of those who experience the Day of the Lord. In addition, those who experience the Day of the Lord call it a day in which no one can stand (Rev 6:17).

God has promised His faithful ones that they will be kept from wrath. Since the wrath of God will affect the whole world, the only way that God can fulfill His promise is to take His faithful ones out of the world. This is the rapture, the snatching up of 1 Thess 4:17.

The question that is before us is the *when* of the rapture, the snatching up. As we have seen, the Day of the Wrath will affect all who dwell on the surface of the earth (Luke 21:35). Jesus, taught that there was an escape, ἐκφεύγω from the Day of Wrath (Luke 21:36). ἐκφεύγω means to become safe from danger by avoiding or escaping.[316] This escape, according to Jesus is to *stand before the Son of Man* (Luke 21:36). The Tribulation is coming on the whole surface of the earth, the phrase *on the face of the whole earth,* where the word *face* is πρόσωπον. πρόσωπον means surface, face.[317] The word *earth* is γῆ, which carries the meaning of the surface of the earth.[318] Finally, the word *all* is πᾶς which means entire, whole.[319] However, according to Jesus, there is an escape from the coming Tribulation. This escape is to stand before the Son of Man, Jesus Christ. We ask the question: where is the Son of Man? The answer is with the Father, in glory. Since the Tribulation will affect the entire surface of the earth, to stand before the Son of Man, must occur somewhere off of the surface of the earth. How can one escape the coming Tribulation by standing before the Son of Man? The answer is that the one who will escape the coming Tribulation must be taken off of the surface of the earth before the Tribulation begins.

The escape from the coming Tribulation is orchestrated by Jesus Himself (1 Thess 1:9, 10). Jesus, will rescue His own from the coming Day of Wrath. Since the whole earth will suffer the torment of the wrath of God; Christians can only be rescued from, kept from the Day of Wrath by being taken off of the surface of the earth before the Tribulation begins. Christians will escape the coming Tribulation because they are not appointed to suffer wrath (1 Thess 5:10) but to receive salvation.

One view of the *when* of the rapture is that the rapture occurs at the Second Coming of Christ. According to this view, Christians will be resurrected from the dead and the living Christians are changed (1 Thess 4:17), the total mass of Christians are then *snatched up*, ἁρπάζω, at the Second Coming of Christ.[320] This view states that Christ will descend to the air and Christians will rise to meet the Lord in the air and then turn around and with Christ descend back to the earth.

In response to this view, we state first of all that there seems to be no logical reason for the Christians to rise in the air to meet the Lord. Is there some spiritual meaning to this? The scholars have not provided an adequate reason for meeting the Lord in the air and then turning abruptly around and returning to the earth. Would it not be more of a declaration to Satan and the mass of unbelievers if all the Christians would be gathered together on the earth waiting for the Lord to descend? Furthermore, there are still the promises of Christ to not only protect the Christian from wrath but to cause the Christian to escape wrath altogether. The rapture at the Second Coming of Christ fails to protect the Christian from wrath and is also a failure for Christ Himself to cause the Christian to escape wrath. Finally, in response to the view that the rapture occurs at the Second Coming of Christ we look again at Jesus' own words in Luke 21: 35, 36 where Jesus said that there is an escape from all that will happen on the earth during the Tribulation. That escape, according to Jesus, is to stand before the Son of Man. Again we are reminded of Jesus' own promise of an escape from *all that is about to happen on the earth* during the Tribulation. A rapture at the Second Coming of Christ, which is *after* the Tribulation is over, will not fulfill this promise. Secondly, even if it is possible to stand in the air or on the clouds, a rapture after the Tribulation where the Christian rises to meet the Lord in the air and then abruptly turns around and returns to the earth does not fulfill Jesus' words of an escape from all that is about to happen on the earth during the Tribulation.

The rapture of God's people is before the Tribulation begins. A rapture that occurs before the Tribulation will fulfill the promises of Jesus to not only keep the Christian from wrath, but would also be the escape for the Christian from all that is about to happen on the earth during the Tribulation. Another reason for a rapture before the Tribulation is the fact that Christ can return at any time (James 5:7-9); in fact, the return of Christ is so near, imminent, it is stated that Jesus is standing at the door (James 5:9). Jesus Himself said that He is coming soon (Rev 22:20). Because the return of Christ can occur at any time, the rapture must occur before the Tribulation begins. If the rapture occurs in the middle of the Tribulation, it is at least 3 ½ years away. If the rapture does not occur until the end of the Tribulation, that is at least 7 years away.[321] In both cases, it is not imminent.

There are several views of a Pre-Tribulational rapture. One view is that the rapture can occur at any time, even up to 20 years before the Tribulation.[322] Another view states that the rapture will occur 10 ½ years before the beginning of the Tribulation.[323] The traditional view is that the rapture will occur approximately seven years before the return of Christ, or just before the beginning of the Tribulation.

Common to almost all of the views of the rapture occurring before the Tribulation, regardless of how many years before is the basic theological understanding that God has two people, the Church and Israel. Not only does God have two people, according to these views, but God relates to these two people by different means, that is by grace to the Church and by Law to Israel.

This theological understanding further states that the rapture closes the Day of Grace.

However, earlier in this study, it has been shown that God has only one people and that He relates to all people from the beginning of time until the end by grace. There is not, therefore, a separate age which is called the Age of Grace. The premise of the understanding that there is an Age of Grace is that there is an age of the Law by which God relates to His people, namely the nation of Israel. According to this view, during the age of the Law, the Law was the means by which God made righteous the nation of Israel. However, as has been shown before, the Law was never given as a means of righteousness (Gal 3:15-25). The Law came approximately 400 or so years after the promise to Abraham (Gal 3: 17) and was never intended by God to replace or set aside the promise (Gal 3:17). The purpose of the Law was never to make righteous (Gal 3:21, 22). The purpose of the Law was to reveal the depth of sin (Gal 3:22) and to lead people to faith in Jesus Christ (Gal 3:24).

Because of the fact that the Age of Grace, in all reality, never ends; the rapture does not close the Age of Grace but is related to the end of the 69th Seven and the beginning of the 70th Seven. The rapture can be said to not do two things. The rapture does not close the Day of Grace, nor does the rapture begin the 70th Seven. As we have said before, the 70th Seven begins when the Anti-Christ establishes a covenant with Israel (Dan 9:27).

When, then, does the rapture occur? The answer is two-fold. Firstly, the rapture will occur in time to rescue God's people from wrath. Secondly, the rapture will occur just before the beginning of the 70th Seven.

The Bible teaches that the Day of wrath is the Great Tribulation (Rev 6:15-17). The rapture will occur just before the beginning of the Tribulation, the Day of Wrath. The reason that the rapture will occur just before the beginning of the Tribulation is that God has promised to rescue His people from wrath (Rom 5:9; 1 Thess 1:10) and He does this by removing them from the place where wrath will fall. Since the Wrath of God will fall on the whole earth (Luke 21:35); God's people will be rescued/able to escape all that which is about to happen, that is the Day of Wrath, the Great Tribulation. The rapture, then, will occur just before the beginning of the Day of Wrath. Jesus has promised that His people will be able to escape the coming wrath and to stand before the Son of Man (Luke 21:36), who is in heaven. What we see from this is that when the Day of Wrath begins, Christians will be before the Son of Man, who is in heaven. So, when the Day of Wrath occurs, Christians will be with Jesus in heaven.

The prophecy of the 70 Sevens is a prophecy that primarily is focused on the nation of Israel (Dan 9:24). The *gap* between the 69th Seven and the 70th Seven is the time when God is focusing on the Gentiles and can be called the Fullness of the Gentiles. The Fullness of the Gentiles is the present age in which we are now living. When the fullness of the Gentiles is over, then the 70th Seven begins. When the present age is over, so is the time of the Fullness of the Gentiles.[324] The 70th Seven is that time when God focuses primarily on Israel (Rom 11:25, 26). The partial hardening[325] of Israel will last *until*, ἄχρι, the full number of Gentiles has believed (Rom 11:25). The word *until*, ἄχρι, means to extend in time with the focus upon the end point.[326] When the time called the Fullness of the Gentiles is over, then all Israel will be saved (Isaiah 27:9[327]; Rom 11:25, 26).[328]

After the Fullness of the Gentiles, there will occur a great revival in Israel[329] (Rom 11:25, 26) where God will focus on bringing Israel to faith in Christ.[330] The revival in Israel will be accomplished, in part, by the preaching of the 144, 000 Jewish evangelists[331] (Rev 7). In addition, the revival in Israel will be the result of the rapture. Prior to the rapture, the teaching of the rapture and of Jesus as the Messiah will be known by some in Israel. When the rapture occurs, this will prove the truthfulness of the Gospel and that Jesus is the Messiah. The validation of the Gospel by the rapture, coupled with the preaching of the 144, 000 Jewish evangelists will be used by God to bring about a revival in Israel. When the rapture occurs and Israel sees that the Christians are gone from this world, many in Israel and around the world will truly consider the Gospel of Jesus Christ for the first time.

The time of the rapture is also stated to be a time when the fig tree

253

sprouts or begins to blossom, but is not yet in full bloom (Matt 24:32). There is

debate as to the meaning of the fig tree. The early Church, however, taught

that the fig tree was a symbol of Israel. The Apocalypse of Peter, states plainly

that the fig tree symbolizes Israel. The Apocalypse of Peter was written

around 120 CE and was part of the Muratorian Canon. The Muratorian Canon

was composed around 180 CE and listed the writings which the many in the

Church at that time acknowledged as canonical.

According to the Apocalypse of Peter, the sprouting of the fig tree is

the time when Israel begins to turn to faith in Christ. This will be around the

beginning of the 70th Seven in the early days of great national revival in Israel.

The sprouting of Israel occurs just before the coming of Enoch and Elias,

according to the Apocalypse of Peter, which maybe the two witnesses which

God sends in the 70th Seven.

At the time of the spouting of Israel, in the early stages of the great

national revival, which begins at the beginning of the 70th Seven, Jesus said

that one is taken and one is left (Matt 24:40, 41). Although there is a view

that *the taking of one and leaving of another* refers to a person taken to

judgment and one spared from judgment,[332] this view must be questioned. The

reason for questioning this view is the Biblical teaching that every human

person, both Christian and Non-Christian will stand before God's judgment

throne (1 Peter 4:17). So, we are left to conclude that the taking of one and the leaving of another refers to the rapture which occurs when Israel sprouts; that is, in the early stages of the great revival in Israel.

The rapture, the gathering of the Christians to be with the Lord, will occur after the revealing of the man of lawlessness, the Anti-Christ (2 Thess 2:3). The revealing, ἀποκκαλύπτω, of the Anti-Christ is when the Anti-Christ is fully known as the Anti-Christ.[333] Before the Anti-Christ is fully known as the Anti-Christ, this person must already be in power. The Anti-Christ will rise to power sometime before his or her true character is fully known. This means that the Anti-Christ will be in power to some extent before the rapture occurs. During the time before the rapture, when the Anti-Christ is in the process of gaining world power, the Anti-Christ will be in the process of consolidating his power. As a part of the Anti-Christ's consolidating of power, he will speak against God. He will also continue the persecution of Christian believers which has been going on since the time of Christ. However, the persecution of Christians by the Anti-Christ will take on a new sense of urgency (Dan 7:25). The persecution of Christians under the Anti-Christ will become more and more of a systematic program of extermination.

The rapture, instead of being seen as a world tragedy, will be seen and broadcast as a cleansing of the world of undesirable elements by the Anti-Christ and others who oppose Christ.[334] The rapture, in the mind of the Anti-Christ will be the removal of the final *roadblock* to His rise to world domination and control. Christians, their teaching on the Last Days and their attempt to expose the Anti-Christ will be a thorn in the side to the Anti-Christ. Because of Christians attempt to expose the Anti-Christ and the Christian refusal to worship the Anti-Christ, the Anti-Christ will already have begun his campaign against Christians before the rapture (Dan 7:25). The rapture, the removal of Christians from the earth, will be seen by the Anti-Christ as the removal of his final opposition. Once the rapture has occurred, the Anti-Christ will make his final move to gain control of the world and to be the object of the world's worship (Rev 13:15).

The rapture, then, will occur, at the end of the Fullness of the Gentiles and just before the beginning of the 70th Seven when the Anti-Christ has gained power in the world. The rapture will occur just before the beginning of the Day of Wrath, when God pours out His punishment on those who refuse to repent. An approximate time for the rapture is that the rapture will occur a little more than 7 years before the return of Christ. The reason for the rapture to occur approximately 7 years before the return of Christ is that the 70th Seven, which is the final seven years before the return of Christ is also the time called the Day of Wrath. Since the Christian is not appointed to suffer the wrath of God, the Christian must be rescued from the wrath of God. The promise of the Lord Jesus is that the Christian will stand before Him during the time of the Day of Wrath.

The conclusion to this chapter is two-fold. Firstly, the Church has had the teaching of an event called *the snatching up, the rapture,* of the Christians from the time of Jesus Christ. Paul included the teaching of the rapture in his preaching of the Gospel (1 Thess 4:17). The Gospel that Paul preached, he received by a direct revelation of Jesus Christ (Gal 1:11-12). So, the verbal, oral teaching of the event has been in the Church since the time of Christ. The written teaching has been in the Church, at least, since Paul wrote 1 Thessalonians in approximately 51 CE. What we see from this is that the teaching of an event whereby Christians are taken out of this world has been a fundamental Christian teaching from the time when Jesus Christ walked on the earth. Secondly, since the word *rapture* is the Latin translation of the Greek, ἁρπάζω, which is used in 1 Thess 4:17 to describe the *snatching up* of the Christians, and the Latin Vulgate has been in the Church since at least 384 CE, the conclusion is that the Church has had a teaching of the rapture from its very inception.

CHAPTER 7

DANIEL'S 70TH SEVEN

God has given in His word a timeline to the Apocalypse. This timeline is found primarily in Daniel, Matthew 24 and Revelation. This timeline was given by God so that we can be ready when the Apocalypse occurs. The Apocalypse is the Second Coming of Jesus Christ. We have taken a cursory view of this timeline up through the 69th Seven as recorded in Dan 9:24-27. In this chapter, we will look at the final seven, the 70th Seven, which is the last seven years before the Apocalypse.

The 70th Seven begins when the Anti-Christ establishes a covenant with the nation of Israel (Dan 9:27). This covenant is the sign that the Apocalypse will occur in 7 years. Thus, when there is a covenant set up between the nation of Israel and the Anti-Christ, the Second Coming of Christ will occur in 7 years.

In the 70th Seven, the time called the Fullness of the Gentiles will be over and the time for the great revival in Israel is about to begin. Thus, as Paul as written, many in Israel will be saved. Yet, this fact does not mean that God has two people. The truth is that God has only one people. While there is the view that God has two people, Israel and the Church, and that God relates to Israel by the Law and the Church by Grace, the Bible is very clear that this is not true. Paul writes that the Law was never given to make a person righteous

259

(Gal 3:21, 22); therefore, the attempt by Israel to become righteous by Law was not in accordance with the truth. The attempt to become righteous by the Law was in reality was a stumbling over the Rock of Ages (Rom 9:30-33). No one, not even those in Israel are made righteous by the Law, the sacrificial system (Gal 2:16). We state the truth again that God has only one people, so that all might understand that the 70th Seven is not a time of Law, but of grace, of the Gospel of Jesus Christ. It is the Gospel that is preached during the Tribulation, the 70th Seven, and not the Law (Rev 14:6). So, although Israel at the beginning of the first half of the 70th Seven reinstitutes the sacrificial system, this is not in accordance with the Gospel or in accordance with righteousness.

The 70th Seven is given more detail by Jesus in Matthew 24. In this chapter, Jesus ties the signs of the end of the Age and His return to Daniel's prophecy of the 70th Seven. We know that Matthew 24 is a more detailed discussion of the 70th Seven because Jesus in Matthew 24:15 connects the signs of the end of the Age and His return with the Abomination of Desolation that Daniel the Prophet foretold. The Abomination of Desolation is set up in the middle of the 70th Seven, 3 ½ years after the beginning of the 70th Seven. The setting up of the Abomination of Desolation occurs 3 ½ years after the Anti-Christ establishes a covenant with Israel (Dan 9:27). In the sequence of events up to this point in the 70th Seven, the Anti-Christ establishes a covenant with Israel that allows Israel to reinstitute the sacrificial system of worship. The Anti-Christ will break that covenant after 3 ½ years or in the middle of the 70th Seven (Dan 9:27). Jesus, in answering the disciples' question of what would be the signs of the end of the Age and His return, connects His return with the setting up of the Abomination of Desolation as foretold by Daniel (Matt 24:15) and the covenant that is made with Israel.

The setting up of the Abomination of Desolation, then, is the key to understanding the signs of the end of the Age and of Jesus' return. What we will do is to begin with Matt 24:15, the setting up of the Abomination of Desolation and work both backward and forward. In working backward, we will discuss some of the major events that will occur in the first half of the 70th Seven. In working forward, we will discuss some of the major events which will occur in the last half of the 70th Seven. This can be done because the setting up of the Abomination of Desolation occurs in the middle of the 70th Seven (Dan 9:27). Thus, the events which Jesus mentions before the setting up of the Abomination of Desolation must occur in the first half of the 70th Seven. The events which Jesus mentions after the setting up of the Abomination of Desolation must occur in the second half of the 70th Seven.

The discussion of Matthew 24 occurs between Jesus and His disciples [335] (Matt 24:1). Jesus, in answering the disciples' question concerning the signs of His return and the end of the age groups the signs of the end of the Age in three different time periods. The first time period is the time from the destruction of the Temple in 70 CE to the beginning of the 70th Seven. Jesus mentions this first time period in Matt 24:2-8. This period is the gap between the 69th Seven and the 70th Seven and is also called the present age. The second time period that Jesus mentions is the first half of the 70th Seven up to the mid-point of the 70th Seven. This period is covered in Matt 24:9-14. The third period is the last half of the 70th Seven until His return and is discussed in Matt 24:16-31.

The first time period we have already discussed previously in the chapter on the *gap*, so we will not discuss those signs here. We will begin with the second time period, which is the first half of the 70th Seven. Jesus, in discussing the signs of the end of the Age and His return during the second time period (Matt 24:9-14) mentions the first sign which is a worldwide hatred of the disciples, i.e. Christians (Matt 24:9). The truth is the world has hated Christ's followers as much as it has hated Christ Himself (John 3:20; 15:18-25). This truth is one that the Church in general seems to either ignore or be ignorant of and is somehow surprised when society acts in ways against Christ. The result of this hatred towards Christians is seen in the fact that more Christians have been martyred for the faith in the last 100 years then in all the years prior.[336]

However, the coming persecution of the followers of Jesus as part of the first half of the 70th Seven is the result of the animosity of both the Anti-Christ (Dan 7:25; Rev 6:9-11; 16:6) and the world against Christ and His followers. The Anti-Christ, in his rise to power, will begin at first in subtle ways to not only continue the persecution of Christ and His followers, but also to increase this persecution. However, after the rapture occurs, there will be many who come to faith in Christ. This coming to faith in Christ will cause the Anti-Christ to become enraged and he will then seek to destroy those who believe in Christ after the rapture.[337]

Jesus knew that He and His followers would be persecuted from the time He walked on the earth until the end. Therefore the sign of persecution which He mentions must be a specific time when His disciples would be persecuted. This specific time of persecution is closely tied to the time when many turn away from the faith (Matt 24:10). Jesus said *at that time*,--the time when the disciples are handed over to persecution--there will be a great turning away from the faith. Paul wrote that one of the signs of the end of the age was that there would be a falling away from the faith (2 Thess 2:3). This falling away from the faith is closely connected, in time, with the coming of the Man of Lawlessness, the Anti-Christ. In other words, the falling away that Paul mentioned is a falling away in the Last Days, in the time near the Second Coming of Christ (1 Tim 4:1). When Jesus told the disciples that there would be coming a time of persecution of God's people that was tied closely in time to the falling away prophesied in the Bible, he was connecting that time of persecution with the Last Days. We see that the time of persecution mentioned by Jesus is one of the signs that would announce the end of the age and of His return that will occur in close time proximity to the 70th Seven and is not a general type of persecution, if there is such a thing. Because Christians are being persecuted now and will be until Christ returns, there is an overlapping of the first period of time, the present age and the second period of time, the first half of the 70th Seven, of the sign of the persecution of Christians.

What we know from Paul is that in the later period there will be a time when many will follow deceiving spirits (1 Tim 4:1) which has been and is even now happening. Paul also stated that in the last days there will be a time of rebellion against God (2 Thess 2:3). This rebellion is closely aligned with the coming of the Anti-Christ, the Man of Lawlessness and is different in intensity of those who have fallen away over the years.

The coming to power of the Anti-Christ will not be seen as a tragedy by the world. As it has already been stated, the world hates Christ and His followers. The only Christians that the world does not hate are the Christians who have watered down the Gospel or who keep the faith within the four walls of their Church building. However, for the Christians who are attempting to be obedient to Christ by spreading the Gospel throughout the world, by growing in holiness and by standing firm for Christ in the world situation where everything but Christ is acceptable, the world's hatred is growing.

In his rise to power, the Anti-Christ will align himself with the truth is relative mentality, at least in the beginning. Because the Anti-Christ is the Man of Lawlessness, one wonders what law or if there is a law that the Anti-Christ will recognize. It is conceivable that the only law which the Anti-Christ will recognize is his own law. In the beginning of his rise to power, the Anti-Christ will be seen by the world as a means of silencing once and for all the voices of the ones who block the world's agenda---the Christian. Many will follow the Anti-Christ simply because of their hatred for Christians and for their hatred for the truth of the Gospel.

When the rapture occurs, this will not be seen by the world as a tragedy. The rapture, instead of being seen as a calamity, will be heralded as a day of rejoicing by the world. The reason for this is because the rapture will rid the world of the troublesome Christians and the world will then be able to do whatever it wants. The rapture will cause such a world situation that it will result in the final step in drawing the world to the Anti-Christ. Part of the reason for this, as has already been stated is the world's hatred toward Christ and His followers. In addition, because the Anti-Christ will claim to have the answers for the world's problems, the world will follow him. Furthermore, the false miracles that the false prophet will be able to do will convince the world that the Anti-Christ is the one with the answers.

The rise to power of the Anti-Christ will be the final fulfillment of the words of the Serpent in the Garden of Eden: In the day you eat from the fruit of the Tree of the Knowledge of Good and Evil, your eyes will be opened and you will be like God; you will know good and evil, right and wrong. And the whole key to this, according to the Serpent, is that since you will be like God, you will not need God anymore. The rise to power of the Anti-Christ is the final rejection of Jesus Christ and of God.

What a day for the world it will be when the morality of Christ, will be removed from the earth! Truly, the rapture will cause the world to rejoice. Gone are the naysayers! Gone are the ones who oppose the world's agenda! The world, without any reminder from Christians, will finally be able to not only decide what is right and wrong but also to do whatever one wants to do (2 Thess 2:7). Perhaps, the day after the rapture occurs, the whole world will celebrate as many people do in New Orleans during Mardi Gras.

There will be, in the mind of the Anti-Christ, another positive that occurs with the rapture. With the Christians out of the way, this will create a world environment in which the Anti-Christ will be able to establish the covenant with Israel. This must mean that the presence of Christians while still in the world will be a hindrance to the Anti-Christ. With Christ's followers still in the world, the Anti-Christ will not be able to come to full power. The reason Christians will be a hindrance to the Anti-Christ will be the preaching, radio programs, television programs, arguing before the world's bodies, of who the Anti-Christ truly is. However, when the rapture occurs, the voices of opposition that would expose the Anti-Christ will be gone. While Christians are still in this world, the voices of Christians will be in some manner a blockage to the rise to power of the Anti-Christ and of his establishing a covenant with Israel. However, the rapture will create a situation in the world where the already eager to follow the Anti-Christ world will be able to fully follow. In addition, the rapture will remove any and all obstacles to the Anti-Christ of rising to power and of beginning his conquest of the world.

At the beginning of the 70th Seven, Israel and the Anti-Christ will have agreed on a covenant together. This covenant, however, lasts only 3½ years. After 3½ years, the Anti-Christ breaks the covenant (Dan 9:27). Why would the Anti-Christ, establish a covenant with Israel and then a mere 3 ½ years later break that covenant? The answer to this question is found in the type of covenant that the Anti-Christ establishes with Israel. The covenant that the Anti-Christ and the nation of Israel agree to has to do in part with the Jewish system of worship.

The Anti-Christ makes a covenant with Israel and then after 3 ½ years break that covenant. The reason for this is in who the Anti-Christ is. The Anti-Christ is the little horn of Dan 7 who speaks boastfully against God (Dan 7:25); who persecutes the saints (Dan 7:25) and will attempt to change set laws and times, that is to make wrong right and right wrong (Dan 7:25). The Anti-Christ is also called the lawless man by Paul (2 Thess 2). The lawless man will oppose and will exalt himself over everything called God or is worshipped (2 Thess 2:4). The lawless man will proclaim himself to be God (2 Thess 2:4). The book of Revelation calls the Anti-Christ the beast coming out of the sea (Rev 13:1). We know that this refers to the Anti-Christ because the beast which comes out of the sea speaks boastfully and blasphemes against God (Rev 13:5, 6). The beast will also slander God's name and those who live in heaven (Rev 13:6). Because of his hatred toward God, the beast will make war against the saints (Rev 13:7). Finally, an image of the beast, of the Anti-Christ will be set up and all the inhabitants of the earth will be forced to worship the image of the Anti-Christ (Rev 13:15). When the Anti-Christ makes a covenant with Israel whereby Israel reinstitutes the sacrificial system, the Anti-Christ is not thinking of helping Israel. In fact, when the Anti-Christ makes this covenant with Israel, he knows within himself that he will break the covenant. In other words, the Anti-Christ deceives Israel.

The Anti-Christ will establish a covenant with Israel and after 3 ½ years will break the covenant (Dan 9:27). The question arises of why the Anti-Christ allows the covenant with Israel to last for 3½ years. The reason is that the Anti-Christ will need time to strengthen his position both with Israel and with the rest of the world. His making a covenant with Israel will be for show, simply a political move that allows him to gain power over the world. After the covenant with Israel is broken, the Anti-Christ will set up the Abomination of Desolation in the temple (Dan 9:27). The setting up of the Abomination of Desolation is the Anti-Christ's move to cause the whole world worship him.

The prophet Daniel said that after the Anti-Christ establishes a covenant with Israel, in the midst of that Seven, that is after 3½ years, the Anti-Christ will put an end to sacrifice and offering (Dan 9:27). What we see from this is that the Anti-Christ establishes a covenant with the nation of Israel that allows Israel to re-institute the sacrificial system of worship. This, in the mind of many, means that the Temple in Jerusalem has to be rebuilt.[338] As everyone knows, the rebuilding of the Temple in Jerusalem is a topic that appears to the human eye to be impossible. The reason for this is that the Dome of the Rock, one of Islam's holiest sites is located on the exact spot where the Temple once stood. To rebuild the Temple, therefore, means either the destruction of the Dome of the Rock, which would probably cause the world wide Muslim community to go to war, or that in some manner Israel and the Muslim world will share the geographical location where the Temple is to be rebuilt.

The manner in which Israel gains the land on which to rebuild the Temple is, of course, in the mind of the Anti-Christ. After all, it is the

Anti-Christ who establishes a covenant with Israel thereby allowing Israel to re-institute the sacrificial system of worship. The Anti-Christ, an astute politician, may also even negotiate an acceptable agreement between Israel and Islam, or the he may bring the Islamic world to its knees in some sort of political or even military manner. Once the Anti-Christ has gained control of the Temple Mount, the land on which the Temple once stood and upon which the Dome of the Rock now stands; he will establish a covenant with Israel, after 3½ years the Anti-Christ then breaks that covenant.

When the Anti-Christ breaks the covenant Israel will be forced to put an end to the sacrificial system. After the covenant is broken and the sacrificial system is ended, then the Anti-Christ will set up the Abomination of Desolation in the temple (Dan 9:27).

As we have already stated, the covenant between the Anti-Christ and the nation of Israel has to do with the sacrificial system and the Jewish nation's worship. The Anti-Christ, once the covenant with Israel has been established finds objection to the covenant. The Bible is very clear what objection the Anti-Christ will have with Israel. The primary objection that the Anti-Christ will have with the Jewish system of worship is not the sacrificial system but the object of Israel's worship. Israel will worship God. The Anti-Christ, who is God's enemy and speaks blasphemy against God (Dan 7:25) will find Israel's worship of God highly objectionable.

The objection that the Anti-Christ will have with the sacrificial system of worship that Israel reinstitutes is the fact that the Anti-Christ wants the world to worship him (Rev 13:15). Because of this desire, the Anti-Christ will not allow anyone or anything else to be worshipped. Thus, the purpose of breaking the covenant with Israel will be the Anti-Christ's attempt to establish himself as god (2 Thess 2:4) and to sabotage Israel's worship of God. Thus, the Abomination of Desolation occurs in the middle of the final seven (Dan 9:27) and will stand in the temple for approximately 3½ years.

The next sign that Jesus mentions as occurring in the first half of the 70th Seven is that the gospel will be preached in the whole world (Matt 24:14). This is also mentioned in John's vision called the Revelation (Rev 6:9-11; 7; 14:6-7; 11). The obedience of Christians in the present age to fulfill the Great Commission (Matt 28:18-20), the Missionary Mandate, which Jesus gave to every Christian, is the foundation upon which the preaching of the Gospel in the Tribulation will be built. The rapture, however, while taking all Christians out of the world, will not end the preaching of the Gospel. The rapture must cause the Anti-Christ and the world such a great amount of distress that even after the rapture the Gospel will still be proclaimed throughout the world.

The book of Revelation also discusses the 70th Seven. The 70th Seven in Revelation is called the Tribulation. The specific structure of Revelation is still a matter of debate. What is known, however, is that Rev 1-3 covers the

271

present age, or the *gap*, between the 69th Seven and the 70th Seven. Rev 4, 5 are events that occur in heaven right before the Tribulation begins. Rev 6-19 covers the period called the Day of the Wrath of God, (Rev 6:17), which is known as the Tribulation[339] and is also known as the 70th Seven, the last 7 years before the return of Jesus Christ. Rev 20-22 covers events after Christ has returned and reclaimed the earth from Satan.

In this study, the major events of the Tribulation will be listed with only a cursory attempt at a structure for Revelation. Fruchtenbaum says that the major events that are listed as occurring in the first half of the 70th Seven are the Seal Judgments (Rev 6:1-8) and the Trumpet Judgments (Rev 8:1-9).[340] He goes on to say that many of the events that occur in the second half of the Tribulation, the 70th Seven, will be the continuation of events that began in the first half of the Tribulation.[341] The Bowl Judgments, according to both Fruchtenbaum[342] and Walvoord[343] occur in the second half of the Tribulation.

Walvoord, in disagreement with Fruchtenbaum regarding the time frame of the Seal Judgments says that the Seal Judgments cover the entire 7 year period of the 70th Seven.[344] According to Walvoord, Rev 6, 7 contain the outline of important events that occur during the first half of the Tribulation. This is seen in the fact that Rev 6 contains the first 6 Seal Judgments. The seventh seal, according to Walvoord, contains the remaining events listed in Revelation.[345] If Walvoord's reasoning is followed, then, the

272

first half of the 70th Seven would contain the first 6 Seal Judgments and the 7th Seal Judgment would cover the second half of the 70th Seven. The reason for this is that the setting up of the Abomination of Desolation is in the middle of the 70th Seven and, in Revelation does not occur until after the 7th Seal is opened (Rev 13).

A further part of Walvoord's reasoning is that at the sounding of the 7th Trumpet, there is a great earthquake, hailstorm and the announcement that the kingdom of the world has become the kingdom of the Lord Jesus (Rev 11:15-19). The question of whether the 7th Trumpet occurs at the end of the first half of the 70th Seven or at the end of the second half of the 70th Seven is dependent upon whether the earthquake that occurs at the sounding of the 7th Trumpet is the same earthquake that destroys the city of Babylon when the angel poured out the 7th Bowl Judgment on the earth (Rev 16:17, 18). A second consideration as to whether the Seal Judgments cover the entire 7 year period is whether the announcement that the kingdom of the world has become the kingdom of Christ occurs in the middle of the Tribulation or at the end of the 70th Seven when Christ has returned to the earth, defeated Satan and the armies of rebels and has reclaimed the earth for God.

At the opening of the first seal, the Anti-Christ rides out to conquer (Rev 6:2). The figure on the white horse, the first of the four horsemen, is the Anti-Christ and not Jesus, although both the Anti-Christ and Jesus ride on white horses (Rev 19:11). The first reason that clearly marks out the first horseman as the Anti-Christ is because the first horseman sets out to conquer the earth and not to redeem it. Here is clearly seen the ultimate purpose of the Anti-Christ. He has as his purpose the conquering of the earth and all who live on it. In addition, the crown of the first horseman is a στέφανος crown, a crown that is given to overcomers or victors.[346] The crown Jesus is wearing is a διάδημα, a diadem crown, which is the crown of sovereignty and is associated with kings.[347] Thus, we see that the rider on the white horse is not Christ, but one who is similar in appearance to Christ, that is the Anti-Christ.

The opening of the first seal and the riding out of the Anti-Christ does not mean that the Anti-Christ magically or all of a sudden pops onto the world's political stage. The Anti-Christ will slowly win the world's support as a politician. The opening of the first seal reveals in a very clear way the purpose of the Anti-Christ. Paul wrote that when the man of lawlessness is revealed, that is fully known, then the end is near (2 Thess 2: 3). When the man of lawlessness is fully known, his purpose will also be fully known. The purpose of the Anti-Christ is to be the god of this world. He will do this by imitating Jesus; he will do this by false miracles; he will do this by—at least the appearance of--dying and then rising to life (Rev 13:3), again in mimicking Jesus' death and resurrection. The Anti-Christ will attempt to be the god of this world by the setting up of the Abomination of Desolation in the

Temple and requiring all people to worship the image (Rev 13:15). Finally, the Anti-Christ will attempt to be the god of this world by instituting the mark of the beast, 666, as a sign of loyalty to the Anti-Christ. Those who refuse to receive the mark, to pledge their allegiance to the Anti-Christ, will not be able to participate in the basic system of life--the economic system (Rev 13:16).

There is a question regarding the identity of the first rider. It is possible that the rider on the white horse is not the Anti-Christ. The reason for this statement is that in all the remaining three horsemen, the riders are not named. What is said is that the 2nd, 3rd, and 4th horsemen are the result of the riding out of the 1st horseman.[348] The question is: why is only the first horseman named while the three remaining horsemen are impersonal results of the first horseman? It is also possible that the identities of the 2nd, 3rd and 4th horsemen are simply unknown.

After the second seal is opened, the second of the four horsemen is freed and rides upon the earth (Rev 6:3, 4). The second horseman has the power to take peace from the earth and to make men kill each other. This horseman brings war upon the earth. War has been a part of the human experience since Cain and Able. The second horseman is not referring to a local or regional war. We are told that the second horseman has the power to take peace from the earth (Rev 6:4). This will not be a regional or local war. The second horseman is referring to a worldwide war. Will there be just one world war remaining or more? Fruchtenbaum says that during the 70th Seven there will be three wars that affect the entire planet.[349] However, there is a view that states that because of the nuclear, biological and chemical stockpiles of weapons, there will be only one more world war.[350] Will another world war be limited in terms of weapons used? Or will the whole arsenal of weapons which are available be utilized? The leaders of many countries in the world are attempting to keep certain nations and individuals from gaining access to nuclear weapons. The reason for this is that many believe that while the majority of world leaders understand the once for all use of nuclear weapons, these certain nations and individuals either do not understand this fact or act as though the once for all use of nuclear weapons is exactly what their ideology or religion requires.

What we do know is that the Anti-Christ, whose purpose is conquest, does not have to do much to cause humanity to kill each other. As a race, humans have invented many ways to kill one another. It also seems that there is in the world an eagerness to kill one another. Life, for the most part is no longer sacred. This is seen in the rise of abortion on demand. It is also seen in the way the elderly are considered a drain on the economy. The false idea of the quality of life raises its ugly head in the discussions regarding those who have physical, mental, emotional challenges. Hitler and the Third Reich had a very limited view of who was worthy to live. The world today is not far from fully embracing this limited view. We also know that with all the weapons that are stockpiled, it will not take much to cause a worldwide catastrophe.

After the second horseman goes out to cause war upon the earth, the third horseman is released. The third horseman is said to bring a world-wide famine upon the earth (Rev 6:5, 6). A scarcity of food is a natural result of war. War will cause the destruction of farms, food processing facilities and all other segments of the chain that puts food in the grocery stores.

When the world is suffering famine, the fourth horseman is released (Rev 6:7, 8). The fourth horseman has the power to kill over one quarter of the world's population. One quarter of the world's population will be killed by famine, sword (war), plague (diseases which will run rampant through a weakened population) and wild animals. The wild animals will attack humans because of the destruction of their food sources.

John then sees the fifth seal being opened. At the opening of the fifth seal, John sees under the altar the souls of those who had been slain because of their stance for God and Christ (Rev 6:9-11). We have already discussed the soul after death earlier in this book, so we will not revisit that topic here. The souls under the altar raise a question as to identity. Since the rapture has already occurred, who are these who are killed for their faith in God during the Tribulation?

In an attempt to answer this question, we state the obvious. The obvious is that in the world there are many people who have an intellectual knowledge of Christianity, the rapture and of Christ. Many of these may think that they are Christian, yet their *faith* is purely intellectual, it is only knowledge. They have not made the life commitment to Jesus Christ as Lord. When the rapture occurs and many of their neighbors, friends, etc. are taken from the earth, this will cause this segment of humanity to reconsider the truth of the Gospel and of Jesus Christ. They will then accept Christ as their Lord and Savior.

In addition, the prophet Joel states that when God pours out His Spirit on the world, which began at Pentecost (Acts 2:17-21), God will continue to pour out His Spirit until the gathering of the nations for judgment (Joel 2:28-3:2). We see in this that not only will the Gospel be proclaimed during the 70th Seven by the witness of the Two Witnesses, but in addition, the rapture will confirm in the minds of many the truth of the Gospel and also that God Himself will be personally involved in the human race during the 70th Seven by the pouring out of His Spirit.

Secondly, during the Tribulation there will be 144, 000 Jewish evangelists who spread the Gospel around the world. With the technology available today, it will not be difficult to present the Gospel message in one place and have people all around the globe hear it. In addition to the Christian knowledge that many have and the preaching of the 144, 000 Jewish evangelists, there will also be the spreading of the Gospel by angels (Rev 14:6-7).

Under girding the preaching of the Gospel during the Tribulation is the truth that even in the midst of wrath, God is merciful (Hab 3:2). The judgments during the Tribulation have as their purpose correction. God's purpose for the judgments is to lead people to repent.[351] This purpose is seen throughout the book of Revelation where it says that after a judgment, the people of the earth refused to repent (Rev 9:20, 21; 16:9, 11, 21). The opportunity is given to repent, yet, the stubborn heart of those who are on the earth refuse, even in the face of end of the world calamity, to repent.

The opening of the sixth seal causes the heavens to be changed (Rev 6:12-14). Before modern GPS navigational systems, the world's travelers depended upon the heavens to guide them. The stars, while moving across the sky, could be depended upon to be in the same relative positions night after night. The heavens, sun, moon and stars are constants in an ever changing world. When the sixth seal is opened, that which was constant is no longer constant.

The seventh seal is opened and it is found to contain the seven trumpet judgments (Rev 8:2).

At the sounding of the first trumpet, one third of the earth's dry surface is destroyed (Rev 8:7).

The second trumpet sounds and a huge mountain is thrown into the sea which destroys one third of the sea including the sea life (Rev 8:8,9). Whether this huge mountain is a meteor or is the result of a volcanic eruption is not known. What is known is that after the first two trumpets have sounded, 1/3 of the earth and 1/3 of the sea is destroyed. In addition to the earth and water being affected, what is also affected is the earth's food supplies. With 1/3 of the earth's surface destroyed, there will not be much farm land to produce food. When 1/3 of the sea is destroyed, the fishing industry will be crippled.

With the sounding of the third trumpet, a great star fell from the sky and destroyed 1/3 of the rivers and other fresh water sources (Rev 8:10, 11). The first trumpet destroys the land, which cripples the earth's farm industry. The second trumpet destroys the sea and in so doing cripples the fishing industry. After the first two trumpets have sounded, the food supply and the earth's ability to provide food has been severely, if not totally, destroyed. It is said that a person can live longer without food than without water. What happens after the sounding of the third trumpet is that the earth's fresh water supply is destroyed. Now, not only are people starving, but they are dying from thirst and from drinking the poisoned water (Rev 8:11).

The fourth trumpet affects the sun, the moon and 1/3 of the stars (Rev 8:12). What happens at the sounding of the fourth trumpet is that the light reaching the earth is limited to 1/3 of what is necessary to maintain life. The fourth trumpet is similar to what happens during the opening of the sixth seal when the sun, moon and stars were changed (Rev 6:12, 13). Again, we see that what many people have depended upon, what they have used to guide their lives is now no longer the source that people can depend upon.

What God is doing is removing anything and everything that people in their rebellion have depended upon to meet their needs and give their lives purpose. What the Serpent said to Eve, and she herself came to believe, was that the fruit of the Tree of the Knowledge of Good and Evil was good for food, (now the food supply in the world is for all practical purposes gone), pleasing to the eye (now the appearance of the earth has been horribly altered) and desirable for gaining wisdom (now the heavenly bodies have been thrown into confusion).

After the fourth trumpet sounded, and people's supports are all gone, the message of God came to the people of the earth that the next three trumpets will be worse than the previous four (Rev 8:13). In the midst of wrath, God remembers mercy. A warning is sounded giving people time to repent.

At the sounding of the fifth trumpet, a demonic invasion of the earth occurs (Rev 9:1-11). These demons are able to torture humans, but not to kill them (Rev 9:5).

The sixth trumpet releases a second demonic invasion which is worse than the first (Rev 9:13-19). The second demonic invasion kills up to 1/3 of the human race (Rev 9:15).

There is in the world a growing fascination with the demonic. Vampires and werewolves are seen nightly on television shows and movies. There is a growing population that is worshipping Satan. The demonic is becoming all the rage. What God does in the sounding of the fifth and sixth trumpets is to give people what they want. When the two demonic invasions occur, people who have a fascination with this evil will know experientially the old saying *that playing with fire will get you burnt.*

After the sounding of the sixth trumpet, we see God's mercy again rejected by people (Rev 8:20, 21). There is no food, no water, the heavens are changed, demons have attacked and killed many, yet, there is still no repentance.

According to Dan 9:27, in the middle of the 70th Seven, the Anti-Christ breaks the covenant he has established with Israel and sets up the Abomination of Desolation. The setting up of the Abomination of Desolation by the Anti-Christ has already been discussed. We will not repeat that discussion; however, a few comments will only be added.

The Devil has, from his rebellion, had a desire to be the god of this world. In fact, the Devil gained the world when Adam and Eve ate from the Tree of the Knowledge of Good and Evil (Luke 4:5-7). He led astray angels who joined him in his rebellion. He deceived Eve in the Garden. He prowls around like a roaring lion, in the present age, to devour and destroy. However, his appearance is as of angel of light (2 Cor 11:14). His true nature and purpose is not fully known. There is coming a day, however, when the true nature and purpose of Satan will be revealed. The full revealing of Satan's purpose and character will be in the middle of the 70th Seven when an image is set up in the Temple and all people are required to worship this image.

The truth is that the Devil can only do that which people want. If he is resisted, he must flee (James 4:7). He succeeds by moving in the shadows, by convincing most that he does not exist. He has convinced the majority that God is withholding the best from them; that God is their enemy. The Devil promises everything (Gen 3), yet his promises lead only to death. In spite of all this, the world is full of people who are eager, willing to do anything and everything to gain his empty promises. When the Devil is fully revealed in the Anti-Christ (Rev 13:2), he will find waiting for him multitudes of willing servants. When the Abomination of Desolation is set up in the Temple, the majority of the world's population will worship and fall down before the image.

Jesus, after discussing the signs of the end of the Age and of His return up to the time of the world-wide preaching of the Gospel, which occurs in the first half of the 70th Seven, then mentions the setting up of the Abomination of

Desolation that Daniel the prophet foretold would occur (Matt 24:15). As it has been mentioned before in this study, the fact that Jesus mentions the setting up of the Abomination of Desolation that Daniel foretold in the context of the end of the age and of His return, proves that as horrendous as the deeds of Antiochus Epiphanes were, his act was not the Abomination of Desolation. The Abomination of Desolation is the act of the Anti-Christ. The Abomination of Desolation is in all actuality the Anti-Christ claiming to be God (2 Thess 2:4). He does this by having an image of himself set up in the Temple and requiring each and every person to worship the image (2 Thess 2:4; Rev 13:13:14-17).

There is a great similarity in the act of the Anti-Christ to the act of Nebuchadnezzar who made a great image of gold and required all to worship the image (Dan 3). The proclamation of both Nebuchadnezzar and the Anti-Christ is that, those who refuse to worship the image will be put to death (Dan 3:6; Rev 13:15). According to both Daniel and Jesus, the setting up of the Abomination of Desolation occurs in the middle of the 70th Seven, the last 7 years before the return of Christ. The middle of the Tribulation period in Revelation is covered in Rev 10-14.[352]

We begin our discussion of the last half of the 70th Seven by setting the context for the events in the second half of the Tribulation. During the first half of the Tribulation, the first half of the 70th Seven, there is the preaching of the Gospel and many people will be turning to faith in Christ. The rapture will of course be the sign to many that Jesus is the Christ and that the Gospel is the truth. When the Anti-Christ sees that the rapture, instead of removing the Gospel from the world, has had just the opposite result, he will become enraged. At the rapture, the Anti-Christ will think that the world is finally freed from Christ and that no one will believe in Jesus from that time on. However, because of the preaching of the Gospel before the rapture occurs and after the rapture has taken place, many people will accept the Truth of Jesus Christ. It will not just be Gentiles who believe, but, many in Israel will turn to Christ. We are told that out of the Tribulation, many will accept Christ (Rev 7:9, 14). This is in part the reason why, in the middle of the 70th Seven, the Anti-Christ breaks the covenant that he made with Israel. The rapture will be one of the means by which the revival in Israel will sweep through the nation. When the Anti-Christ breaks the covenant that he established with Israel, this will be seen by Israel as a tragedy. Yet, in all reality, it will be another step in the beginning of the great revival of the Jewish people. Thus, Paul's statement that after the Fullness of the Gentiles, all Israel[353] will be saved will be fulfilled.

Although the persecution of Christians has occurred since the time of Jesus and intensifies up to the rapture, it is after the Anti-Christ sets up the Abomination of Desolation that he begins a systematic campaign to rid the world, once and for all, of all who would confess the Name of Jesus (Matt 24:21). To rid the world of all who believe in Jesus as the Christ is in part the reason why the Anti-Christ takes complete control of the world's economic system and requires all to either buy or sell to have the mark (Rev 13:16).

The mark of the beast, 666, is not simply a credit card or a chip implanted on the forehead or right hand (Rev 13:16). The mark is also a sign of loyalty and allegiance to the Anti-Christ (Rev 13:15, 16). Christians, those who have confessed Jesus as Lord, will not accept the mark. The ones who do not accept the mark are then clearly marked out as enemies of the Anti-Christ and can then be hunted down and killed.

Jesus, describes the time after the setting up of the Abomination of Desolation as a time of great distress, a time that is unequaled from the beginning of the world and never to be equaled again (Matt 24:21). While the whole 70th Seven is called the Tribulation,[354] the final 3 ½ years, the second half of the 70th Seven is called by Jesus as the Great Tribulation (Matt 24:21).[355] The prophet Daniel also describes the final 3 ½ year period, the second half of the 70th Seven as a time of distress such as not happened from the beginning of the nations (Dan 12:1). This time of unequaled distress will begin when the Abomination of Desolation is set up and will end 3 ½ years later (Dan 12: 7, 11).

The 3½ years after the Abomination of Desolation is set up will see

286

two major events. The first major event to occur after the setting up of the Abomination of Desolation is the Great Tribulation (Matt 24:15-21). The second major event is return of Christ.

The Great Tribulation ushers in the Bowl Judgments (Rev 15:7). The Bowl Judgments contain the seven last plagues (Rev 15:1). With the Bowl Judgments, God's wrath is said to be complete (Rev 15:1).

The first bowl is poured out and affects only those who have the mark of the beast, the sign of loyalty to the Anti-Christ (Rev 16:2).

When the second bowl judgment is poured out, the remaining oceans are destroyed. (When the second trumpet was blown, only 1/3 of the oceans were destroyed). At the second bowl judgment, the remaining oceans are destroyed (Rev 16:3). While it was possible that after the second trumpet there might still be a fishing industry that was able to supply some food to the world, at the second bowl, the entire oceans are destroyed, in that destruction, the fishing industry is also completely destroyed.

The third bowl judgment destroys the remaining fresh water supply (Rev 16:4). There is now no water at all to drink.

With the fourth bowl judgment, the world no longer has the protection of the ozone layer that helps filter our harmful rays from the sun (Rev 16:8). This will cause painful burns and sores on people.

The sad state of the human heart is seen in the fact that even now, near the end, people refuse to repent, but still raise their fist and curse God (Rev 16:9). The truth is the Tribulation is not necessary. If people would only reject the Devil, sin and return to God, then there would be no Tribulation. However, because people have rejected God and chosen the fruit of the Tree of the Knowledge of Good and Evil, God sends the Tribulation as a means to turn the hearts of humanity back to God.

At the fifth bowl judgment, the wrath of God is poured out on the throne of the beast, Satan (Rev 16:10). The kingdom of the beast will be plunged into darkness. In the darkness, people will be suffering from hunger, thirst, sores, pains and they will still refuse to repent.

The sixth bowl judgment dries up the Euphrates River (Rev 16:12). At that time, demons go out to the armies of the world to gather them together at Armageddon (Rev 16:13-16). The reason that they are gathered together at Armageddon is because Satan knows that Christ will soon return to claim the earth.

The seventh bowl judgment is the sign of the return of Christ. At the seventh bowl judgment, there is a great earthquake and huge hailstones fell from the sky (Rev 16:18-21). Still, the human heart is unrepentant, for they cursed God (Rev 16:21).

At the seventh bowl judgment, the city of Babylon is destroyed (Rev 16:19). At the destruction of the city of Babylon, there is a great mourning, for the destruction of Babylon means the end of consumerism, capitalism, the enriching of oneself and the exploitation of others economically (Rev 16:11-20). The Judgments of God destroys everything that people have placed before God; those things that have become more important to people than God. All that is left after the judgments of God is God Himself. Even then, the unbeliever still will not want God.

At the destruction of the city of Babylon, there is a great roar in heaven (Rev 19:1). At this great roar, Jesus Christ will return to the earth with the armies of heaven (Rev 19:11-16). The Apocalypse will now have occurred.

The second major event that will occur after the Abomination of Desolation is set up is the Second Coming of Jesus Christ, the Apocalypse (Matt 24:29, 30). Jesus said that *immediately after the distress of those days,* the Son of Man will appear (Matt 24:29, 30). Immediately after the Great Tribulation, Jesus will come again.

After the Great Tribulation, the second half of the 70th Seven, the Apocalypse will occur, that is the revealing, the Second Coming of the Lord Jesus Christ (Matt 24:29, 30). The Second Coming of Christ will be an event that is witnessed by everyone on the earth (Matt 24:30). When Christ returns, He will bring with Him all His people (Matt 24:31).

At this point as we are discussing the Second Coming of Christ, I want to compare and contrast the Second Coming with the rapture. The teaching of the when of the rapture in the book of Revelation is within chapters 4, 5 of Revelation. The reason for this is that Rev 1-3 talk about the present age. Rev 6 is the beginning of the Tribulation, the Day of the wrath of God (Rev 6:16, 17). Because Jesus Christ has promised His people that they will be spared from, rescued from wrath, this means that those who are Christian at the time of the rapture must be taken from the place where God's wrath will fall and that is the entire earth.

There has been much debate over whether Rev 4:1 is a reference to the rapture. I will not go into a great detail of this debate. I will say that for Rev 4:1 to be a reference to the rapture, then John must symbolize in some way, all Christians. There is no Biblical basis for this.

On the other hand of the debate, however, are common elements in Rev 4:1 and other Scriptures that refer to God snatching up of His people. In Rev 4:1 there is the voice like a trumpet that calls John to heaven. In 1 Thess 4:16, 17 there is the voice of an archangel, the trumpet call of God and God's command, presumably to rise both from the grave, as Jesus called Lazarus to come out of the tomb (John 11:43) and to rise in the air. Also in Rev 11:12, in reference to the Two Witnesses who witness in the earth, are killed and their bodies lie in the street for 3 ½ days, there is a loud voice from heaven saying *come up here.*

The common elements between Rev 11:12, 1 Thess 4:16, 17 and Rev 4:1 do not necessarily mean that Rev 4:1 is a reference to the rapture. However, the common elements of these three Scriptures does lead to a possibility that Rev 4:1 refers in some way to the rapture.

The Second Coming of Christ and the rapture, the snatching up Christians (1 Thess 4:17) are thus to be differentiated in that at the rapture, the Christian rises to meet the Lord in the air while at Christ's Second Coming, the followers of Christ come with Him to the earth (Rev 19:14). When Jesus Christ returns, the Second Coming, He will come with *all* His holy ones (1 Thess 3:13). Holy Ones are from the Greek, ἅγιος, which means holy.[356] ἅγιος is used to refer to Christians (Rom 1:7; 1 Cor 1:2; 2 Cor 1:1; Eph 1:1; Phil 1:1; Col 1:2). ἅγιος is also used in reference to angels (Mark 8:38), although in Mark 8:38 the word *angels* is used in connection to ἅγιος. The point, however, in 1 Thess 3:13 is that when Christ appears, He will come with *all* His holy ones, both Christians and angels. The word *all* is important. Paul does not say that when Christ appears He will appear with some of His holy ones, but with *all* of His holy ones. The statement of Paul is in agreement with John's vision when he saw Jesus returning with the armies of heaven (Rev 19:14).

At the Second Coming of Christ, Jesus will come on the clouds (Matt 24:30). When the Lord Jesus returns, every eye will see Him descend from the heavens (Rev 1:7). His Second Coming will be with power and great glory (Matt 24:30). The glory of the Lord is like the sunrise (Hab 3:4). This is one reason why every eye will see Him when He returns. His return will be like the sunrise which no one will be able to miss. At His Second Coming, Jesus will bring with Him the armies of heaven (Rev 19:14). The sky will be filled with the Lord and all His holy ones. At the Second Coming of the Lord Jesus, the armies of the world will be gathered together to make war against the Lamb and His holy ones (Rev 19:19).

The Second Coming of Jesus Christ is a day when the world is prepared for Christ's return. The reason for this is that the armies of the world are gathered together to make war against Christ. The day of Christ's Second Coming will not catch the world by surprise. This day will not come suddenly. The world will be ready for Christ's return. When Christ returns, He will come on the clouds and every eye will see Him (Rev 1:7). It is inconceivable that the world's news agencies will not be there with cameras pointing towards the heavens televising the return of Christ. The return of Christ will not come as a surprise. The world will be ready for Him.

However, Paul writes that there is coming a day that will catch the world by surprise. This day will come like a thief in the night (1 Thess 5:2). This day will occur when the world is talking about peace (1 Thess 5:3). The day that Paul is writing about will come suddenly and for many unexpectedly.

The word, suddenly is αἰφνίδος, which is also used in Luke 21:34 where Jesus is warning His followers to stay vigilant for the Day of His coming or they will be surprised when it occurs.

Because the day of Christ's return will be a day in which every eye will see Him; a day when the armies of the world are gathered together to try and prevent Christ from reclaiming the earth; a day in which no one will be surprised; there must be another day in which the world is caught by surprise. This day must be the rapture—a day when the world is taken by surprise, a day the world is not prepared for. This day is also a day when the Christian, if involved in the affairs of this world, will also be taken by surprise. We see from the description of Christ's Second Coming and the day when the world is taken by surprise, the rapture, that these must be two different days.

Another difference between the rapture and the Second Coming of Christ is that at the rapture, the Lord descends and meets His people in the air (1 Thess 4:17); while at the Second Coming, Jesus descends to the earth with His people (Rev 19:19).

The signs that the world is rapidly approaching the Apocalypse are all around. Global warming is affecting the weather patterns all around the world. Not only are the glaciers melting which is causing a destruction of the environment in the Arctic, Antarctica, and the climates and environment of all the northern countries; there is also growing concern of the potential flooding

293

of the world's coastlines by the water that flows into the world's oceans by the melting glaciers. Melting glaciers are not the only area affected by global warming. Global warming is changing weather patterns all across the world. Both summers and winters are being changed so that the weather patterns are more and more extreme.

In addition to global warming, there is also the growing concern over greenhouse gases, which in the minds of many is the cause of global warming. However, greenhouse gases are doing more than just causing global warming. The world is more polluted now than ever. The air quality in many cities, at times, is unbearable. The world's farmlands are wearing out and need more and more artificial fertilizers to produce a crop. Fresh water is at a premium and may not exist anymore.

While medicine is making gains in many areas, there is the existence of super germs that are becoming more resistant to known antibiotics. Most of the world still does not have health care and where there is health care, the cost of medicine is growing at such a rate, that eventually only a few will be able to afford it.

The constant stress of the increase cost of simply living is causing more and more people to become ill; more and more families to break up with the result of more and more people becoming angry. Some of these angry people will take out their anger on others and thus the need for more and more prisons to house the growing prison population. The increase of drug use and addiction of alcohol, over the counter, prescription and illegal drugs is producing a population that is unable to function. The growth and spread of terrorism around the world is producing a hopelessness that eats away at the soul.

The world situation, the many problems facing the world, people desperate for answers, coupled with the growing animosity of many towards Christ is the setting, the environment in which the Anti-Christ will not only rise to power, but will have the people's support.

The Tribulation and the wrath of God poured out in judgment is something that can be avoided by the individual and the world as a whole. All that is needed is to repent and to accept Jesus Christ as Lord and Savior. Many people claim and will claim as the Day draws nearer that God is to blame, that God is the source of evil because of the judgments. However, the judgments of God poured out during the Tribulation are simply God's response to a heart that is unwilling to live for Him.

The timeline to the Apocalypse, the return of Christ is near the end. What will your response be?

As John writes at the end of his vision in the Book of Revelation, I also write "Amen. Come Lord Jesus!"

NOTES

---

[1] C. Westermann, trans. by Hugh Clayton White, *Basic Forms of Prophetic Speech* (Philadelphia: The Westminster Press, 1967), 26.

[2] A. Heschel, *The Prophets* (New York: Harper & Row, 1962), 15.

[3] Josephus, *The Antiquities of the Jews,* Book 10, Chapter 11.

[4] A. Heschel, *The Prophets,* 15.

[5] *Ibid,* 15.

[6] *Ibid,* 24. See also Josephus, *Antiquities of the Jews,* Book 10, Chapter 11.

[7] As an example of this see Jeremiah 49-51 where God through the prophet addresses the Gentile nations. This is followed by Jeremiah 52 where the fall of Jerusalem is prophesied.

[8] A. Heschel, *The Prophets,* 14, 15.

[9] D. Baly, *God and History in the Old Testament* (New York: Harper & Row, 1976), 5.

[10] *Ibid,* 75.

[11] A. Heschel, *The Prophets,* 24.

[12] J. Bright, *Covenant and Promise* (Philadelphia: The Westminster Press, 1976), 15.

[13] *Ibid,* 26.

[14] φερόμενοι is a present passive participle of φέρω. Φέρω means to so influence others as to cause them to follow a recommended course of action (J. Louw & E. Nida, *Greek-English Lexicon of the New Testament, Based on Semantic Domains,* New York: United Bible Societies, 1989, 465).

[15] *Ibid,* 440.

[16] θεόπνευστος, means pertaining to a communication which has been inspired by God (J. Louw & E. Nida, *Greek-English Lexicon,* 418).

[17] The later date will be discussed further on in this study.

[18] Josephus, *Antiquities of the Jews,* Book 10, Chapter 11.

[19] The identity of the Little Horn of Dan 7 and of Dan 8 will be discussed later on in this study.

[20] J. Boice, *Foundations of the Christian Faith* (Downers Grove: InterVarsity Press, 1986), 38.

[21] There are a number of views regarding the transmission of the Scriptures from God to the human authors. This study will not go into the various views. The Bible says that all Scripture is God-breathed. The Scriptures do not go into the detail as to the method of transmission. The Bible simply states the fact that the Scriptures are God-breathed. The unfortunate result of the debate over the *how* of the inspiration of the Bible by God is that the *fact* of the inspiration of the Bible is forgotten or minimized. The inspiration of the Scriptures by God leads to the understanding that the Bible is a result of God's creative act. The Bible as a creative act of God is seen in the connection of the speaking of God and creation. To use anthropomorphic terms, there is a close connection between speaking and breathing. Since the speaking of God

results in a creative act (see the many statements in Gen 1 where it is stated that God said and it was) and breathing and speaking are intimately connected, it leads to the understanding that the breathing of God also results in a creative act.

[22] ἀποκάλυψις means to cause something to be fully known, to reveal, to disclose, revelation (J. Louw & E. Nida, *Greek-English Lexicon*, 339.

[23] J. Boice, *Foundations of the Christian Faith*, 40.

[24] The word *record* denotes God's activities in the past, present and future.

[25] Josephus, Book XII, Chapter 1, *Antiquities of the Jews*.

[26] J. Montgomery, *The Book of Daniel* (Edinburgh: T & T Clark, 1972), 292.

[27] *Ibid*, 290.

[28] *Ibid*, 291.

[29] *Ibid*, 289.

[30] *Ibid*, 288.

[31] *Ibid*, 288.

[32] *Ibid*, 290.

[33] *Ibid*, 291.

[34] R. Hammer, *The Book of Daniel* (Cambridge: Cambridge University Press, 1976), 98, 99.

[35] A. Bloomfield, *The End of the Days: The Prophecies of Daniel Explained* (Minneapolis: Bethany Fellowship, 1970), 63.

[36] The New International Version states *to anoint the most holy place* in Dan 9:24. Bloomfield states that what is meant is to anoint the   most holy one, A. Bloomfield, *The End of the Days*, 61. The Hebrew for this phrase is: קדשים קדש קדשים is masculine, which would lead toward the most holy one. However, literally the meaning is the most holy. The reality is however, it is God's presence that makes anything and all things holy. Nothing is holy in and of itself.   If Dan 9:24 is translated the most holy place, the place is holy only because God is there. It is God who makes the place holy by His presence. This being said, it makes little difference if the most holy place is understood or the most holy one. The most holy one makes the most place holy by His presence. When the presence of the Most Holy One is not in the place, the place is no longer holy. In addition, Heb 9:23-28 states that the earthly temple is only a copy, shadow of the real temple, which is in heaven and that the real holy place can only be cleansed by the blood of Christ. Therefore, it is to be understood that the most holy place and the most holy one are intimately related and tied together.

[37] J. Louw & E. Nida, *Greek-English Lexicon*, 453.

[38] For a more detailed discussion of this see further on in this study.

[39] Jesus died for sinners. He bore the sin of the world on His body on the Cross. This means that the statement that the Jews killed Jesus is only partially accurate. The truth is that every single person killed Jesus. It is the sins of everyone that killed Jesus.

[40] See the discussion above concerning the purpose of the Law and its relationship to Christ.

[41] The use of the term *salvation* is an attempt to describe the on-going experience that the Believer in Christ undergoes. In no way does this study hold the position that saved means an end to the experience of salvation or an end to the work of the Holy Spirit in the life of the Christian Believer. The term salvation is simply a comprehensive term, an umbrella term, if you will, under which the whole past, present and future work of the Holy Spirit is brought together.

[42] John R.W. Stott, *The Cross of Christ*, (Downers Grove: InterVarsity Press, 1986), 167.

[43] These two perspectives frame the theological discussion of justification and righteousness. These two perspectives are termed the imputation of righteousness, which is God's declaration that the believing sinner is righteous and the impartation of righteousness whereby God not only declares the believing sinner righteous but also gives to, imparts to the believing sinner the righteousness of Christ.

[44] E. Brunner, *The Christian Doctrine of the Church, Faith and the Consummation*, (Philadelphia: The Westminster Press, 1962), 200.

[45] J. R. W. Stott, *The Cross of Christ*, 182.

[46] J. Wesley, *Wesley's Notes on the New Testament, Vol. II*, (Kansas City, Missouri: Beacon Hill Press of Kansas City, 1983), see Wesley's comments on Rom 5:18 where he writes: justification to life means that the sentence of God, by which a sinner under sentence of death is adjudged to life.

[47] R.E. Cushman, *John Wesley's Experimental Divinity*, (Nashville: Kingswood Books, 1989), 62.

[48] J. Wesley, *Salvation by Faith*, Sermon, *The Works of John Wesley, 11* (CD-Rom; Franklin, TN: Providence House Publishers, 1995), Vol. 5, 10.

[49] *Ibid*, 10.

[50] J. Wesley, *Scripture Way of Salvation*, Sermon, *The Works of John Wesley, 11* (CD-Rom; Franklin, TN: Providence House Publishers, 1995), Vol. 6, 44.

[51] Justification and righteousness mean that the person is right with God (J. Louw & E. Nida, *Greek-English Lexicon*, 452).

[52] E. Brunner, *The Christian Doctrine of the Church, Faith and Consummation*, 196.

[53] John R.W. Stott, *The Cross of Christ*, 149.

[54] J. Louw & E. Nida, *Greek-English Lexicon*, 583.

[55] W. F. Arndt and F. W. Gingrich, *A Greek-English Lexicon of the New Testament and Other Early Christian Literature*, 476.

[56] The phrase *has become* is the translation of the Greek ἐγενήθη. Ἐγενήθη is an aorist verb. The aorist signifies that the action is attained, is completed (Dana and Mantey, *A Manual Grammar of the Greek New Testament*, New York: Macmillan Publishing, 1955), 193.

[57] G. Osborne, *Romans* (Downers Grove: InterVarsity Press, 2004), 200.

[58] A. Fruchtenbaum states that the most holy refers to the Temple of the Messianic Kingdom (A. Fruchtenbaum, *The Footsteps of the Messiah*, Tustin, CA: Ariel Publishers, 2003), 192. However, see the discussion in footnote 36 concerning the intimate connection between the most holy place and the most holy one.

[59] J. Louw & E. Nida, *The Greek-English Lexicon*, 543.

[60] *Ibid*, 543.

[61] A. Lococque, Translated by David Pellauer, *The Book of Daniel* (Atlanta: John Knox Press, 1979), 195.

[62] *Ibid,* 196.

[63] *Ibid,* 191.

[64] A. Bloomfield, *The End of the Days,* 64.

[65] A. Fruchtenbaum, *The Footsteps of the Messiah,* 194.

[66] The phrase *after the 62 sevens* does not mean after the first 62 sevens. There are three sub-divisions of the 70 sevens. The first sub-division is found in the first seven during which the city of Jerusalem will be rebuilt (Dan 9:25). The second sub-division is the 62 sevens that follow the rebuilding of Jerusalem and ends with the cutting off of the Anointed One (Dan 9:25). Thus when Dan 9:26 says *after the 62 sevens* it means after the 62 sevens that follow the first seven. In other words the phrase *after the 62 sevens* means after the first 69 sevens. This is seen in that the first seven is followed by the 62 sevens for a total of 69 sevens.

[67] Bloomfield calls the time of the *gap* between the 69th Seven and the 70th Seven the *Time of the Fullness of the Gentiles* (A. Bloomfield, *Before The Last Battle: Armageddon,* Minneapolis: Dimension Books, 1971, 162. He disagrees with the view that calls the time of the *gap* between the 69th Seven and the 70th Seven, the Times of the Gentiles. He states that the times of the Gentiles is the last 3 ½ years before Christ's Return, or the last half of the 70th Seven (Bloomfield, *Before the Last Battle,* 161).

[68] R.L. Harris, ed. *Theological Wordbook of the Old Testament, Vol. I* (Chicago: Moody Press, 1981), 334.

[69] A. Fruchtenbaum, *The Footsteps of the Messiah,* 188.

[70] Fruchtenbaum states that the little horn of Dan 8 is the Anti-Christ. A. Fruchtenbaum, *The Footsteps of the Messiah,* 214; while F. Beare states that the Anti-Christ is Antiochus Epiphanes, (*The Earliest Records of Jesus,* Nashville: Abingdon Press, 1962), 216.

[71] *Sibylline Oracles,* 3, 381-400.

[72] Josephus, *Antiquities of the Jews,* Book 10, chapter 11; A. Lacocque, *The Book of Daniel,* 190; R. Hammer *The Book of Daniel* (Cambridge: Cambridge University Press, 1976), 85.

[73] Josephus, *Antiquities of the Jews,* Book 12, Chapter 5.

[74] *Ibid,* Book 10, Chapter 11.

[75] *Ibid,* Book 10, Chapter 11.

[76] To confirm this statement, let the reader simply listen to the news and talk to the person on the street. When this is done, what will be discovered is that very few people view God as loving and as one who cares for them.

[77] J. Louw & E. Nida, *The Greek -English Lexicon,* 758.

[78] R. Trench, *Synonyms of The New Testament* (Grand Rapids: Eerdmans, 1980), 244.

[79] B. McGinn, *Anti-Christ: Two Thousand Years of The Human Fascination with Evil* (San Francisco: HarperSanFrancisco, 1994), 51.

[80] A. Bloomfield, *Before the Last Battle: Armageddon,* 119.

[81] B. McGinn, *Anti-Christ: Two Thousand Years of The Human Fascination with Evil,* 279.

[82] *Ibid,* 33.

[83] J. Louw & E. Nida, *The Greek-English Lexicon,* 543.

[84] R. Trench, *Synonyms of the New Testament,* 106.

[85] B. McGinn, *Anti-Christ: Two Thousand Years of The Human Fascination with Evil,* 9.

[86] *Ibid,* 52.

[87] The War Scroll is one of the scrolls found in the caves of Qumran, commonly called the Dead Sea Scrolls.

[88] The War Scroll, 13, 10.

[89] F. Waters, *Book of The Hopi* (New York: Ballantine Books, 1963), 408.

[90] Koran 23:61.

[91] Sibylline Oracle, Book 3, lines 63-92.

[92] The Revelation of Esdras, location 6542-47.

[93] Whether this world changing event is the end of the world as recorded by some or is a time of renewal as recorded by others is a matter of debate. For more information regarding the debate over the Mayan Long Calendar and 2012, all one has to do is to visit any bookstore.

[94] The names of the gods and goddesses of Greek and Roman mythology such as: Cronos, Gaia, Ouranos, Titans, Aphrodite, Demeter, Hestia, Dione, Pluto, and others are names of *humans* who lived immediately after the Tower of Babel and the confusion of languages, *The Sibylline Oracle* Book III, lines 105-160. In addition, some of the names of the kings on the Sumerian King List reappear in other writings as gods or heroes of legends (C. Leonard Woolley, *The Sumerians,* New York: W.W. Norton & Co., 1965, 29). Further, *The Book of Jubilees* states that there were/are female demons. These female demons are called *Sirens* (*The Book of Jubilees* 5:1, 2). What is interesting is that the same name *Sirens* is used in Greek and Roman mythology to describe non-human females who had powers beyond human ability. Another fact to be understood is that since there are female demons, there are female angels; since the demons are fallen angels.

[95] The *seed* of the idea of the Greek and Roman mythological stories of gods and goddesses cavorting with human men and women is from Gen 6:1,2. For a defense of this position, see the discussion to follow.

[96] There exists in many cultures, many statues and other cultural expressions that are similar to statues found in other cultures that, at this point, archeologists state had no contact with each other. The similar designs in statuary and other cultural expressions is said by some to have been given by ancient aliens. The coming to earth of angels, both Godly and Fallen, who shared knowledge with human beings would explain the similar design of many cultural expressions found in cultures around the world who had no contact with each other after the Tower of Babel.

[97] *The Book of Jubilees* 22:17; *Enoch* 19:1; 1 Cor 10:20.

[98] *The Book of Jubilees,* 4:15.

[99] *Enoch* 7: 1, 2.

[100] *Enoch* 9:6.

[101] *The Book of Jubilees* 8:3, 4.

[102] *The Book of Jubilees* 8:4.

[103] C. Leonard Woolley, *The Sumerians*, 189.

[104] *Ibid*, 189.

[105] *The Book of Jubilees* 4:15.

[106] *The Testament of Reuben* 5:6 in *The Testament of the Twelve Patriarchs.*

[107] *Antiquities of the Jew*, Book 1, Chapter 3, par 1.

[108] See *Enoch* 6:1-8; *The Book of the Secrets of Moses*, 10:18; *The Book of Jubilees*, 5:1,2 which all state that angels took human women as wives. In addition, Charles cites Bousset who writes in *Religion des Judenthums* 382, 560 that there is a teaching in Persia which claims that before the coming of Zoroaster, demons corrupted the earth and allied themselves with women (R.H. Charles, ed., *The Apocrypha and Pseudepigrapha of the Old Testament, Vol. 2* Berkeley: The Apocryphile Press, 2004), 191.

[109] LXX is the Greek translation of the Hebrew Bible, the Old Testament. LXX is called the Septuagint.

[110] *Antiquities of the Jews*, Book 1, Chapter 3, section 1.

[111] W. Holladay, *A Concise Hebrew and Aramaic Lexicon of The Old Testament* (Grand Rapids: Eerdmans, 1971), 241.

[112] One example of a giant that is recorded in Scripture is Goliath. Goliath was a man over nine feet tall (1 Sam 17:4).

[113] *Enoch* 10:1-16; *The Book of Jubilees* 4:24; 7:21-28.

[114] There is ample evidence to show that the ancient aliens were angels, as seen in the discussion and footnotes above.

[115] R. H. Charles, *A Critical and Exegetical Commentary on the Revelation of St. John* (Edinburgh: T&T Clark, 1975), 245.

[116] W. Barclay, *The Revelation of John, Vol. 2* (Philadelphia: The Westminster Press, 1960), 59.

[117] *Ibid*, 65.

[118] *Ibid*, 64; V. Eller, *The Most Revealing Book of the Bible: Making Sense of Revelation* (Grand Rapids: Eerdmans, 1974), 110; R. H. Charles, *A Critical and Exegetical Commentary on the Revelation of St. John*, 247.

[119] A. Bloomfield, *Before the Last Battle: Armageddon*, 127.

[120] A. Bloomfield, *The End of the Days: The Prophecies of Daniel Explained*, 115.

[121] A. Bloomfield, *Before the Last Battle*, 125.

[122] See the discussion above concerning the Fallen Angels who came to earth, shared knowledge with the human race. Many of the cultures that met these Fallen Angels called them Aliens who came to earth from space.

[123] B. McGinn, *Anti-Christ: Two Thousand Years of The Human Fascination with Evil*, 52.

[124] J. Louw & E. Nida, *The Greek-English Lexicon*, 6.

[125] *The Revelation of Esdras*, location 6542-47 states that the adversary of the human race will rise up from Tartarus.

[126] A. Bloomfield, *Before The Last Battle: Armageddon*, 125.

[127] R. Trench, *Synonyms of the New Testament*, 109.

[128] T. McCall and Z. Levitt, *Satan in The Sanctuary* (New York: Bantam Books, 1973), 79.

[129] Satan sought to place his throne equal with God states *The Book of the Secrets of Enoch*, 29: 4; Isa 14:12-23.

[130] See also *The Testament of Asher* 7:1-3 in *The Testament of the Twelve Patriarchs*.

[131] A. Fruchtenbaum, *The Footsteps of the Messiah*, 194.

[132] Many of the points in this discussion are found in the book by H. Wayne House, *Charts of Christian Theology and Doctrine* (Grand Rapids: Zondervan, 1992), 15, 16 which is based on the study of Richard Belcher, *A Comparison of Dispensationalism and Covenant Theology* (Columbia, SC: Richbarry Press, 1986).

[133] J. Louw & E. Nida, *Greek-English Lexicon*, 749; L. Berkhof, *Systematic Theology* (Edinburgh: The Banner of Truth Trust, 1984), 427.

[134] Gen 3:15 is called the Proto-Evangelium.

[135] Neither Adam nor Eve took responsibility for their own action. Adam blamed both God and Eve (3:12) and Eve blamed the Serpent (Gen 3:13).

[136] See the *Revelation of Moses* which states: Adam said to Eve: Why did you work mischief against us and bring upon us great wrath, which is death, holding sway over all the race? (location 6357-61); see also J. Boice, *Foundations of The Christian Faith* (Downers Grove: InterVarsity Press, 1986), 206.

[137] The Hebrew חשׁב means to impute, to count, to consider, R. Laird Harris, *Theological Wordbook of The Old Testament, Vol. I* (Chicago: Moody Press, 1981), 330.

[138] The word righteous is translated from the Hebrew צדק which describes the righteous standing of God's heirs to salvation, this righteousness, actually possessed by the Messiah (Jer 23:6), is bestowed by him, thus pointing toward the NT doctrine of Christ our righteousness. The righteousness of God's heirs of salvation is the righteousness of the Messiah attributed to them by God through faith in the redemptive work of Messiah in which God declares them righteous only because of the grace provided through that redemptive work, R. Laird Harris, *Theological Wordbook of The Old Testament, Vol. 2* (Chicago: Moody Press, 1981), 754.

[139] Heb 11 is the chapter on faith, but not just faith in general, but the faith that leads to righteousness (Heb 11:39-40). As has already been discussed, righteousness is by faith, not Law. In addition, Heb 11 lists the great cloud of witnesses of the faith. Both Abraham (Heb 11:11) and David (Heb 11:32) are both listed in the cloud of witnesses who had faith that leads to righteousness.

[140] Paul said the giving of the Law was 430 years after the establishment of the covenant of grace to Abraham. For the number of 430 years see also Ex 12:40-41.The number 400 years is found in Gen 15:13.

[141] J. Louw & E. Nida, *Greek-English Lexicon*, 126.

[142] W. Arndt & F. W. Gingrich, eds. *A Greek-English Lexicon of The New Testament and Other Early Christian Literature* (Chicago: The University of Chicago Press, 1979), 241.

[143] J. Louw & E. Nida, *Greek-English Lexicon*, 126.

[144] R. Trench, *Synonyms of The New Testament*, 2.

[145] J. Louw & E. Nida, *Greek-English Lexicon*, 126.

[146] House, *Charts of Christian Theology and Doctrine*, 15.

[147] *Ibid*, 15.

[148] Fruchtenbaum, *The Footsteps of the Messiah,* 375.

[149] House, *Charts of Christian Theology and Doctrine,* 15.

[150] The two divisions of humanity in this particular sentence refers to the division of the world by some in the Jewish community into two groups: Jews and Gentiles.

[151] J. Louw & E. Nida, *Greek-English Lexicon,* 638.

[152] Dispensational Theology is the branch of Christian theology which states that God has divided salvation history into periods or dispensations. In these various dispensations, God relates to His people differently and with different means. Thus, in the Old Testament dispensation (this study prefers the term age for dispensation), God gave the Law as a means of righteousness. However, as has been shown in this study, this cannot be true for the Law was never given to make a person righteous (Gal 4:21). This being the case, the foundational thought of Dispensational Theology is seen to be suspect.

[153] Ladd says that the true people of God are those who accept Jesus as Messiah and constitute the *spiritual Israel* (G. E. Ladd, *A Theology of The New Testament,* Grand Rapids: William B. Eerdmans, 1974, 342); see also J.P.M. Sweet, *Revelation* (Philadelphia: The Westminster Press, 1979), 147.

[154] Gen 3:15.

[155] Gen 12:1-4.

[156] Acts 2:1-13.

[157] G. Ladd, *A Theology of the New Testament,* 347.

[158] *Ibid,* 347.

[159] G. Osborne, *Romans,* 99; Ambrosiaster, *Commentary on Paul's Epistles,* Gerald Bray, ed., *Ancient Christian Commentary on Scripture* (Downers Grove: InterVarsity Press, 1998), 102.

[160] The Greek, μεταμορφόομαι, means to take on a different physical form or appearance (Louw & Nida, *Greek-English Lexicon,* 587). The root of μεταμορφόομαι is μορφή. Μορφή is a word that describes the nature or character of something, with the emphasis upon the internal and external form (Louw & Nida, *Greek-English Lexicon,* 586). Trench adds further clarity to the understanding of μορφή when he says that μορφή refers to the essence of thing (Trench, *Synonyms of The New Testament,* 265). What is to be understood from this is that when Jesus was transfigured on the Mount, His outward appearance reflected His inner character. The external and inner combined to express the very nature of Jesus.

[161] J. P. Sweet, *Revelation,* 58.

[162] J. Walvoord, *The Revelation of Jesus Christ* (Chicago: Moody Press, 1966), 48.

[163] R. Mounce, *The Book of Revelation* (Grand Rapids: William B. Eerdmans, 1977), 82.

[164] *Ibid,* 82.

[165] Walvoord, *The Revelation of Jesus Christ,* 50; R.H. Charles, *A Critical and Exegetical Commentary on The Revelation of St. John* (Edinburgh: T & T Clark, 1975), 33.

[166] J.P.M. Sweet, *Revelation,* 73.

[167] *Ibid,* 73.

[168] Walvoord, *The Revelation of Jesus Christ,* 102.

[169] R.H. Charles, *A Critical and Exegetical Commentary on The Revelation of St. John*, 33.

[170] *Ibid*, 51.

[171] *Ibid*, 52.

[172] G. Osborne, *Romans*, 305.

[173] J. Louw & E. Nida, *Greek-English Lexicon*, 597.

[174] *Ibid*, 598.

[175] *Ibid*, 638.

[176] For a detailed discussion on the meaning of the word *hardened*, see my book, *Spiritual Portrait of A Believer*.

[177] G. Osborne, *Romans*, 306.

[178] J. Louw & E. Nida, *Greek-English Lexicon*, 1.

[179] *Ibid*, 597.

[180] *Ibid*, 104.

[181] *Ibid*, 357.

[182] G. Berry, *A Dictionary of New Testament Greek Synonyms*, 25.

[183] J. Louw & E. Nida, *Greek-English Lexicon*, 597.

[184] The Temple was destroyed in 70 CE by the Romans.

[185] R. Laird Harris, *Theological Wordbook of The Old Testament*, Vol. 2, 936.

[186] This study will not enter the discussion between Creation and Evolution. The plain teaching of the Word of God is that God created the world and all that is in it.

[187] The word *fall* denotes the fall from grace, the fall from the purpose of God, the fall from a personal relationship with God and the loss of Paradise.

[188] H. Morris, *The Genesis Record: A Scientific and Devotional Commentary on the Book of Beginnings* (Grand Rapids: Baker Book House, 1988), 119.

[189] *Ibid*, 119.

[190] J. M. Boice, *Foundations of the Christian Faith* (Downers Grove: InterVarsity Press, 1986), 401.

[191] J.R.W. Stott, *The Cross of Christ*, 188.

[192] E. Brunner, *The Christian Doctrine of the Church, Faith and the Consummation*, 140.

[193] *Ibid*, 145.

[194] *Ibid*, 146.

[195] T. Epp, *Flesh and the Spirit in Conflict: Practical Studies in Galatians* (Lincoln, Nebraska: Back to the Bible Broadcast, 1968), 12.

[196] L.S. Chafer, *Major Bible Themes* (Grand Rapids: Zondervan, 1974), 99.

[197] Brunner calls the new birth the creation of the person through God's historical self-communication. (E. Brunner, *The Christian Doctrine of the Church, Faith and Consummation*, 269).

[198] J. R. W. Stott, *The Cross of Christ*, 192.

[199] E. Brunner, *The Christian Doctrine of the Church Faith and Consummation*, 420.

[200] *Ibid*, 420.

[201] *Ibid*, 428.

[202] *Ibid*, 291.

203 *Ibid*, 434.
204 *Ibid*, 277.
205 G. Berry, *A Dictionary of Greek New Testament Synonyms*, 17.
206 J. Louw & E. Nida, *Greek-English Lexicon*, 438.
207 R. Trench, *Synonyms of the New Testament*, 381.
208 J. Louw & E. Nida, *Greek-English Lexicon*, 348.
209 *Ibid*, 347.
210 *Ibid*, 349.
211 *Ibid*, 349.
212 *Ibid*, 394.
213 *Ibid*, 160.
214 H. E. Dana & J. R. Mantey, *A Manual Grammar of the Greek New Testament*, 230.
215 E. Brunner, *The Christian Doctrine of the Church, Faith and Consummation*, 418.
216 *Ibid*, 418.
217 J. Louw & E. Nida, *Greek-English Lexicon*, 438.
218 G. Berry, *A Dictionary of New Testament Greek Synonyms*, 17.
219 J. Louw & E. Nida, *Greek-English Lexicon*, 745.
220 H. Dana & J. Mantey, *A Manual Grammar of Greek New Testament*, 168.
221 *Ibid*, 166.
222 J. Louw & E. Nida, *The Greek-English Lexicon*, 541.
223 J. Louw & E. Nida, *The Greek-English Lexicon*, 139.
224 C. Cataldo, *A Spiritual Portrait of A Believer: A Comparison Between the Emphatic 'I' of Romans 7, Wesley and the Mystics* (Newcastle upon Tyne: Cambridge Scholars Publishing, 2010), 301.
225 G. Osborne, *Romans* (Downers Grove: InterVarsity Press, 2004), 162.
226 *Ibid*, 162.
227 C. Cranfield, *A Critical and Exegetical Commentary on The Epistle to the Romans* (Edinburgh: T &T Clark, 1975), 319.
228 *Ibid*, 325.
229 G. Osborne, *Romans*, 162, 163.
230 *Ibid*, 157.
231 C.F.H. Henry, *God, Revelation and Authority, Vol. IV* (Waco: *Word* Books, 1979), 503; J.R.W. Stott, *The Contemporary Christian* (Downers Grove: InterVarsity Press, 1992), 375-392.
232 *Ibid, 498.*
233 G.E. Ladd, *A Theology of the New Testament,* (Grand Rapids: Eerdmans, 1974), 480.
234 J. Dunn, *The Theology of Paul's Letter To The Galatians,* (Cambridge: Cambridge University Press, 1993), 47.
235 P. Tillich, *Systematic Theology: Three Volumes in One,* (New York: Harper and Row, 1967), 394.
236 *Ibid.*
237 *Ibid*, 395.

[238] G.E. Ladd, *A Theology of the New Testament*, 480.

[239] T. Epp, *Flesh and Spirit in Conflict*, 75.

[240] See the Book *Spiritual Portrait of A Believer*, by C. Cataldo, Newcastle upon Tyne: Cambridge Scholars Press, 2010 for a detailed discussion of this question.

[241] J. Louw & E. Nida, *Greek-English Lexicon*, 691.

[242] The Greek word is: ἐκπίπτω. Ἐκπίπτω means to abandon a former relationship or association, to fall away (J. Louw & E. Nida, *Greek-English Lexicon*, 449).

[243] This study will not enter the discussion of once saved, always saved.

[244] J. Louw & E. Nida, *Greek-English Lexicon*, 221.

[245] By Western Church is meant primarily the Catholic and Protestant Churches. The Eastern Church, composed of the various Orthodox Churches, do not use the Latin in their translations of the Bible.

[246] J. Louw & E. Nida, *Greek-English Lexicon*, 3.

[247] In the Hebrew what the witch says she sees is gods coming up from the earth. The witch did not mean that she saw God Himself coming up from the ground. What the witch saw was someone who had in some way changed and in appearance was closer to the appearance of God. This teaches us that after death, the righteous do in fact lay aside the old and in some way the new shines through.

[248] The Greek is ψυχή. Ψυχή refers to the inner person (J. Louw & E. Nida, *Greek-English Lexicon*, 321).

[249] J. Louw & E. Nida, *Greek-English Lexicon*, 263.

[250] Sheol is the Hebrew equivalent to the Greek Hades, J. Louw & E. Nida, *Greek-English Lexicon*, 6.

[251] *Ibid*, 6.

[252] *Ibid*, 6.

[253] *Ibid*, 267.

[254] *Ibid*, 268.

[255] *Ibid*, 221.

[256] W. Arndt & Walter Bauer, *A Greek-English Lexicon of the New Testament and Other Early Christian Literature*, 109.

[257] R. H. Charles, *A Critical Commentary on the Revelation of St. John*, 90.

[258] B. Metzger, *Breaking the Code: Understanding the Book of Revelation*, 42.

[259] J. Louw & E. Nida, *Greek-English Lexicon*, 10.

[260] *Ibid*, 106.

[261] J. Moulton & George Milligan, *The Vocabulary of the Greek New Testament* (Grand Rapids: Eerdmans, 1982), 443.

[262] The Greek is ἔθνη, which means nations (J. Louw & E. Nida, *Greek-English Lexicon*, 130.

[263] *Ibid*, 613.

[264] *Ibid*, 597.

[265] *Ibid*, 730.

[266] *Ibid*, 703.

[267] *Ibid*, 10.

[268] *Ibid*, 613.

[269] *Ibid*, 10.

[270] δοῦλος means slave, *Ibid,* 741.

[271] ἐλεύθερος means free person, *Ibid,* 742.

[272] *Ibid,* 597.

[273] Walvoord is one who holds the view that Rev 3:10 refers to the rapture, J. Walvoord, *The Revelation of Jesus Christ,* 87.

[274] While the promise was made to the church at Philadelphia, since the 7 churches of Revelation are both individual churches and types of churches, the promise is made to faithful Christians of every time and place.

[275] New International Version of the Bible.

[276] J. Walvoord, *The Revelation of Jesus Christ,* 87.

[277] B. Metzger, *Breaking the Code: Understanding the Book of Revelation,* (Nashville: Abingdon Press, 1993), 42.

[278] R. Mounce, *The Book of Revelation,* 119.

[279] New International Version.

[280] H. E. Dana & Julius R. Mantey, *A Manual Grammar of the Greek New Testament,* 102.

[281] To inspect the various meanings see J. Louw & E. Nida, *Greek-English Lexicon,* 75; J. Moulton & G. Milligan, *The Vocabulary of the Greek New Testament,* 189-190.

[282] For a more detailed explanation of the various meanings of not only ἐκ but of prepositions in general see H. E. Dana & J. R. Mantey, *A Manual Grammar of the Greek New Testament,* 98, 99.

[283] I by no means mean to state that a Christian is not in the church when they are in prison. The idea here is of location. At one point in time they were in one location and at another point in time they were in another location.

[284] J. Louw & E. Nida, *Greek-English Lexicon,* 761.

[285] R. Trench, *Synonyms of the New Testament,* 130.

[286] W. Arndt & F. Wilbur Gingrich, *A Greek-English Lexicon of the New Testament,* 579.

[287] J. Louw & E. Nida, *Greek-English Lexicon,* 490.

[288] Both the Hebrew אכל and the Greek, καταναλίσκω, which is the Greek translation found in the LXX, both mean to consume, devour, as in the eating of a meal. For the Hebrew see R. Laird Harris, ed., *Theological Wordbook of the Old Testament, Vol. I,* 39. For the Greek see J. Lust, *A Greek-English Lexicon of the Septuagint, Part II* (Stuttgart: Deutsche Bibelgesellschaft, 1996), 239.

[289] J. Louw & E. Nida, *Greek-English Lexicon,* 468.

[290] *Ibid,* 379.

[291] J. Louw & E. Nida, *Greek-English Lexicon,* 159.

[292] *Ibid,* 483.

[293] *Ibid,* 809.

[294] W. Arndt & W. Gingrich, *A Greek-English Lexicon of the New Testament,* 816.

[295] J. Moulton & G. Milligan, *The Vocabulary of the Greek New Testament,* 634.

[296] J. Louw & E. Nida, *Greek-English Lexicon,* 721.

[297] J. Wesley, *Explanatory Notes Upon The New Testament;* G. Osborne, *Romans,* 135; K. Barth, *The Epistle to The Romans,* 164; Ambrosiaster, *Commentary on Paul's Epistles,* Gerald Bray, ed., *The Ancient Christian Commentary on Scripture: Romans,*

132.

[298] J. Louw & E. Nida, *Greek-English Lexicon,* 241.

[299] J. Louw & E. Nida, *Greek-English Lexicon,* 645.

[300] *Ibid,* 642.

[301] The word translated passed away is παρέρχομαι, which means to out of existence, to cease (*Ibid,* 159).

[302] E. Brunner, *The Christian Doctrine of the Church, Faith and the Consummation,* 283.

[303] G. Osborne, *Romans,* 152.

[304] For a more detailed explanation of the differences between ζωή and βίος, see R. Trench, *Synonyms of the New Testament,* 91.

[305] For a more detailed discussion of forgiveness and the wiping away of the record of sins, see Chapter 5 of this book.

[306] J. Louw & E. Nida, *Greek-English Lexicon,* 556.

[307] *Ibid,* 124.

[308] *The Sibylline Oracles,* Book IV, lines 162-175.

[309] R. H. Charles, *A Critical and Exegetical Commentary on the Revelation of St. John,* 90.

[310] W.F. Arndt & W. Gingrich, *A Greek-English Lexicon of the New Testament,* 564.

[311] R. H. Charles, *A Critical and Exegetical Commentary on the Revelation of St. John,* 200.

[312] *Ibid,* 200.

[313] G. Osborne, *Romans,* 242.

[314] *Ibid,* 242.

[315] J. Walvoord, *The Revelation of Jesus Christ,* 139.

[316] J. Louw & E. Nida, *Greek-English Lexicon,* 240.

[317] *Ibid,* 703.

[318] *Ibid,* 10.

[319] *Ibid,* 613.

[320] L. Morris, *The First and Second Epistles to the Thessalonians* (Grand Rapids: Eerdmans, 1982), 214.

[321] A. Fruchtenbaum, *The Footsteps of the Messiah,* 154.

[322] *Ibid,* 155.

[323] A. Bloomfield, *Signs of His Coming,* 159.

[324] N. Geldenhvys, *The Gospel of Luke* (Grand Rapids: Eerdmans, 1983), 537.

[325] At the present time, there are members of the Jewish community who have and are accepting Jesus as the Messiah. This number is small in proportion to both the number of Gentiles accepting Christ and to the total number in the Jewish community.

[326] J. Louw & E. Nida, *Greek-English Lexicon,* 645.

[327] The context of Isaiah 27 is Isaiah 24-35 which describe the Day when the Lord will devastate the earth. It is in the context of the devastation of the earth, that the revival in Israel will occur. The day when the Lord will devastate the earth is called the Great Tribulation.

[328] K. Barth, *The Epistle to the Romans,* 414.

[329] G. Osborne, *Romans,* 306.

[330] A. Bloomfield, *Before the Last Battle,* 163.

[331] A. Fruchtenbaum, *The Footsteps of the Messiah,* 221; C. Buxton, *Expect These Things* (Old Tappan: Fleming H. Revell, 1971), 105.

[332] R. Gundry, *Matthew: A Commentary on His Literary and Theological Art* (Grand Rapids: Eerdmans, 1982), 494.

[333] ἀποκαλύπτω means to make fully known, J. Louw & E. Nida, *Greek-English Lexicon,* 339.

[334] See 2 Tim 3; 2 Pet 3:3 and Jude 18.

[335] In this situation, although Jesus is addressing the 12 disciples, the disciples here represent the whole church, R. Gundry, *Matthew,* 474; W. Bundy, *Jesus and the First Three Gospels* (Cambridge: Cambridge University Press, 1955), 459.

[336] See the Christian Martyr Website for verification of this statement.

[337] A. Bloomfield, *Before the Last Battle,* 164.

[338] R. Gundry, *Matthew* (Grand Rapids: Eerdmans, 1982), 482.

[339] J. Walvoord, *The Revelation of Jesus Christ,* 137.

[340] Fruchtenbaum says that Rev 6-18 covers the Tribulation and that Rev 6-9, 17 discuss the First Half of the Tribulation, the first half of the 70th Seven, A. Fruchtenbaum, *The Footsteps of the Messiah,* 203.

[341] *Ibid, 273.*

[342] *Ibid, 273.*

[343] J. Walvoord, *The Revelation of Jesus Christ, 138.*

[344] *Ibid, 135.*

[345] *Ibid, 138.*

[346] J. Louw & E. Nida, *Greek-English Lexicon,* 76.

[347] *Ibid, 77.*

[348] B. Graham, *Approaching Hoof Beats: The Four Horsemen of the Apocalypse* (Minneapolis: Grason, 1983), 122.

[349] A. Fruchtenbaum, *The Footsteps of the Messiah,* 216.

[350] B. Graham, *Approaching Hoof Beats: The Four Horsemen of the Apocalypse,* 128.

[351] *Ibid, 76.*

[352] Fruchtenbaum, *Footsteps of the Messiah,* 237.

[353] Barth says that *all Israel* refers to the whole Church, K. Barth, *The Epistle to the Romans,* 416. In disagreement is Palmer who writes that to interpret *all Israel* as the Church is not exegetically fair to Paul's use of the word *Israel* in Rom 9-11, E. Palmer, *Salvation by Surprise: A Commentary on the Book of Romans* (Waco: Word Books, 1975), 134 and Osborne who states that *all Israel* does not refer to every single Jewish person that has ever lived, but to the nation of Israel at the end of history, G. Osborne, *Romans,* 306.

[354] A. Fruchtenbaum, *The Footsteps of the Messiah,* 203; A. Bloomfield, *Before the Last Battle,* 154; H. Lindsay, *The Late Great Planet Earth* (New York: Bantam Books, 1973), 132; C. Buxton, *Expect These Things,* 37.

[355] Fruchtenbaum calls the entire 7 year period the Great Tribulation and not just the second half of the 70th Seven, A. Fruchtenbaum, *The Footsteps of the Messiah,* 173.

[356] J. Louw & E. Nida, *Greek-English Lexicon,* 745.

BIBLIOGRAPHY

Arndt, William and F. Wilbur Gingrich, eds. *A Greek-English Lexicon of The New Testament and Other Early Christian Literature* (Chicago: The University of Chicago Press, 1979).

Baly, Denis. *God and History in the Old Testament.* New York: Harper & Row, 1976.

Barclay, William. *The Revelation of John, Vol. 2.* Philadelphia: The Westminster Press, 1960.

Barth, Karl. Translated by Edwyn Hoskins. *The Epistle to the Romans.* Oxford: Oxford University Press, 1968.

Beare, Frank. *The Earliest Records of Jesus.* Nashville: Abingdon Press, 1962.

Berkhof, Louis. *Systematic Theology.* Edinburgh: The Banner of Truth Trust, 1984.

Berry, George. *A Dictionary of Greek New Testament Synonyms.* Grand Rapids: Zondervan, 1979.

Bloomfield, Arthur. *Before The Last Battle: Armageddon.* Minneapolis: Dimension Books, 1971.

Bloomfield, Arthur. *The End of The Days: The Prophecies of Daniel Explained.* Minneapolis: Bethany Fellowship, 1970.

Boice, James. *Foundations of the Christian Faith.* Downers Grove: InterVarsity Press, 1986.

Bray, Gerald, ed. *The Ancient Christian Commentary on Scripture: Romans.* Downers Grove: InterVarsity Press, 1998.

Bright, John. *Covenant and Promise.* Philadelphia: The Westminster Press, 1976.

Brunner, Emil. Translated by David Cairns. *The Christian Doctrine of the*

Church, Faith and the Consummation. Philadelphia: The Westminster Press, 1962.

Bundy, Walter. *Jesus and the First Three Gospels.* Cambridge: Cambridge University Press, 1955.

Buxton, Clyne. *Expect These Things.* Old Tappan: Fleming H. Revell, 1971.

Cataldo, Chet. *A Spiritual Portrait of A Believer: A Comparison Between the Emphatic 'I' of Romans 7, Wesley and the Mystics.* Newcastle upon Tyne: Cambridge Scholars Publishing, 2010.

Chafer, Lewis. *Major Bible Themes.* Grand Rapids: Zondervan, 1974.

Charles, R.H., ed. *The Apocrypha and Pseudepigrapha of the Old Testament, Vol. 2.* Berkeley: The Apocryphile Press, 2004.

Charles, R.H. *A Critical and Exegetical Commentary on The Revelation of St. John.* Edinburgh: T & T Clark, 1975.

Cranfield, Charles. *A Critical and Exegetical Commentary on The Epistle to the Romans.* Edinburgh: T &T Clark, 1975.

Cushman, Robert. *John Wesley's Experimental Divinity.* Nashville: Kingswood Books, 1989.

Dana, H.E. and Julius R. Mantey. *A Manual Grammar of the Greek New Testament.* New York: Macmillan Publishing, 1955.

Dunn, John. *The Theology of Paul's Letter To The Galatians.* Cambridge: Cambridge University Press, 1993.

Eller, Vernard. *The Most Revealing Book of the Bible: Making Sense of Revelation.* Grand Rapids: Eerdmans, 1974.

Epp, Theodore. *Flesh and the Spirit in Conflict: Practical Studies in Galatians.* Lincoln, Nebraska: Back to the Bible Broadcast, 1968.

Fruchtenbaum, Arnold. *The Footsteps of the Messiah.* Tustin, CA: Ariel Ministries, 2004.

Gelednhvys, Norval. *The Gospel of Luke.* Grand Rapids: Eerdmans, 1983.

Graham, Billy. *Approaching Hoof Beats: The Four Horsemen of the Apocalypse.* Minneapolis: Grason, 1983.

Gundry, Robert. *Matthew.* Grand Rapids: Eerdmans, 1982.

Hammer, Raymond. *The Book of Daniel.* Cambridge: Cambridge University Press, 1976.

Harris, R. Laird, ed. *Theological Wordbook of the Old Testament, Vol. I.* Chicago: Moody Press, 1981.

Harris, R. Laird, ed. *Theological Wordbook of the Old Testament, Vol. II.* Chicago: Moody Press, 1981.

Henry, C.F. H. *God, Revelation and Authority, Vol. IV.* Waco: Word Books, 1979.

Heschel, Abraham. *The Prophets.* New York: Harper & Row, 1962.

Holladay, Willliam, ed. *A Concise Hebrew and Aramaic Lexicon of The Old Testament.* Grand Rapids: William B. Eerdmans, 1971.

House, H. Wayne. *Charts of Christian Theology and Doctrine.* Grand Rapids: Zondervan, 1992.

Lacocque, Andre. Translated by David Pellauer. *The Book of Daniel.* Atlanta: John Knox Press, 1979.

Ladd, George. *A Theology of the New Testament.* Grand Rapids: William B. Eerdmans, 1974.

Lindsay, Hal. *The Late Great Planet Earth.* New York: Bantam Books, 1973.

Louw, Johannes and Eugene Nida. *Greek-English Lexicon of the New Testament based on Semantic Domains.* New York: United Bible Societies, 1989.

Lust, J. *A Greek-English Lexicon of the Septuagint, Part II.* Stuttgart: Deutsche Bibelgesellschaft, 1996.

McCall, Thomas and Zola Levitt, *Satan in The Sanctuary.* New York: Bantam Books, 1973.

McGinn, Bernard. *Anti-Christ: Two Thousand Years of the Human Fascination with Evil.* San Francisco: HarperSanFrancisco, 1994.

Metzger, Bruce. *Breaking the Code: Understanding the Book of Revelation.* Nashville: Abingdon Press, 1993.

Montgomery, James. *The Book of Daniel.* Edinburgh: T & T Clark, 1972.

Morris, Henry. *The Genesis Record: A Scientific and Devotional Commentary on the Book of Beginnings.* Grand Rapids: Baker Book House, 1988.

Morris, Leon. *The First and Second Epistles to the Thessalonians.* Grand Rapids: Eerdmans, 1982.

Moulton, James & George Milligan. *The Vocabulary of the Greek New Testament.* Grand Rapids: Eerdmans, 1982.

Mounce, Robert. *The Book of Revelation.* Grand Rapids: William B. Eerdmans, 1977.

Osborne, Grant. *Romans.* Downers Grove: InterVarsity Press, 2004.

Palmer, Earl. *Salvation by Surprise: A Commentary on the Book of Romans.* Waco: Word Books, 1975.

Stott, John R.W. *The Cross of Christ.* Downers Grove: InterVarsity Press, 1986.

Stott, John R.W. *The Contemporary Christian.* Downers Grove: InterVarsity Press, 1992.

Sweet, J.P.M. *Revelation.* Philadelphia: The Westminster Press, 1979.

Tillich, Paul. *Systematic Theology: Three Volumes in One.* New York: Harper and Row, 1967.

Trench, Richard. *Synonyms of The New Testament.* Grand Rapids: Eerdmans,

1980.

Walvoord, John. *The Revelation of Jesus Christ.* Chicago: Moody Press, 1966.

Waters, Frank. *Book of The Hopi.* New York: Ballantine Books, 1963.

Wesley, John. *Wesley's Notes on the New Testament, Vol. II.* Kansas City, Missouri: Beacon Hill Press of Kansas City, 1983.

Wesley, John. *Salvation by Faith,* Sermon, *The Works of John Wesley, 11.* CD-Rom; Franklin, TN: Providence House Publishers, 1995.

Wesley, John. *Scripture Way of Salvation,* Sermon, *The Works of John Wesley, 11.* CD-Rom; Franklin, TN: Providence House Publishers, 1995.

Westermann, Claus, translated by Hugh Clayton White. *Basic Forms of Prophetic Speech.* Philadelphia: The Westminster Press, 1967.

Woolley, C. Leonard. *The Sumerians.* New York: W.W. Norton & Co., 1965.